FEEDING THE CRISIS

RACHEL GARST &
TOM BARRY

Feeding
the
CRISIS

U.S. Food Aid
and Farm Policy in
Central America

University of Nebraska Press
Lincoln & London

Library of Congress Cataloging-in-Publication Data
Garst, Rachel.
Feeding the crisis : U.S. food aid and farm policy
in Central America /
Rachel Garst and Tom Barry.
p.   cm.
Includes bibliographical references.
ISBN 0-8032-1217-8 (alkaline paper)
ISBN 0-8032-6095-4 (pbk.)
1. Food relief, American – Central America.
2. Agricultural assistance, American – Central America.
3. Agriculture and state – Central America.
1. Barry, Tom, 1950-
11. Title.
HV696.F6G37   1991
363.8′83′09728–dc20
90-31524   CIP

Contents

Preface

When people are hungry they become dissatisfied and unhappy. Eventually, this unrest could lead to political instability. Upheaval in the third world inevitably has an effect on the United States, which depends on these countries for natural resources. Clearly, U.S. food efforts contribute to the world's economic and political stability.

AID policy statement,
"Feeding the Hungry"

PREVIOUSLY REGARDED as insignificant banana republics, the countries of Central America have become world-class hot spots in the past decade. The Pentagon has responded to the crisis with vast amounts of military aid and frequent military maneuvers. The State Department has supplied even greater amounts of economic aid to support "friendly" governments in the region.

The United States Department of Agriculture (USDA) is an important participant in the U.S. build-up. Since 1979, the year when the Nicaraguan revolution focused U.S. attention on Central America, U.S. food aid has flooded into this food-short and poverty-stricken region. But the U.S. government is not just shipping surplus food to Central America, it is also working to change the farm policies and practices of this largely agricultural region.

At first glance, generous servings of food aid and attempts to reform farm policies in Central America seem positive and humanitarian. This attention to the problems of hunger and agricultural production appears to be dealing with the very causes of social turmoil and underdevelopment in Central America.

But has this response really been in the best interests of Central Americans? After almost two years of interviews, research, and extensive travel throughout the region, we conclude that the results, on the whole, have not been positive. In fact, we have found that U.S. food aid and associated farm programs are feeding the crisis in Central America. Food aid and agricultural development assistance—commonly regarded as the most beneficial and positive aspects of U.S. involvement in Central America—are hurting rather than helping. Not part of the solution, they are actually part of the problem.

At the outset of this investigation, we had already heard reports that made us question the positive picture painted by food-aid proponents. First, there was the growing body of literature critical of the effects of U.S. agricultural and food aid on developing countries. Second, our own experience in the region had raised additional doubts. We had heard that U.S. food had been handed out by soldiers on counterinsurgency missions. We read AID project papers that advocated increased agroexport production and reduced support for the local basic grains sector. We had heard reports of corruption, and we had even been offered cans of food-aid rations for sale in the streets.

Food aid seemed problematic, yet at the same time we noted points in its favor. Something, obviously, had to be done to assist the region's refugees and displaced. The economic crisis was also undermining the already precarious levels of subsistence of many Central Americans. Without food aid to maintain market supplies and keep prices down, many families would be squeezed out of the buying market altogether. We spoke to church and development workers who had plainly humanitarian motives, and did not doubt their goodwill and sincerity. Throughout the region, we saw a hunger and human desperation that made us shudder, and we were therefore reluctant to criticize aid that could ease that hunger.

Through our research, we hoped to clarify our own understanding and to produce a book that would offer a much-needed perspective about the U.S. role in food distribution and production in Central America. We set out by asking ten basic questions about the objectives and consequences of U.S. food aid and agricultural policy in the region. These questions, which we try to answer in the pages that follow, are:

− How much food aid is going to Central America, and who is benefiting?
− What are the objectives of the U.S. food-aid program, and are these being met?

- What is the United States doing to reduce hunger and improve the production of basic foods?
- How does Congress regulate the U.S. food-aid program, and are these regulations being respected?
- Are recipient countries putting U.S. food aid and agricultural assistance to good use?
- What is the effect of aid inflows on local farming and marketing?
- What is the effect of distributive aid on popular organization and political attitudes?
- Is U.S. food aid to Central America being used for direct political or military ends?
- How is this assistance affecting prospects for long-term stability in Central America?
- What is the appropriate role for food aid in this region?

We found few others asking these same questions. Still fewer had answers for us, especially when it came to questions regarding the capability of Central American governments to guarantee sufficient food supplies for their citizens. Although several U.S. government officials we interviewed did express concern over agricultural issues, most were too involved in administrative details to be worried about the overall food and farming picture and the long-term consequences of U.S. assistance. Or given their commitment to promoting U.S. agriculture and interests, the precarious state of Central American food security was simply not one of their concerns.

Nor was food aid's effect on nutrition and development an easy topic to research. The whole distributive aid world is characterized by wishful thinking. Program planners, assuming that giving free food to hungry people must be doing some good, rarely conduct rigorous evaluations of their programs and usually do not have a clear idea of their actual effects. Within Central America, we found literally hundreds of uncoordinated distribution programs. In field visits we were obviously only scratching the surface of a mammoth network of enormous variety. The most common feature of these diverse programs, however, was that, whatever was touted in the program descriptions, the reality usually looked very different.

Yet in our visits, by reading others' evaluations, and through interviews with more than 150 government employees, agricultural experts, farmers, planners, and social workers—both up and down the isthmus and in Washington—we were finally able to piece together some answers to our questions. And the picture we have constructed is not a flattering one. Although more investigative work is needed, we found enough problems in the programs we looked into to make us doubt the claims currently being made on food aid's behalf and to call for a serious reevaluation.

Feeding the Crisis focuses on the four Central American countries—Costa Rica, El Salvador, Guatemala, and Honduras—that have received the bulk of the increased food aid to the region. The first chapter presents an overview of the U.S. food-aid program and of its economic, political, and humanitarian motives. Next we look at the ways food aid functions as a form of U.S. aid. In the third chapter we begin our examination of the ways U.S. food aid and farm policy are intertwined with a discussion of the effects of U.S. food aid on local food production. The fourth chapter continues this discussion by examining how the U.S. government is using food aid as a tool to alter food production and distribution systems in the region.

In the fifth chapter we turn to a study of distributive food-aid programs. Here we examine the appropriateness of food aid as a solution to the problems of hunger and malnutrition. We next examine the use of food aid, particularly food-for-work, as a tool for social and economic development. The seventh chapter examines the explicitly political and military uses of food aid. The Conclusion offers our conclusions and recommendations.

Acknowledgments

We are grateful to the many United States and local government officials, food-aid program directors, and field workers who generously shared with us their time and knowledge. We also want to thank our colleagues who acted as readers and otherwise contributed their skills and our friends and families, who supported us in times of stress. This book would not have been possible without the backing of the Inter-Hemispheric Education Resource Center and its staff. Special thanks are due Debra Preusch for her research assistance and administrative support and Jenny Beatty for her word-processing and production skills. The book was made possible by grants from the Presbyterian Hunger Program, Conventional Friars, Sisters of St. Joseph of Peace, Dominican Sisters, Ann Roberts, and several anonymous donors. Any mistakes are our own.

ABOUT THE RESOURCE CENTER

The Inter-Hemispheric Education Resource Center is a private nonprofit research and policy institute in Albuquerque, New Mexico. Founded in 1979, the Resource Center produces books, policy reports, and audiovisuals about U.S. foreign relations with Third World countries. Among its most popular materials are *The Central America Fact Book*, an overview of the region, and the *Bulletin*, which examines important but little-studied issues and reaches several thousand subscribers quarterly. For a catalog of publications, please write to The Resource Center, Box 4506, Albuquerque, New Mexico 87196.

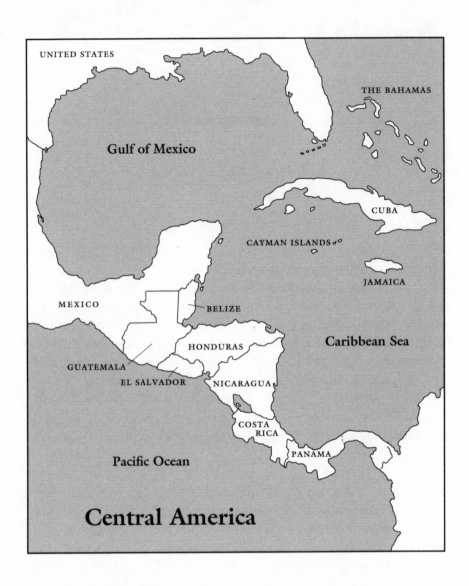

1

The Food Rushes In

The Embassy is concerned about public relations.
USDA is promoting U.S. commodities. AID is into
development. Everybody wants to get something dif-
ferent out of food aid.

GUILLERMO ALVARADO
AID official in Honduras
7 July 1987

CENTRAL AMERICA is awash in U.S. food aid. Poverty and hunger are nothing new in the region. It was not, however, until the Nicaraguan Sandinistas sent Anastasio Somoza scurrying into exile that Washington decided Central America urgently needed U.S. food support.

Before 1979, the fateful year of the Nicaraguan revolution, all Central American countries except Belize received some small level of U.S. food donations, mostly for distribution programs serving the poor. But with the political turmoil of the 1980s, the level and character of that assistance changed dramatically. All food aid to Nicaragua was discontinued by the Reagan administration, while the food assistance shipped to those countries surrounding the new leftist regime skyrocketed. In 1984 the National Bipartisan Commission on Central America (Kissinger Commission) recommended increased use of food aid and agricultural credits to help stabilize and pacify the region.[1]

Food aid from the United States for Guatemala, Honduras, El Salvador, and Costa Rica increased more than tenfold from 1979 to 1987. Government-to-government food aid (mostly Title I) in particular rose sharply and currently saves these four countries up to $120 million a year in hard cash while

TABLE I

U.S. Food Aid to Central America, FY 1979–87 (Millions of Dollars)

| Fiscal Year | Government-to-Government/Resale Programs | | | Distributive Programs | | |
	Title I/III	416 Sugar* Quota	Total	Title II	416* Regular	Total
1979	1.8	——	1.8	10.5	——	10.5
1980	2.96	——	2.96	8.7	——	8.7
1981	17.0	——·	17.0	19.3	——	19.3
1982	45.1	——	45.1	14.0	——	14.0
1983	78.9	——	78.9	18.5	——	18.5
1984	87.4	——	87.4	15.6	——	15.6
1985	74.7	——	74.7	17.3	0.3	17.6
1986	57.9	3.8	61.7	19.1	3.6	22.7
1987	66.0	9.7	75.7	17.2	5.8	23.0

Sources: USDA, *Food for Peace Annual Report on Public Law 480* and CCC export records.
Note: Figures represent export value of commodities shipped.
*Preliminary

covering nearly 30 percent of their total agricultural imports from the United States.[2] (See table 1.)

Distributive aid, though far outstripped by Title I programs, has more than doubled over the past ten years. Distributive food aid (mostly Title II) is especially significant for its direct impact on people's lives, political attitudes, and customs. By 1983 a full one-quarter of the Central American people were receiving food aid, mostly U.S.-labeled products.[3] In El Salvador calculations for 1987, based on AID and World Food Program figures, show 37 percent of the population receiving donated food aid.[4]

THE FOOD-AID BONANZA

In Central America the signs of U.S. food aid are everywhere. Most apparent is the large influx of wheat. From the pizza parlors dotting San Salvador to the women selling wheat tortillas in the Costa Rican marketplaces, wheat products are gaining a prominent place in the region's diet. Television commercials and billboards advertise the delicious, nutritious qualities of white sandwich bread. Pastries and rolls are now sold in the most isolated mountain villages by

Varieties of U.S. Food Assistance

The main U.S. food-aid legislation, Public Law 480, is based on the 1954 Agricultural Trade Development and Assistance Act. As it stands today, this law has two major aid mechanisms: Title I (a concessional sales program) and Title II (donations for free distribution). In addition to PL 480, a small portion of food aid is donated from the surplus stocks of the the Commodity Credit Corporation (CCC) under Section 416 of the Agricultural Act of 1949. Section 416 foods are once again distributed under two main mechanisms: the Sugar Quota Set Aside and the regular donations program. Note that in both PL 480 and Section 416 two very different types of programs both come under the general heading of food aid.

Government-to-Government: We use this term to refer to aid going to recipient governments for resale on the domestic market for local currency. Though it is known by many as program food aid, we prefer the term government-to-government aid to highlight the economic support this type of aid provides to the recipient government. Governments acquire the food either through purchase on soft credit terms or through outright donation. Under PL 480

Title I, which represents some three-quarters of total U.S. food aid both world-wide and in Central America, the recipient governments buy the food on concessional credit terms. Under the Section 416 Sugar Quota Set Aside, the United States has in recent years donated surplus CCC commodities to Central American governments (with the exception of Nicaragua) to compensate them for reductions in their U.S. sugar import quotas. Finally, the government of El Salvador has been donated powdered milk for resale under the little-known Section 206 of PL 480 Title II.

Distributive: This term refers to food aid that is donated to humanitarian or development agencies for free distribution to the poor and malnourished. Most distributive aid is channeled through nongovernmental organizations (NGOs) or through the United Nations World Food Programme (WFP), though in special cases (for example, El Salvador) donations have been made straight to government agencies in the recipient country. The main channel of U.S. distributive food aid is the regular PL 480 Title II donations program. In recent years Title II shipments have been supplemented by surplus CCC foods donated under Section 416 regular.[5]

vendors going from house to house on their rickety bicycles. In Costa Rica, *campesinos* are eating noodles and *tortipan* (wheat-flour tortillas) instead of the customary corn tortillas and rice. Urban restaurants or shops often no longer carry locally produced corn products, though wheat-flour products are always to be had.

Corn is also part of the U.S. food-aid program, but most goes to large agribusinesses for animal feed. In the past decade, fried chicken has become an important part of the urban diet. Chances are good that the chickens sold in the supermarkets and the fried chicken at the ever more popular fast-food outlets were raised on a diet of U.S. food aid. The oil used to fry the chicken is also largely supplied by U.S. food-aid programs, as is the tallow in the soap used to wash sticky fingers after the meal.

On street corners, women wave bags of powdered milk and cans of processed cheese at passing motorists. Local food processors are buying up powdered milk right out of agency warehouses, using it to produce everything from ice cream to "fresh" milk. In almost every town, one can see long lines of women waiting in front of the local government health centers: not for medical care—the centers often have no medicines—but for food handouts. First, however, they must receive "nutritional education": this week, perhaps a pancake-making class; next week, the art of preparing a white sauce.

In line, beneficiaries while away the time by complaining about who got into the program unfairly or whispering about the sacks of donated food one of them saw carried into the shopkeeper's store in the middle of the night. The nuns down the road are also giving out food, the women say, and there you don't even need to have a baby to get in. They just give you the food and remind you to go to mass. While the women wait in line, their school-age children bring the teacher not an apple, but a stick of wood to help boil up the wheat-soy mix at snacktime.

Tiny U.S. flag emblems, reminding the recipients of the U.S. people's generosity, are seen everywhere: on the sign at the distribution center, adorning the gunnysack in which a refugee family carries its few possessions, or glinting from the can a woman is using to carry water home from the nearby river. In an isolated mountain village one suddenly comes across a warehouse piled high with bags of powdered milk or discovers a mound of rusty food cans by the side of a pigsty. Work crews, paid in food, can often be seen repairing a road, repainting park benches, or reforesting a hillside. Inside the local military base, stacked in a corner one spies boxes marked "Puerto Rican school-lunch program," although how exactly they arrived in this most unlikely place remains a mystery. The commander prefers to talk about all the food and health care being given to the peasants "rescued" from the guerrillas and now being held at the army base for reeducation.

We encountered each of these scenes in the course of our investigation. As food aid increases, these scenarios are becoming a fixed part of Central American society. Yet for all food aid's current ubiquity, surprisingly little is known about the origins of these strange situations or the exact source of the flour in the bread consumed by more and more Central Americans.

OBJECTIVES OF FOOD AID

Perhaps because it is called "aid" and consists of such a necessary item as food, most people assume that food assistance is a good thing, probably helpful and certainly not harmful. The Central American governments are often not sure how much total food aid they are receiving, but they almost always welcome more. Development planners dream up various uses for this aid, even though their programs look much better on paper than in practice. The agencies actually distributing the food often have no clear idea of just what objectives they are trying to achieve. But donations are available and people are hungry, so it seems logical and humane to put the two together.

The U.S. Agency for International Development (AID), Washington's overseas development arm, is in charge of most food aid. AID representatives describe their food-aid program in bland generalities, stressing whenever possible its humanitarian or development aspects. Food aid to Central America, report local agency field missions, offers crucial assistance to these poor and war-torn nations, softening the effects of their economic crises and contributing to development, recovery, and peace. As proof, one is offered press handouts detailing how many thousands of metric tons of food boosted local market supplies and how many were distributed to such-and-such a number of the needy. All this food, reaching so many people—goes the implication—can do nothing but good.

Many U.S. citizens also have a positive view of such food aid. The term calls up a benign, romantic vision of a nation of plenty sharing its bounty with the suffering poor abroad. Images arise of a ragged little girl clutching a glass of milk, hands reaching up to lift U.S.-marked sacks off a truck, a childlike skeleton being fed from a bowl of gruel. These visions are encouraged both by the advertising of some of the agencies dealing in food aid—"You can save Maria or you can turn the page"—and by the rhetoric of U.S. government agencies responsible for managing the program.

On the thirtieth anniversary of the U.S. food-assistance program, President Reagan declared that the creation of the U.S. Food for Peace program was "one of the greatest humanitarian acts ever performed by one nation for the needy of other nations."[6] In a similar vein, AID administrator Peter McPherson said, "Eliminating world hunger is the central focus of the Agency for International Development."[7]

The true goals of the U.S. food-aid program, however, are more complex and self-interested. Current food-aid legislation and program documents list at least five different, often conflicting, objectives:

– Develop and expand export markets for U.S. agricultural commodities.
– Combat hunger and malnutrition.
– Provide humanitarian relief to victims of disasters.
– Encourage economic development in the developing countries, particularly those making efforts to expand their agricultural production.
– Promote in other ways the foreign policy of the United States.

This great diversity of aims makes food aid unique among U.S. aid programs; no other foreign assistance effort attempts to satisfy so many different interests simultaneously. The farm sector backs this program because it helps hold down commodity surpluses, thereby sustaining farm prices—a purely economic motive. Churches and nongovernmental organizations (NGOs) use these government donations in their overseas relief and development efforts. The foreign-policy establishment regards food aid as just another weapon in its diplomatic, political, and military arsenal.

FOOD FOR PEACE/FOOD FOR WAR

When the U.S. food-aid program was established in 1954 it had little to do with humanitarianism. Surplus food, not world hunger, was what induced the U.S. Congress to pass the PL 480 food-aid legislation. Overproduction by U.S. farmers had been a problem for the agricultural economy since the beginning of the century. Depression or war seemed the only way to keep supplies down and prices up.[8] In the early 1950s at the end of the Korean War, surplus commodity stocks held by the government were at an all-time high. As a way to reduce those stocks, Congress passed Public Law 480, the Agricultural Trade Development and Assistance Act, better known as just PL 480.[9]

Three and a half decades later, PL 480 has helped shape both the world's diet and its politics. When Congress instituted food aid, it was considered a temporary program that would probably wither away once commodity surpluses were reduced. But once under way, it found its own political and economic momentum. When its role in surplus disposal was overshadowed by the sharp increases in U.S. commercial exports in the 1960s and 1970s, PL 480 began to incorporate other objectives. Humanitarian and developmental concerns have been more closely integrated into the food-aid program. There has also been the expanded use of food aid as an instrument of foreign policy.

Liberal democrats have long been the strongest proponents of food aid and its use as a foreign policy tool. When PL 480 came up for review in 1957, Senator Hubert Humphrey conducted hearings on the program and supported its reauthorization in a policy report entitled "Food and Fiber as a Force for Freedom." Humphrey called upon the Eisenhower administration to make more "imaginative use of our food resources as an instrument of peace and freedom." Early on, Humphrey recognized the value of food power in global politics. During the 1957 hearings, he expounded: "I have heard here this morning that people may become dependent upon us for food. I know that was not supposed to be good news, because before people will do anything, they have got to eat. And if you are really looking for a way to get people to lean on you and to be dependent upon you, in terms of their cooperation with you, it seems to me that food dependence would be terrific."

In the early 1960s the Kennedy administration, adopting Humphrey's policy recommendations, began to wield the full political power of U.S. food aid. "Food is strength," declared Kennedy, "and food is peace and food is freedom and food is a helping hand." The new Democratic president appointed Congressman George McGovern to direct the invigorated PL 480 program, soon renamed Food for Peace.

Kennedy recognized that world hunger and underdevelopment were political, not just moral issues. In the drive to keep the Third World tied to the United States and world capitalism, food aid could be an important resource. During the Kennedy administration, not only was Washington's own food-aid program strengthened, but major support was also given to the newly created World Food Programme (WFP), a multigovernment food-aid program operating under the auspices of the United Nations Food and Agriculture Organization (FAO). The United States both supported the WFP's creation and became its largest contributor.[10]

During the 1960s, food aid evolved as a flexible instrument of U.S. policy in the Third World. When PL 480 came up for reauthorization in 1966, surplus disposal was deleted from the list of official PL 480 objectives. New clauses were introduced to strengthen PL 480's utility as a political and developmental resource. For example, countries receiving Title I import assistance were required to adopt "self-help measures" designed to spur economic growth and increase agricultural production.

The intended developmental focus of PL 480 soon took a backseat, however, to the increased politicization and militarization of Food for Peace. Politics, not nutritional need, guided the yearly allocation process. The bulk of PL 480 resources went to a handful of key U.S. allies, including such countries as Egypt, Pakistan, South Korea, Turkey, India, South Vietnam, and Cambodia.[11]

During the period of U.S. military intervention in South Vietnam, food aid, already a foreign-policy instrument, became a direct instrument of war. The governments of South Vietnam and Cambodia, which received the great bulk of total Title I allocations in the early 1970s, were permitted to use the local currency generated from this food aid for military expenses. Food aid was also being used to feed troops and support pacification programs. In 1973, when Congress began to grow weary of the war and started cutting back on military aid, Title I food aid to South Vietnam and Cambodia suddenly rose from about $100 million to over $450 million for the following year, thereby substituting for lost military assistance.[12] In fiscal year 1974, in the midst of the first "world food crisis" that led to a sharp reduction in the size of the PL 480 program, over two-thirds of Title I aid went to South Vietnam and Cambodia.[13] Finally, public outrage and congressional concern forced an end to the use of PL 480 for military purposes. In 1975, as U.S. troops were pulling out of Vietnam, Congress attempted to restore some balance to the Food for Peace program by modifying PL 480.

The new legislation mandated that 75 percent of Title I food assistance be given to poor, food-short countries, with the remaining quarter left for distribution to any country (this is known as the 75/25 clause).[14] Congress also stipulated a minimum tonnage level for the amount of aid to be distributed directly to needy people under the smaller Title II program. Two years later, the Carter administration succeeded in inserting a human-rights provision in the food-aid legislation that prohibited Title I assistance to the government of any country that "engages in a consistent pattern of gross violations of internationally recognized human rights . . . unless such agreement will directly benefit the needy people in such country."[15]

Congress has continued to make revisions and additions to PL 480. Some changes try to halt the more blatant of its political uses, some foster U.S. commercial interests, and others strengthen the program's humanitarian or development focus. Yet the nagging tension between aid conceived as a benefit to the people of the recipient country and aid as a direct instrument of foreign policy has never been resolved. The 75/25 clause, to this date the only food-aid legislation imposing need criteria, is just not that effective: a full one-quarter of Title I assistance still goes to relatively wealthy, politically important U.S. allies; and as for the aid earmarked for poor countries, within that group there is plenty of room to pick and choose. In addition, the strong role of AID and the State Department in PL 480 management, and the low degree of oversight exercised by Congress, all result in the continued allocation and use of PL 480 for foreign-policy purposes.

To this day Title I food aid continues to be concentrated on a small number of countries, most of them of strategic interest to the United States. Over the period 1977–84, for example, half the value of all Title I shipments went to just five countries, and a full quarter went to Egypt alone.[16] The degree to which these allocations are linked to foreign policy concerns is perhaps best illustrated by the close overlap between the countries receiving Title I food aid and those receiving a special type of grant known as Economic Support Funds (ESF), which is allocated on the basis of security and foreign policy considerations. Over the period 1980–83, for example, fourteen of the top thirty Title I recipients were also among the top thirty recipients of ESF.[17]

THE GATEKEEPERS OF FOOD AID

U.S. food-aid legislation leaves substantial decision-making power in the hands of those who administer the programs. Perhaps because the program started largely as a method for reducing agricultural surplus rather than as a direct foreign aid program conceived solely as such, Congress has left the program largely in the hands of executive branch administrators and set down only basic allocation guidelines. Most of these focus on general political criteria as to the type of nations Congress feels deserve U.S. support. These political conditions, written into PL 480, stipulate that:

– The recipient nation should be a "friendly country" that is not "dominated or controlled by a foreign government or organization controlling a World Communist movement."

– Food aid should not go to countries regarded to be "an aggressor, in a military sense, against any country having diplomatic relations with the United States."

– No agreement will be signed with "the government of any country which engages in a consistent pattern of gross violations of internationally recognized human rights, including torture, . . . prolonged detention without charges causing the disappearance of persons by the abduction and clandestine detention of those persons, or other flagrant denial of the right to life, liberty, and the security of person, unless such agreement will directly benefit the needy people in such country."[18]

These preconditions help identify what countries Congress would consider unacceptable as candidates for U.S. food aid, but they do not give any guidance as to which of the eligible countries should be aided. In terms of positive criteria, the legislation gives mixed signals, for it refers both to furthering United States foreign policy and also to humanitarian and need criteria such as in the 75/25 rule.

Congress, meanwhile, has left these allocation decisions largely in other hands. Owing to PL 480's history as a surplus disposal and market development program, congressional oversight of allocations has been delegated to internal committees mostly concerned with agricultural issues. Funding for PL 480 food loans is handled by the Agricultural Committee in the Senate and the Agricultural and Foreign Affairs Committee in the House and by the respective agricultural appropriations committees of both chambers. The role of these committees, however, is largely to give final approval to allocation decisions made by the executive branch. Furthermore, the initial allocations they approve each year can be changed during the course of the year by program administrators without further congressional approval.

This decision-making structure, by leaving so much in the hands of government administrators, leaves the door open to extensive foreign policy uses of this program. A wide variety of government agencies ranging from the U.S. Department of Agriculture to the National Security Council (NSC) participate in program decision making, but those most concerned with foreign policy appear to dominate the process.

What aid is given to what country is decided through an executive-branch interagency working group, which is part of the Food Aid Subcommittee of the Development Coordination Committee. Here decisions are reached by consensus among representatives of AID, USDA, the State Department, the National Security Council, and the Office of Management and Budget.[19] The first matter decided each year is the overall size and commodity composition of the program. Although year-to-year PL 480 levels are fairly stable, especially since the introduction of congressionally mandated minimum tonnage levels,

USDA must determine the availability of individual commodities, and over the medium run the program still relies on the size of the U.S. farm surplus. Once the exact size of the aid pie is known, agencies begin to calculate the size of the pieces.

Of great influence in aid requests are the recommendations of individual AID and embassy missions. AID missions work directly with nongovernmental organizations, the World Food Programme, and local governments to determine food-aid needs and help define projects, and to relate food-aid projects to other foreign-assistance programs. USDA field representatives, for their part, bear the responsibility of ensuring that scheduled aid shipments will neither disrupt nor undercut previously existing levels of commercial imports from the United States or any other food exporter.

The State Department, AID, and the National Security Council all bring geopolitical concerns to the food aid negotiating table. In 1985, for example, the NSC issued at least two National Security Decision Documents (NSDDs) concerning food aid. The NSC, in its NSDD 167, advocated adopting a new type of Title I food aid called Food for Progress that would be based on a country's "commitment to reform and implementation of policy decisions." The NSC emphasized that "U.S. strategic and foreign policy interests must be served by the Food for Progress program." NSDD 156 declared that the NSC would chair an interagency group with representatives from "State, Treasury, USDA, DOT, OMB, CIA, CEA, AID, the Peace Corps, and the White House Congressional Affairs Office to further define the Food for Progress initiative."[20]

FAVORED NATIONS

Although all the diverse interests and objectives of the U.S. food-aid program are at work in Central America, the political objectives of food aid predominate. Washington's concern with the political turmoil in Central America—not just the Nicaraguan revolution but grass-roots insurgencies in Guatemala and El Salvador—is clearly reflected in a tremendous increase in food aid to this region in the 1980s.

By the second year of the Sandinista government, Nicaragua was cut off from U.S. food aid altogether; meanwhile, aid to its U.S.-allied neighbors swelled. The increase in Title I aid to Central America has paralleled the rise in military and economic aid to this region.[21] In particular, in every country Title I aid began almost hand in hand with security-linked ESF assistance—as well it might, since both programs offer the same type of openhanded dollar support. Most of the increase in food aid to Central America has gone to El Salvador, where a powerful guerrilla movement has been battling U.S.-backed governments since the beginning of the decade. The United States is deeply involved in the Salvadoran civil war; this tiny country, the size of Vermont, is currently the top recipient of U.S. military aid in Latin America.

The U.S. embassy in El Salvador is also using food aid as another way to maximize aid levels for the beleaguered Salvadoran government. U.S. government officials described to us how at one point, U.S. Ambassador Edwin Corr demanded that USDA staff approve the embassy's escalating requests for food aid to El Salvador. Concerns by USDA officials that requested levels were not really needed and would probably compete unfairly with local agricultural production were dismissed. Insisting that the Salvadoran government desperately needed the financial support that would be provided through this aid, Ambassador Corr reportedly sent his inflated aid request to Washington without the customary USDA approval. As one USDA official complained to us, "Food aid in Central America is local-currency driven. Nothing else seems to matter but to find new sources of local currency for the government budget."

As a result of these foreign-policy pressures, El Salvador is currently the largest Title I recipient in Latin America and among the top five worldwide.[22] The Congressional Research Service recently calculated that for FY 1989 El Salvador will be the largest per capita recipient of Title I aid in the world: $6.49 worth of food aid per Salvadoran, versus an average Title I aid level $1.69 for all the countries participating in the program. El Salvador is also the largest recipient of Title II distributive aid in Latin America, even though many other countries suffer higher infant mortality rates and have comparable levels of malnutrition.[23]

The inflated food-aid allocations for El Salvador make evident the uses of the PL 480 program for foreign policy purposes, even at the sacrifice of other program aims such as supporting agricultural development. From a market-development perspective as well, this small and war-torn country would not be a strong candidate for concessional sales. Indeed, such is the administration's interest in making foreign policy use of PL 480 that it has even ridden roughshod over the human-rights restriction placed by Congress on the PL 480 program; El Salvador, along with Guatemala, is one of the worst human-rights violators in the Western Hemisphere.[24] In order to continue aid to these two repressive governments, Washington has evaded this legal restriction either by simply denying these human-rights violations or by claiming that these countries are not "consistent" violators because the number of people being assassinated and disappearing is declining.[25]

PL 480 aid to Guatemala, like that to El Salvador, is largely motivated by the wish to support a U.S.-allied government battling an internal insurgency. In the early 1980s, Congress restricted this support owing to widespread human-rights violations, including the routine use of massacre and torture, carried out by the military regime then in power. This human-rights obstacle was largely removed, however, when the military government allowed the election of a civilian president in late 1986. Today the elevated levels of food and economic aid to Guatemala are portrayed as the reward for democracy— despite continuing human-rights violations under the civilian regime.[26]

Congressional limitations on aid to Guatemala in the early 1980s were not, however, entirely respected by administration aid officials. In one case they used the food-aid loophole to get around congressional limitations on ESF support to this country, limitations that had been imposed in response to serious human-rights violations. As a Congressional Research Service report describes it, "The Administration was able to circumvent, to a degree, the congressional prohibitions against the provision of balance-of-payments aid to Guatemala through the substitution of PL 480 Title I food loans for ESF aid." As ESF funds were cut back in response to Guatemalan human-rights violations, the amount of PL 480 requested for FY 1985 rose from $11.4 million to $21.0 million, and in the end $19.7 million was actually approved. The Congressional Research Service report notes that this maneuver was in part made possible by Congress's habit of not reviewing PL 480 allocations, since this program is usually "seen as a vehicle for food aid or a mechanism for increasing U.S. agricultural exports."[27]

Honduras and Costa Rica, two key countries in U.S. efforts to destabilize the Nicaraguan revolution, have also been given unprecedented sums of U.S. food aid in the 1980s. Honduras, which in the early 1980s signed on as a central player in the contra war against Nicaragua in exchange for large amounts of U.S. economic and military aid, received a food aid reward as well: PL 480 shipments rose from $3.4 million in FY 1980 to $16.1 million just three years later. In the case of Costa Rica, rising U.S. support was motivated not just by an interest in using this country as a base for a second contra front, but also by concern over potential social unrest in the wake of a 1981 financial crisis. Despite yearly USDA determinations that this country, for all its financial problems, could still afford to import its food needs on commercial terms and thus did not require any special assistance,[28] PL 480 Title I shipments rose from nothing in FY 1981 to $23 million in FY 1984 and continued at high levels throughout the 1980s. In this case, foreign-policy interest in maximizing the financial support given by Title I actually undercut normal U.S. commercial exports.

These aid flows to Central America, motivated mostly by foreign-policy concerns, have resulted in disproportionate allocations going to this tiny region. In FY 1986 nearly 10.7 percent of worldwide Title I allocations went to the United States' four Central American allies, whose combined population of 20 million persons represented less than 0.003 of the world total.[29]

SUMMARY

U.S. food aid flows through many spigots, and most of them are open all the way in Central America. The food aid flooding into the region has little to do with hunger and a great deal to do with satisfying geopolitical appetites. This political orientation of food aid is nothing new. It has been evolving ever since food aid became a major part of the U.S. foreign aid program.

In 1990, PL 480 once again comes up for congressional review. It has evolved from a surplus-disposal measure to a multipurpose program that enjoys strong support around the nation and in Washington. Owing to its humanitarian image, the U.S. food-aid program enjoys wide public support. For the giant grain companies, food aid means over a billion dollars in annual sales. The food-aid program reduces farmers' concern about surplus production and low commodity prices. The U.S. Department of Agriculture regards PL 480 as a way to increase agricultural trade and market agricultural commodities and to encourage countries to adopt farm policies in keeping with U.S. trade interests.

For the State Department, food aid is a way to reward friendly governments and punish those that stray from Washington's political orbit. For the Pentagon, it is an essential part of counterinsurgency campaigns. The Agency for International Development, which administers the program, regards food aid as a flexible source of foreign aid that can mold recipient governments to the agency's own political and economic priorities or support beleaguered allies. Nongovernmental organizations and churches rely on food aid as the base of their humanitarian programs.

Food aid has flooded into Central America, and the evidence is everywhere. In agriculture, in politics, in health ministries, in changing consumption patterns, and in refugee camps, food aid is making itself felt throughout the region. Given the magnitude of this influence, it is now time for a closer examination. In the following chapters we will look closely at the uses—and effects—of Food for Peace in a region rocked by war and political crisis.

2

Food as Money

Like ESF, the food loan program operates basically
as a supplemental balance of payments support pro-
gram. . . . The recipients of this aid are countries
of high significance to current U.S. policy in the
region.

Congressional
Research Briefing on food aid
to Central America

GOVERNMENT-TO-GOVERNMENT food aid to Central America—best
viewed as economic aid that happens to arrive in the form of agricultural
commodities—represents the great bulk of food aid to this region. Eight out
of ten bags of U.S. food aid are sold to governments and private businesses—
not donated to the poor and needy. The main purpose of this type of aid is not
to reduce malnutrition, but to help stabilize the economy.

The workings of Title I food aid are little known, either by Central Americans or by U.S. taxpayers. Most people assume that all food aid is donated to
the poor and hungry. The reality is quite different. Title I food aid is not
donated and does not come in bags labeled "Furnished by the people of the
United States of America. Not to be sold or exchanged." In fact, it is shipped
into the country for the express purpose of being sold and is therefore more
likely to end up in the stomachs of the middle and upper classes than in the
bellies of hungry *campesinos*. Some Title I "food aid" is not even food, but
tallow for soap making or corn and soybean meal for animal feed.[1]

In this chapter we examine the exact workings of Title I and other forms of
government-to-government food assistance. In recent years this type of semi-

commercial food aid has accounted for about 80 percent of all U.S. food aid to Central America and about 10 percent of all official U.S. nonmilitary aid to the region.[2] Despite its magnitude, the mechanics of government-to-government food aid are a mystery to most U.S. citizens who support this program with their taxes, and also to the Central Americans who are its supposed beneficiaries.

Government-to-government food aid refers to U.S. agricultural commodities that are either sold at concessional rates or given to recipient governments for resale on internal markets. These commodities were in the past often purchased by government marketing institutes (also known as grain-stabilization institutes), but increasingly they are being purchased directly by private processing firms, such as wheat mills, or by poultry or cattle feeders. Instead of paying the U.S. exporter as in a normal commercial transaction, these private importers pay their own government. The recipient government (although it eventually must pay back the Title I loan) benefits by saving immediate import dollars and also through the funds generated by the sale of the aid to the private importers. Government-to-government food aid, then, is in essence a form of economic support for foreign governments. (See fig. 1.)

This type of food aid increased dramatically in Central America in the 1980s. During the first twenty-five years of the Title I program, from 1954 to 1979, Central American countries received only $10 million in this type of aid. Yet from 1980 to 1988, over $600 million in government-to-government food aid was shipped to the region. Nicaragua, categorized as an unfriendly nation, no longer receives any U.S. food aid, nor has it been permitted even to make cash purchases from the United States. When relations soured with General Noriega, Panama too was crossed off the food-aid list. Yet the four main U.S. allies in the region—Costa Rica, El Salvador, Guatemala, and Honduras—all have warehouses brimming with subsidized U.S. imports.

In a certain sense this food aid is invisible to the region's residents; most people don't even know that these special import programs exist. Food imported under Title I is indistinguishable from food imported commercially: both end up in the hands of private businesses. Although it may be hard to spot, this type of food aid is having an important influence on Central America. Title I food commodities are common ingredients in Central American diets, a major source of profit for local food-processing industries, and a significant form of economic support for Central American governments. (See fig. 2.)

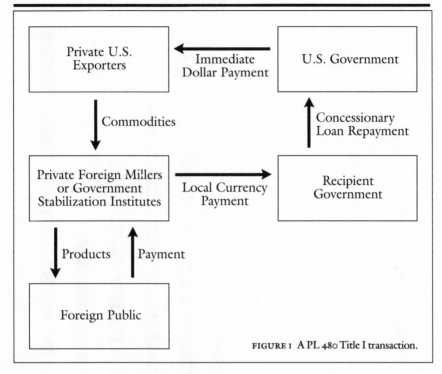

FIGURE 1 A PL 480 Title I transaction.

HUNGRY FOR MONEY

For the most part, the poor and hungry do not benefit from government-to-government food aid. A Congressional Research Service briefing on food aid to Central America, noting the great increase in Title I aid to this region in the eighties, concluded: "The move from grant to loan aid in this area means that, to a substantial degree, U.S. food aid in Central America is being distributed through the marketplace to those who have the money to purchase it rather than through grant aid to needy individuals." The aid does help keep food prices down, but mostly for foods like bread, milk, chicken, and vegetable oil—products consumed more by the urban middle and upper classes than by the truly poor. In Honduras, where almost all Title I imports are in the form of wheat, the urban rich consume twenty-seven times as much wheat per capita as the rural poor.[3]

AID officials explain government-to-government food aid as an element in its economic-stabilization policy. Economic stabilization refers to AID efforts to keep foreign governments and economies afloat through injections of economic aid. Stabilization aid is used to ease balance-of-payments crises and

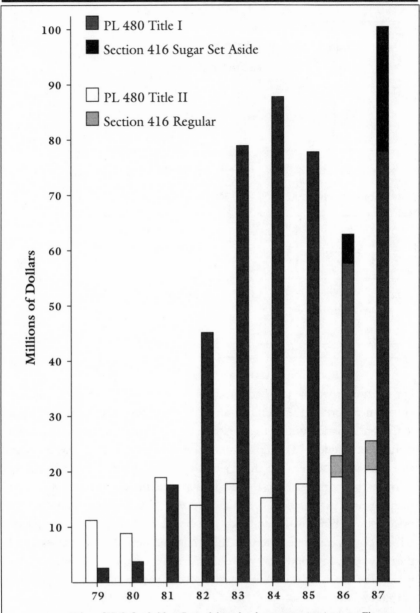

FIGURE 2 Value of U. S. food aid to Central America, by program, FY 1979–87. Figures, which represent commodities shipped, include Title II food aid to the United Nations World Food Programme but exclude Nicaragua. Source: USDA, *Food for Peace Annual Report on Public Law 480*, various years.

PL 480 Title I

The largest U.S. food-aid program, Title I of Public Law 480 does not provide food per se but rather allows very concessional financing terms for the import of agricultural commodities from the United States. Its basic function is to save importing countries dollars they would have spent on commercial food purchases, thereby freeing foreign exchange for other uses. In addition, this aid program contains a resale mechanism to provide importing country governments with immediate budgetary support.[4]

The program works as follows: First, private or public sector importers in the recipient country make purchases from private U.S. exporters through an open bidding process, paying normal commercial prices.[5] These U.S. exporters are paid immediately by the USDA's Commodity Credit Corporation (CCC), while in the recipient country the food importers pay their Central Bank, in local currency, for the U.S. products. This local currency enters the budget of the recipient country.

The recipient government must eventually pay the United States back for the loan, but at very easy and extended terms. Title I import loans carry up to a ten-year grace period, at as little as 2 percent interest. This grace period is followed by a re-payment schedule over as many as thirty years at as little as 3 percent interest. Sometimes a 5 percent down payment is required at the time the loan is signed. Since Title I imports are made at normal commercial prices, the real savings for the recipient country comes in the very concessional financing terms of these loans. Under a special Title I/III program, repayments are forgiven for countries that agree to a program of policy reform.[6]

The funding for the Title I program, handled by the CCC, must be appropriated each year by Congress. Programming for each country is done year by year, with levels for each commodity set in dollars (meaning that the exact volume imported will vary depending on changing prices).

In the field, the program is managed by AID together with USDA. They calculate what amounts of which commodities are needed, negotiate sales agreements and local-currency uses, and monitor program implementation. The commodities, subject to officially declared "availability," are supplied by U.S. private exporters (CCC surpluses can be sold only to the Title II donation program). Title I covers exports of mostly wheat and wheat flour, followed by corn, sorghum, vegetable oil, and rice. This program also finances the sale of nonfood items such as tallow and cotton.

alleviate budget shortfalls, maintain imports and production, and thus keep economies and governments functioning. It is often combined with pressure for countries to undertake structural-adjustment measures to bring down budgetary deficits and promote export production.[7] Since the early 1980s, when the United States became worried about the economic and political stability of the Central American countries, nearly 75 percent of all nonmilitary U.S. aid to Central America has gone for economic stabilization.[8]

The two main instruments of economic stabilization are Economic Sup-

TABLE 2

U.S. Aid to Costa Rica, El Salvador, Guatemala, and Honduras by Main
Program Categories, FY 1987 (Millions of Dollars)

Country	PL 480 Title I	PL 480 Title II	Development Assistance	Economic Support Funds	Peace Corps	Military Assistance	Total
El Salvador	42.0	6.4	133.0	281.5	0.0	111.5	574.4
Guatemala	22.7	8.5	38.0	115.5	3.1	5.5	193.3
Honduras	12.7	5.4	42.7	131.8	5.2	61.2	259.0
Costa Rica	17.2	0.1	18.3	142.5	3.0	1.7	182.8
Total	94.6	20.4	232.0	671.3	11.3	179.9	1,209.5

Source: USAID, Office of Planning and Budgeting, *U.S. Overseas Loans and Grants, Obligations and Loan Authorizations, July 1, 1945–September 30, 1987* (Washington, D.C.: Agency for International Development, 1989).

port Funds (ESF) and Title I food aid. Economic Support Funds are dollars awarded to countries of particular foreign-policy interest to the United States. Because of its foreign-policy objective, the ESF program is technically a form of security assistance.[9] ESF and Title I food aid are very similar in their workings and effects, and both are employed by AID to ease the economic hard times of the Central American governments. They help in two main ways: (1) by softening the foreign exchange or balance-of-payments crisis, that is, providing extra dollars for imports, and (2) by opening up new sources of local currency for financially strapped governments—putting quick money in the budget.

BALANCING PAYMENTS WITH COMMODITIES

Since the early 1980s Central America has been in the throes of a balance-of-payments crisis. Simply put, the dollars these countries have been able to earn on their exports or capture through foreign aid and investment have not been sufficient to cover import needs and debt repayments. Sagging and unstable commodity markets, combined with the rising cost of industrial and fuel imports, left area countries with their dollar coffers empty.[10]

In the case of Central America, normal balance-of-payments difficulties have been complicated by the region's political instability and armed insurgencies. As guerrilla movements gathered strength in Nicaragua, El Salvador, and

Guatemala in the late 1970s and early 1980s, the local private sector, fearful of losing its power and privileges, tried every way it could to shift its dollar profits safely abroad. Hundreds of millions of dollars flowed out of the region and into foreign bank accounts.

Both political and economic factors contributed to the region's acute economic crisis. In a typical vicious circle, the economic difficulties gave rise to new political problems. In the 1980s, as the dollar shortage became more acute, Central American countries found themselves unable to import even the basic productive goods—fuel, raw materials, machinery, fertilizers—needed by their import-dependent economies to maintain production and exports. The resulting widespread shortages and unemployment only worsened the problems of poverty and political instability.

Washington has tried to stave off this crisis—and keep its allies, especially El Salvador, from crumbling as a result of political and economic tensions—by pumping unprecedented sums of economic aid into the region. To supplement the dollar support provided by ESF, Washington policymakers have also authorized healthy amounts of government-to-government food aid. Title I eases the press for foreign currency by allowing each of the region's governments to save $10 to $45 million a year in hard dollar outlays.[11]

Title I assistance to Central America has been on exceptionally advantageous terms. Both El Salvador and Honduras enjoy the longest payback period (forty years) and lowest interest rates (2 percent during the grace period and thereafter 3 percent) allowed by law. These soft terms mean that over the long run these countries will realize a nearly 70 percent savings on their food imports compared with the cost of paying for the goods up front.[12] The long payback period is especially attractive because it is not the recipient government that has to pay back the loans but some future administration.

Moreover, in Central America AID and USDA officials, in order to channel maximum Title I credits to these countries, have been sidestepping the legal stipulation known as the Usual Marketing Requirement (UMR). This requires that Title I assistance be additional to, not substitute for, the recipient country's normal commercial imports, usually calculated on the basis of a previous five-year average. In the case of Central America, the agencies do fill in the space dedicated to the UMR in each Title I sales agreement, but instead of reporting true import levels, they simply write in the word "zero." By allowing U.S. aid to replace commercial imports, this maneuver is obviously designed to maximize these countries' dollar savings.

Dollars saved on food imports can then be allocated to other ends, ranging from debt repayment to productive inputs to arms purchases. Whatever alternative use a Central American government chooses for its savings, food aid helps take off the pressure. Generous Title I import financing also means that governments are better able to guarantee steady supplies of major food commodities, thereby avoiding the political turmoil that food shortages and inflation often cause.

PAYING THE BILLS

In addition to balance-of-payments support, food aid also serves as a type of budgetary support for governments. The local currency (national money) generated when the food is sold to private importers is an important source of government revenue. Local-currency income is very much like tax revenue in that it is generated locally and can be used to cover budgetary expenses.

In times of economic recession and austerity in Central America, local currency generated from food-aid resales is a boon to financially strapped governments. If a country like El Salvador receives $40 million in government-to-government food assistance, this means a quick infusion of an extra $40 million worth of *colones* into the national budget. This extra income helps Central American governments to cover budget deficits and also to sponsor new projects recommended by AID.

In El Salvador, Title I local currencies in recent years represent approximately 3.5 percent of total government spending.[13] In Honduras, from 1982 to 1985, Title I revenues averaged 1.5 percent of the central government budget, 2.2 percent of domestic revenues, and 32 percent of the net budget of the Ministry of Natural Resources (Ministry of Agriculture).[14] In Guatemala, government-to-government food aid from the United States represented about 17 percent of the Guatemalan government's 1987 budget deficit.

Although Title I local currency officially belongs to the recipient government, AID tries to direct its use and thereby shape the country's budget priorities. Rarely does any foreign government give aid carte blanche. Rather, most donors try to maintain some influence over the way their aid is used. At the very least donors try to guard against corruption and misuse on the part of the recipient regime. Often they try to specify the uses to which their assistance can or cannot be put—for example—requiring financial aid to be spent on products from the donating country or prohibiting the use of development aid in war-related programs. In the Title I program, recipient governments must agree to spend their local currency only on programs approved by AID. The activities funded are supposed to be in addition to ongoing government programs.[15]

In practice, however, the use of local currencies to shape government spending patterns has not been very effective. When referring to local-currency generations, AID officials often say these funds are "fungible," meaning that this local currency, while nominally applied to AID-specified uses, in reality cannot be easily traced. Recipient governments often keep their food-aid money in the same account as other funds, making it impossible to track exact uses. When their reporting deadlines roll around, governments simply attribute certain line items in their budget to the PL 480 contribution. Furthermore, even if the funds are spent as specified by AID, it is difficult to ensure that this financing is truly additional. Often it substitutes for what the government might have spent in any case. In Honduras an AID-sponsored study found that tax revenues slated for the Ministry of Natural Resources declined in direct proportion to the increased flow of PL 480 local currency to that office. Rather than adding to the funding available for agricultural programs, food-aid money was simply freeing domestic revenues for other uses.[16]

AID monitoring of local currency has never been strong. The U.S. General Accounting Office (GAO) reported in a 1984 survey of Central American economic assistance that "AID officials told us they do not attempt to closely control or monitor local currencies."[17] Numerous other GAO audits on the region have also reported weaknesses in AID's monitoring and controls.[18] Part of the problem may be that AID, interested in providing theses countries with maximum economic support, is just not that interested in close controls and monitoring, especially since these require substantial administrative and personnel resources.

In consequence, not all local currency is used as stipulated by official agreements. An economist working at SETEFE, a special Salvadoran government office formed by AID to manage the country's "extraordinary budget" (composed of Title I, ESF, and other aid resources), told us of high levels of mismanagement and corruption, with considerable resources being diverted to the war effort.[19] Javier Vargas, an economist at Costa Rica's grain-stabilization institute, also commented on the diversion of local currency: "It could be a good program if the government saw it as a soft loan. But as it is, there is no planning for the future. Resources are just slipping through the government, and most of the money is lost through waste, corruption or theft. Local currency should be used for long-term investment in the future. Instead, we are becoming more dependent and indebted."[20]

One possible beneficiary of the fungibility of food-aid revenues is the military. At a time when other government ministries are being cut back, the ministries of defense in Guatemala, Honduras, and El Salvador have seen their annual budgets steadily expand. Reports by congressional members of the Arms Control Caucus have pointed out that it is likely that the injection of large sums of local currency each year into the national budget permits governments to fund these increased military expenditures.[21] Military and security expenses in El Salvador equaled $230 million in 1986, contributing substantially to the country's $240 million budget deficit. Over 20 percent of that deficit was covered by Title I local currency.[22]

For donors interested in economically stabilizing a recipient country, food aid is an ideal mechanism because it is not as controversial and expensive as direct dollar assistance. Furthermore, the two-step-removed character of local-currency financing helps veil the exact uses to which these funds are put from congressional and public scrutiny. For recipient governments, the local currency generated from food-aid resales represents an easy source of budget revenue and one that is more politically feasible than tax reform. The oligarchies in Central America have blocked most efforts to increase income, property, and export taxes. As a result, the tax rates in countries like Guatemala are among the lowest in the world, leaving their governments crippled and ineffective.[23] Street protests and business shutdowns organized by the powerful private sector in El Salvador and Guatemala have toppled several tax-reform efforts. In dire need of more revenue, Central American governments have grown increasingly dependent on outside assistance, including government-to-government food aid.

FOOD AID AS A POLICY LEVER

Food-aid agreements attempt to shape government policy in two ways: by stipulating how a country must spend its local currency, and also by making participation in Title I conditional upon the recipient country's promising to undertake certain "self-help" measures. The self-help measures are negotiated yearly between AID and the recipient government and are formalized in official Title I "sale agreements." Later "memorandums of understanding"

Section 416 Sugar Quota Set Aside

In 1986 Congress established a temporary Section 416 donation program to compensate sugar-exporting countries for a series of cutbacks in their U.S. sugar sales quota. Under this unusual program, the CCC donated surplus Section 416 commodities to governments of thirty-nine countries affected by the cutbacks, in proportion to the losses taken by each country. The recipient governments then resold the products on their internal markets, just as in Title I, to generate local currency to support their budgets. In 1986, the first year of the program, there was virtually no control over the uses given to resale profits. But in 1987 AID did attempt to tighten up this aspect, asking countries to sign currency-use agreements similar to the ones used in Title I, though without being very strict about exactly what uses were proposed.

By 1988 the sugar set aside program was already being cut back—in part because CCC stocks were running low.[24] The amounts given did not completely compensate the income losses from the sugar quota cuts but were still significant, especially taking into account that the Section 416 SQ shipments were outright donations, with little or no restriction on local-currency uses. The value of the food aid that was delivered through this temporary program up through 1988 ranged from $4.4 million for Costa Rica to $18 million for Guatemala.[25]

---

indicate exactly how the governments should spend the local currency generated by the sale of food aid.

Many Title I evaluations have studied to what degree Title I really works as an instrument of policy reform. The results have been mixed. In cases where Title I assistance is awarded on largely political grounds, AID often seems more interested in giving openhanded support than in using Title I as an instrument of leverage to promote reforms. But even where reforms are truly sought, Title I still has its limitations. This "additionality" is difficult to ensure without close supervision and monitoring, which in turn requires substantial administrative resources. Frequently, Title I local currencies and self-help measures do not appear to significantly alter normal government spending patterns.

The self-help approach also has the limitation common to all attempts at aid conditionality: the magnitude of the policy changes a government is willing to undertake in exchange for aid depends on its need for the resource being offered as well as the attractiveness of that offer. Food-aid programs, for all their advantages, may not always be at the top of a government's shopping list: this is tied aid that covers the import of only certain items, and it also has fairly high administrative and reporting requirements. There is a limit, therefore, to what a government may be willing to do in exchange for Title I aid, particularly if alternative resources are available. For these reasons, food-aid conditions have generally centered on limited and specific agricultural-sector measures felt to be of benefit to the importing country as well as to the United States.

The list of self-help measures became a standard part of food-aid agreements in the mid–1970s when Congress became concerned that countries receiving U.S. food aid were doing little to improve their own abilities to produce and buy food and thus were in danger of becoming dependent on continuing U.S. assistance. Self-help measures have thus focused on developing recipient countries' agriculture by establishing agricultural input industries, improving transport and storage facilities as well as marketing and distribution systems, creating a favorable climate for private investment, providing adequate incentives to producers, establishing institutions for agricultural research, creating farmer training programs, and so forth. Measures have also included programs to control population growth and to improve the health of the rural poor.

Though many of the self-help measures refer to the development of agriculture in general or are designed largely to benefit the United States (such as animal and plant pest-control programs), there has also been a clear congressional intent for these measures to improve local food production and the living standards of the rural poor. The preamble of the PL 480 law states a major goal of the act is "to enhance food security in developing countries through local food production." The body of the law refers to "increasing per capita production" and suggests as a self-help measure "devoting land resources to the production of needed food rather than to the production of nonfood crops." In Central America, Title I sales agreements—in reference to the global considerations that are to guide the implementation of all self-help measures—typically contain the following general language:[26]

Self-Help Measures
to improve the production, storage, and distribution of agricultural commodities. The following self-help measures shall be implemented to contribute directly to the developmental progress in poor rural areas and enable the poor to participate actively in increasing agricultural production through small farm agriculture.

Local Currency
The proceeds . . . will be used . . . in a manner designed to increase the access of the poor in the recipient country to an adequate, nutritious, and stable food supply. In the use of proceeds for this purpose, emphasis will be placed on

directly improving the lives of the poorest of the recipient country's people and their capacity to participate in the development of their country.

But although the aims of reducing poverty and increasing food supply remained inscribed in the law and in the preamble to food-aid agreements, over the past decade the content of those agreements has somehow shifted. In Central America, AID is currently using Title I self-help measures not just to support general agricultural and agribusiness development, but also to support broader macroeconomic reform and privatization programs, policies that actually undermine the welfare of the poor. Basic grains production, meanwhile, is largely ignored in favor of the promotion of new export crops. Somehow, the benign-sounding term "policy reform" today means something very different than it did in the past.

One reason for this change is that worldwide debt problems and the rise of monetarism in the West caused AID's view of economic development to shift dramatically in the 1980s. Instead of the previous concern with basic needs, grain production, and the rural poor, AID's new watchwords are the free market, exports, and the private sector. Furthermore, instead of concentrating largely on specific infrastructural and productive projects, much more attention is now being paid to the overall macroeconomic environment.

Food-aid conditionality is also being approached differently. AID has begun to package this aid together with other types of assistance in order to strengthen the agency's ability to use these programs in promoting policy change. Title I assistance, notes AID, "increases, sometimes substantially, the magnitude of the total assistance package we are able to offer governments, and thus increases our ability to influence their decisions."[27] Furthermore, AID is now coordinating its own assistance with international financial institutions like the International Monetary Fund (IMF) and the World Bank. All three together are using their aid leverage to demand major economic and political reforms oriented toward increasing the role of market forces and decreasing the role of the state. These reforms are part of what foreign financial institutions call "structural adjustment programs."

FOOD AID AND STRUCTURAL ADJUSTMENT

Structural adjustment refers to an economic strategy to revise the macroeconomic policies of Third World debtor nations, in order to bring these countries' balance of payments into line and enable them to pay off their external debts. Such changes are now routinely demanded by international financial institutions such as the IMF and World Bank, and increasingly by AID as well, as a condition for their economic support. Food aid, along with other forms of U.S. economic assistance, is currently used to support structural adjustment around the world and in Central America.

Adjustment advocates argue that the Central American nations are facing financial crisis largely because they have pursued erroneous economic policies, in particular the maintenance of overvalued exchange rates and excessive public-sector spending. In consequence, these countries need strong measures to hold down imports, boost exports, and thereby free up funds to meet mounting debt payments. A main thrust of the adjustment approach is to get internal prices into line with international prices, starting with a currency devaluation to make imports more expensive (to hold them down) and making exports cheaper in foreign markets (to stimulate sales). A national adjustment program generally also calls for reduced social service budgets, cutbacks in public-sector employment, privatization of state-operated enterprises, removal of protectionist tariffs, and increased incentives for exports and private-sector investment.

Though many of the measures advocated by the international banks make sense, the strong-arm approach they have employed throughout the Third World has frequently been criticized as one-sided, overly ideological, and insensitive to the acute social and economic problems of these countries. The international banks, interested primarily in debt repayment, impose measures that force the entire burden of adjustment on crisis-ridden debtor countries while ignoring the problems caused by the economic policies and practices of lender nations and the whole structure of world trade.[28] The export price reductions brought by currency devaluations are expected to boost exports of traditional commodities, such as coffee, in a world market that has a limited demand for these products and is often ruled by export and import quotas.[29] The stress on nontraditional exports such as assembly industries or vegetable production pushes these countries into extremely competitive markets (where only some will come out ahead) and exploits their lack of environmental and labor regulations.

Much of the theory of adjustment is based on abstract free-market economic models that may not work in economic systems characterized by monopolies and by inequalities in technology, knowledge, and power, where states indeed play important regulatory roles. In addition, adjustment assumes economic efficiency to be the only valid determinant of decisions, to the detriment of other worthy political and social goals.

The adjustment programs now being imposed in Central America are subject to many of these weaknesses. These economies suffered greatly in the late 1970s and early 1980s owing to declining terms of trade as well as capital flight brought on by political unrest and war. Governments held on to previous exchange rates as long as possible, substituted state expenditures for private investment, and borrowed heavily abroad, but eventually these efforts collapsed.

El Salvador and Honduras, given their military importance to the United States, were partially bailed out. El Salvador in particular receives generous U.S. economic and military support not linked to any painful adjustment requirements. Aid given for political reasons, especially to ensure the survival of a beleaguered government of strategic interest to the United States, can hardly be conditioned on reform; El Salvador knows that it will receive U.S. aid whether it complies with policy reforms or not.

Both Costa Rica and Guatemala, in contrast, were forced to turn to adjustment packages supported by the IMF, the World Bank, and AID. These adjustments included devaluation, cuts in public spending, and a loosening of market controls. AID has also insisted on support for private enterprise.

Some restructuring was obviously needed. As one economist noted: "Because of the magnitude of the income losses imposed on the region by international and military events, there was no economic alternative to a reduction in consumption, growth, and employment."[30] Yet given the ongoing political crisis in the region, painful adjustment measures may well not be the medicine needed right now. With the basic causes of the region's social conflicts unresolved, free-market economic policies alone are unlikely to renew investor confidence and growth. Central American economic recovery, argue many regional economists, depends largely on a resolution of the region's political conflicts, and structural adjustment packages will likely inflame rather than diminish this unrest.[31]

Nor does AID's faith in the entrepreneurial capabilities of the Central American private sectors—up to now characterized more than anything by corruption, union busting, capital flight, speculation, and opposition to basic economic and social reforms—seem justified. Finally, the burden of structural adjustment is being borne largely by the poorer social sectors. For example, deficits are being attacked by cutting social services, not by reducing defense expenditures or raising taxes.

Although economic readjustment may or may not be able to establish the basis for renewed long-term growth, all agree that in the short run free-market policies can have dire consequences for the Third World poor. Currency devaluation, often the first step in these programs, discourages imports by making them that much more expensive in terms of local currency. Prices of imported goods (including such basic items as fuel, fertilizer, food, and industrial components) rise, lowering both consumption and import-dependent production. In other words, devaluation brings both inflation and a fall-off in production. Real wages, and employment, decline dramatically—especially in the short run. The state, meanwhile, is cutting back on subsidies and social services. The country may well end up more able to pay its debts, but literally at the cost of rising malnutrition and death rates among the poor.[32]

Despite the negative consequences structural adjustment has on poverty and nutritional levels, AID is now using Title I, a program designed to "directly improve the lives of the poorest," as leverage to help impose these adjustment packages.[33] In Guatemala, a recent AID "Action Plan" noted the use of Title I in support of policy reform: "Title I local-currency generations will be used in a coordinated fashion with ESF generations to support the GOG [government of Guatemala] economic and financial adjustment packages to be put into place in May 1986."[34]

In Costa Rica, AID has taken a particularly active role in promoting economic adjustment. It has stipulated that the government must eliminate all export taxes, adopt a new monetary law, establish a special line of government credit for the private sector, and divest itself of certain holdings. The use of Title I food-aid conditionality in achieving these measures is explicit. AID reports that "we will also attempt to enhance the use of PL 480 in the policy dialogue particularly concerning agricultural prices and GOCR credit policy which constrains productivity in the sector."[35]

Food aid's new role in structural adjustment is not limited to acting as leverage, however. Given the negative impact of structural adjustment on food security of lower-income groups, food aid in recent years has also been identified as a cushioning agent. The dollar and budgetary support offered by Title I can help reduce balance-of-payments and budget deficits. In the period of inflation brought on by devaluation and import restrictions, Title I can help hold down food prices. Title II donations, for their part, can help sustain the income and nutrition levels of the poor.

Obviously, these approaches hold an element of political as well as humanitarian interest. Of particular note is the targeting of adjustment-motivated food aid particularly for urban populations. Most Title I commodities (wheat, vegetable oil, feed grains, and tallow) go to produce items consumed primarily by urbanized populations.[36] Adjustment-motivated food distribution programs, for their part, are often specifically directed to the urban poor. Although it is true that structural-adjustment programs usually hit urban low-income sectors harder than they do the rural poor (which typically are less dependent on wage income), it is also true that in most Third World countries the living standards of the rural poor remain far below those of urban slum dwellers. Urban sectors are targeted not just because they are affected by adjustment but also because of their greater political volatility.

In Guatemala City, a massive food-for-work program, the first ever in urban areas, is being used to soften the impact of a U.S.-backed structural adjustment program on the city's shantytown dwellers.[37] A recent AID evaluation of food aid in Guatemala concluded, "The political context, in which a new, more democratic government must increase taxes and cut spending to restore economic growth and financial stability, justifies use of Title II to alleviate consequences of structural adjustment on the poor."[38]

United States food assistance means more food and money for the "friendly" countries of the Central American isthmus. Yet food aid, like most bilateral assistance, also brings with it certain impositions on national sovereignty. Aid is used to help support the adoption of foreign economic and political models. Any economic model, however, is necessarily molded by the development ideology then in vogue, as well as by the donor country's economic and political interests. Twenty years ago it was basic needs and local market-oriented industry; today it is the free market, the private sector, and an all-out export push.

Yet increasingly, some national leaders are beginning to challenge the conditions of aid, saying the agreements amount to "blackmail" and foreign intervention in the internal affairs of their countries. Not only do these adjustment measures affect the poor, but as will be described in the following chapters, they also have serious consequences on small-farm agriculture and national food security. The ministries of agriculture are starting to question

Title I in regional forums. In Costa Rica, associations of *campesinos* and small farmers are urging their government to reject U.S. food aid and all its attendant conditions. What many critics object to is not so much that national economic policies must be adjusted as that outside institutions like AID specify the exact type of adjustments a country has to make.

IMPORTS FOR THE PRIVATE SECTOR

Central American governments are the most favored beneficiaries of U.S. food aid, but U.S. grain exporters and local food-processing firms are also doing well by PL 480. From the food-aid negotiations that occur in the United States to the self-help measures and local-currency expenditures, private business is an honored guest at the food-aid table.

Using food aid to support the private sector—both at home and abroad—is a tradition of the Food for Peace program. Before the 1980s, Central America received little Title I food aid. In other parts of the world, however, Title I food aid has long had a role in boosting private business interests. First and most obviously, Title I is an export-promotion program that increases sales for U.S. exporters while expanding the market for future commercial sales. Imported Title I wheat has helped change eating patterns throughout the Third World, creating permanent markets for U.S. grain companies. Under the Cooley loan program (a mechanism to channel local currency), Title I repayments financed the construction of mills used to process the U.S. wheat. Companies like Cargill, Continental Flour, and General Mills were among those that benefited. Another plus for U.S. business has been the Cargo Preference Act, which stipulates that at least 75 percent of U.S. food aid be transported on U.S.-flagged ships, which generally charge higher prices than their international competitors.

In Central America the private sector can be found at each stage of the Title I food aid process. Even before the food aid arrives in Central American ports, the region's businessmen are already fully involved. Local wheat millers, for example, first tell USDA what grade and quantity of wheat they want. Then, along with local government officials, they travel to the United States to negotiate the purchase.

When the cargo ships unload their huge containers of U.S. food aid, buyers from the private sector are also there to transport the food to their ice cream factories, wheat mills, and poultry businesses. On paper the food passes through government hands, but in practice government officials never even see the goods. Official involvement, except in those increasingly rare cases when local grain-stabilization institutes handle the transaction, is limited to receiving the private sector's local-currency payments.

The main financial advantage for the Central American importers is that they do not need dollars to buy the wheat, milk powder, oil, and corn feed they import under food-aid programs. Instead they pay their governments in more readily available local currency. Without the Title I program, wheat importers, for example, would have to apply for rationed dollars doled out by the Central Bank or resort to buying high-priced dollars on the black market. The food-aid program, then, allows companies to skirt the problem of the scarcity and high cost of dollars.

In Honduras, a wheat miller confided that he wouldn't be in business if it weren't for U.S. food aid: "Dollars are just too hard to find." Or as an AID official reported, "If the millers had to pay with dollars for all the wheat they are now importing, they couldn't do it—and the result would be a lot less wheat for Hondurans." In Guatemala, the buyer for the country's largest wheat mill said he believes termination of the Title I program would cause wheat prices to rise because millers would have to resort to the black market to find the dollars they needed to import wheat commercially. This would in turn mean a sudden rise in price for wheat-based products and a probable drop in demand. "Without PL 480 we would have forty times more problems," he asserted. "But we will always be in business because the government would be under such political pressure to keep the population supplied with bread."[39]

The second main advantage of importing through U.S. aid programs is the current low prices of U.S. commodities compared with prices for local grains. The poultry sector, for example, can save large amounts of money by importing cheap yellow corn from the United States instead of buying it locally. Agribusiness profits depend on how much the government allows them to charge consumers for the chicken, eggs, flour, and milk that they produce with these U.S. imports. Given the poor record of Central American governments in imposing price controls and the manifest eagerness of agribusiness to avail themselves of U.S. food-aid programs, windfall profits are obviously accruing to these importers.

In El Salvador, for example, our interviews revealed a major dispute between the two major cattlemen's associations over who would be allowed to buy what percentage of Title I and Section 416 imports. In Honduras, an AID-contracted study found that wheat importers had not been required to pass the full savings from imported wheat on to their consumers. Although the international wheat price had fallen, internal bread and pasta prices did not follow suit. Another bonus for the millers was the flat rate the government was charging for internal transport (unloading, port charges, and freight), considerably below the real cost of these services.[40]

Central American millers and poultry farmers also experience a few disadvantages from their participation in food-aid programs. Bureaucratic delays in the program management are their main complaint. Red tape in Washington or in national capitals spells delayed shipments. Purchases must be made on dates specified by the U.S. government, reducing an importer's ability to shop around or to hold out for the best possible price. Importers also complain that Title I agreements are generally concentrated in the latter part of the fiscal year, requiring those who rely on the program for most of their import needs to invest in expensive storage facilities. Under Section 416 donations there is the additional problem of the low quality of the surplus stocks being dumped. Despite these complaints, however, we heard of no companies withdrawing from the program.

NURTURING BUSINESS

The attractive purchasing terms for Title I commodities are only the beginning of food aid's support for the private sector. Title I self-help conditions often stipulate that governments change their policies to improve conditions for the private sector. In addition, an increasing amount of the local currency generated by food aid is being plowed back into private-sector lending programs.

During the 1980s the concept of private-sector support, pushed by the Reagan administration with substantial bipartisan backing, came to dominate management of the food-aid program. Food assistance, like most aspects of U.S. foreign aid, has been remodeled to better serve private enterprise, both at home and abroad. New provisions of Public Law 480 specify that foreign currencies accruing to recipient governments should be used "to foster and encourage the development of private enterprise." Governments are also obligated to create "a favorable environment for private enterprise and investment, both domestic and foreign."[41]

In Central America we have seen this "private-sector support" philosophy at work in the following ways:

- The channeling of increasing quantities of food aid directly to the private sector instead of these imports being handled by state marketing institutes.[42]
- The use of food aid as leverage to privatize these grain-stabilization institutes
- The allocation of increasing amounts of local currency for lending to the local private sector instead of for supporting government development efforts.
- The insistence that recipient governments increase financial incentives for agroexport production, which diverts resources away from support for basic grains production.

In Guatemala, AID stipulated that the government channel all Title I commodities to the private sector rather than through the local stabilization institute and that it undertake a series of economic development projects that promote private-sector participation. The Honduran government, to be eligible for U.S. food aid, was required to increase the role of the private sector in the marketing of grains and to divest itself of part of the grain-stabilization institute. In Costa Rica, AID required the government to adopt a plan of export promotion for nontraditional produce. In El Salvador, the government was obligated to promote private-sector investment in agribusiness and pressured to pass a new export-promotion law.[43] These private-sector support measures, set forth in Title I sales agreements, complement other measures to aid businesses that are sustained by AID Development Assistance and Economic Support Funds.

Congress etched the private-sector focus of food aid into law with the 1985 Food Security Act. Section 108 of this law establishes a mechanism by which Title I local currencies are channeled back to the U.S. government, which then makes them available to local private-sector lending programs. Worldwide, at least 10 percent of the global value of Title I agreements must now go to this program.[44] The U.S. government directs this local currency to intermediate financial institutions (IFIs), usually private banks and financial companies, for lending to promote private investment and to finance private-enterprise facilities that, among other things, help increase the consumption of U.S. agricultural commodities.[45]

In Central America, Section 108 private-sector support agreements are already operable in Guatemala and Costa Rica. The 1987 Title I agreement with Costa Rica, for example, specified that nearly $5 million of the total $16

Government Guaranteed Credit

Government-to-government food aid is not just a foreign assistance program but also serves to promote U.S. exports. The spectrum of U.S. agricultural export programs ranges from the concessional food-aid programs at one end to strictly commercial sales on the other. Midway between the two are the Export Credit Guarantee Programs of the Commodity Credit Corporation (CCC), which, while not exactly aid, are still a boost to a poor country's import abilities.[46]

CCC export credit guarantee programs are designed to increase commercial sales of U.S. agricultural commodities by enabling U.S. exporters to offer importing countries more favorable financing terms than they would get under purely private sales transactions. Under these guarantee programs, when a U.S. financier extends credit to cover a sale abroad, the CCC (backed by the U.S. Treasury) guarantees to make repayments if the foreign importer defaults. Countries are given three years to pay for the food they import under this program, a very long period for this type of nonproductive import.

Like Title I credits, CCC credit guarantees underwrite U.S. farm exports while doubling as economic aid to friendly gov-

ernments. Although the CCC guarantees serve primarily to promote commercial trade, foreign-policy considerations still do play a role in their allocation. In its country "Strategy Statements" for Central America, AID lists CCC credits as balance-of-payments support for these nations. One of the stabilization measures recommended for Central America by the Kissinger Commission was the increased use of CCC export credit guarantees.[47] Food brought into Central America through CCC credit guarantee programs rose rapidly in the 1980s. CCC guarantees currently cover as much as 30 percent of all U.S. agricultural exports to Central American countries.[48]

One USDA representative we interviewed judged CCC credits "very political" in that there is a great deal of pressure in Washington to keep these programs going to Central America even though these countries are not the best commercial prospects. "These programs are done with mirrors," he said, "but you can be sure that the U.S. taxpayer is paying for them somewhere down the line. . . . Without this credit, the Central Bank wouldn't have the dollars to allow imports of U.S. agricultural commodities. Under this program, the U.S. exporters always get their money— otherwise they wouldn't be selling to Central America."[49]

million program be channeled to private enterprise through Section 108. Of this Section 108 money, 95 percent was scheduled "to foster and encourage the development of private enterprise institutions and infrastructure" while 5 percent was used for "technical assistance to agribusiness," especially USDA projects to increase U.S. export sales.[50]

SUMMARY

Most U.S. food aid, as we have seen, is not shipped to Central America with humanitarian intent. Instead, about 80 percent of food assistance to this region is a form of financial aid, whose principal objective is to support governments. Resale food aid provides the Central American governments with both balance-of-payments and budgetary support, freeing up funds they can direct to nearly any use. Secondarily, this semicommercial food aid provides important benefits for wheat millers and other agroindustrialists.

Title I assistance is often used as a lever to induce recipient governments to institute policy changes. But this conditionality is often not that effective, and to the degree that it is, many of the conditions currently imposed run contrary to the stated objectives of Title I legislation. Instead of focusing on agricultural development, as the legislation directs, Title I in Central America is being used, in conjunction with other aid programs, to push through controversial macroeconomic reforms that actually undermine the welfare of the poor. Program conditions, and resources, are also largely directed toward private-sector support.

Understanding the complicated workings of government-to-government food aid—the resale process, local-currency generation, and the conditionality of food-aid agreements—is essential to grasping the ramifications of the boom in U.S. food aid to Central America. In its impact on local food production and distribution systems, U.S. food aid may be having its most profound effect. It is to this subject that we turn in the following two chapters.

3

Food Aid versus Food Security

What a Honduran has to eat from local food production is going down. Food aid is creating a dependency on the United States that is going beyond what is rational. What happens if tomorrow the U.S. has a bad crop and can't supply the grain Honduras needs? The U.S. will be transferring its own problems to Central America.

DR. JUAN ANTONIO AGUIRRE
representative of the Interamerican Institute
for Agricultural Cooperation (IICA)
in Honduras.

THE FOOD FOR PEACE annual report proclaims: "A primary objective of PL 480 since its inception has been to alleviate hunger worldwide: in the short term, by providing food; and in the long term, by increasing food production in deficit areas and promoting economic activity." Solutions to the problems of hunger and inadequate food production in Central America are clearly needed. Food aid, however, does not appear to be an appropriate response to the serious problems of poverty and import dependence affecting the food security of this region.

Central America, a major exporter of food products to the United States, currently does not produce enough food for its own people, though this region has more than enough land resources to meet its basic food needs.[1] After all, Central America easily satisfies U.S. appetites for coffee, sugar, bananas, cotton, and beef. Yet despite its agricultural richness, little by little this region has been losing its own food self-sufficiency.

For decades now, Central American grain output has barely kept up with population growth, and as per capita food consumption slowly increased in the 1960s and 1970s, consumer demand began to outstrip production. Food imports made up the difference. In the twenty-three years from 1963 to 1986, the region's grain imports increased five times over.[2] From 1970 to 1986, Central American cereal production increased some 45 percent and cereal imports jumped 125 percent. Today imported cereal, especially wheat but also corn, beans, and rice, contributes about one-fifth of the region's annual consumption of basic grains.[3] In addition, Central America is importing ever larger quantities of powdered milk and vegetable oil.

The increasing import dependence of the Central American countries is cause for concern. According to the United Nations, "The ultimate objective of world food security should be to ensure that all people at all times have both physical and economic access to the basic food they need." The concept of food security thus implies a reliable supply of food. For Central America, local food production, supplemented by food imports only in real emergencies, would be the surest way to guarantee this supply. A country like Japan or the United States, with large and fairly stable foreign-exchange earnings, can import a large portion of its food and still be reasonably food secure. But for a poor country dependent on unstable commodity export earnings, a reliance on imported food may be a luxury it can ill afford.

Nor can Central America be considered food secure when the majority of its population goes hungry. The hunger endemic in Central America is directly related to the poverty of most of its people. Whereas the families of the rich landowners and industrialists consume many times their food requirements, most Central American households are simply unable to grow or buy enough food to meet their biological needs. Even before the economic crisis of the 1980s, at least half of all Central American families were trying to survive on a diet insufficient to cover their basic needs, and two out of three Central American children exhibited stunted growth due to malnutrition.[4] Landlessness and unemployment, compounded by low wages, were the chief causes of this poverty-induced malnutrition.

Today, with the loss of jobs and falling real wages brought on by economic crisis and adjustment measures, nutritional levels are declining even further. One measure of this is the recent reduction in the apparent per capita consumption of basic grains.[5] Simply put, millions of Central Americans, never able to afford an adequate diet, are now eating less than ever.

For the Central American nations to achieve food security, they must both improve their food production and provide a means of livelihood for all of their population. Food security requires that governments take the measures—be they land redistribution, pricing policies, nutritional programs, agricultural development projects, or investment in social services and jobs— necessary to ensure that all citizens, no matter what their income, receive a minimum level of food.

Food aid does play a role in Central American food security. But as we will show in the next two chapters, that role is decidedly mixed. While helping to make up immediate shortfalls, this aid is also allowing governments to avoid needed reform, encouraging import dependence, and undercutting local production. The long-term result of all this aid will be not food security, but greater dependence and hunger.

A DUAL AGRICULTURAL SYSTEM

Central America is predominantly an agricultural region. But agroexport production, not local food production, has traditionally controlled the region's best land. Not only do agroexporters monopolize the most fertile lands, particularly the rich coastal plains, they also have preferential access to credit, irrigation, technical assistance, and other forms of government support.[6]

Local food production, by contrast, is relegated to the region's worst and most marginal lands. Except for rice, grown on medium-sized commercial farms, the important task of producing staple foods has been left mostly to peasant farmers laboring by hand on tiny plots. Since the Spanish Conquest, agroexport production has been pushing the small farmers who produce the region's corn and beans farther and farther into the eroded highlands and isolated jungle regions of the Central American isthmus. Without sufficient land and largely bereft of government support, the *campesinos* of Central America are increasingly unable to raise enough grains even to meet their own family food needs, much less supply the internal market. Indeed, the low income of the Central American peasantry is a major cause of the poverty and hunger endemic in this region, which is clearly concentrated in the rural areas.

This dual structure of Central American agriculture—the best lands owned by a few large agroexport growers and the worst lands owned (or rented) by a multitude of small grain farmers—lies at the heart of the region's food-security crisis, affecting both grain supply and family income. Large farmers, who are notorious for leaving significant portions of their land idle, simply cannot be bothered with less profitable grain farming as long as export cropping is where the real money is to be made. The peasant sector, excluded from these export options and in any case preferring to minimize risk by at least growing enough corn and beans to meet family food needs, thus supplies the bulk of Central American grain production.

Central American peasant grain producers, however, have low productivity (at least compared with the giant mechanized farms of the United States) and even lower incomes. Though they labor hard over their crops and get maximum use out of every bit of land, the peasants' plots are often small and scattered, and their land is steep and eroded from overuse. Fertilizer costs are so high that many producers cannot afford to use it, and credit to finance input purchases is usually just not to be had. Lack of technical advice, poor storage facilities, and transport problems further undermine this sector's hope of advance.

Central American governments have always been more concerned about increasing exports and currying the favor of rural oligarchs than about meeting the basic needs of the peasantry.[7] Not only are most Central American peasants extremely poor, most are also illiterate and, except in Costa Rica, have had little success in organizing themselves to pressure for more land and other government support. Indeed, in El Salvador and Guatemala nearly every attempt at peasant organization has been met with bloody repression. The *campesinos'* most pressing and immediate demand for land just seems too threatening to the large landowners that dominate these countries. Land-distribution measures have therefore been extremely limited, consisting mostly of the colonization of isolated jungle regions.

Although relatively uninterested in rural poverty, Central American governments have shown sporadic concern with the problems of meeting internal demand for grains. In the late 1960s and 1970s these governments, often with the support of foreign donors, took a variety of measures to strengthen basic grains production. Tariffs and import controls were set up to shield local producers against outside competition. A type of regional protectionism was set up as well: area governments signed an agreement to buy from each other before turning to extraregional suppliers. Grain-stabilization (marketing) institutes were established to regulate internal supplies and prices. Agricultural development banks and agricultural extension agencies were founded to serve small and medium-sized farmers as well as large ones. The Guatemalan government even passed a law, largely ignored, requiring large farms to plant 10 percent of their land in grains.

These measures proved only a partial solution to the region's food supply problems, however, and did little indeed for the deeper problems of rural poverty and malnutrition. The peasantry's main problem, lack of land, was not adequately addressed, and the new credit and extension services were quickly monopolized by the larger farmers. Peasant farmers proved willing to use fertilizer; indeed, many found it necessary to squeeze yet another crop from their exhausted and eroded fields, but too often they had neither the income nor the credit opportunities to finance its purchase. Though grain production continued to rise in line with population, this was largely due to the colonization of new lands, not to increases in productivity and yields.

Nor were the measures to protect and stabilize producer prices very effective. With consumers clamoring for cheap food and industries trying to keep wage costs down, the temptation was to abandon protectionist import controls and open the door to imports anytime prices began to rise. Meanwhile, the grain-stabilization institutes, designed to bid up depressed harvest-season producer prices and then release their purchases to consumers throughout the year, never adequately fulfilled their price-stabilizing and support function. Budgetary constraints often kept them from buying enough grain to have a real impact on the market. They also often slid into offering across-the-board consumer subsidies that quickly bled their coffers dry. Often the institutes' customers were not so much poor consumers as agroindustries that basically used them as cheap warehousing.

After decades of mismanagement and neglect, the problems of rural Central America are now coming to a head. As peasant colonizers slash and burn the lasts bits of tropical jungle, the agricultural frontier, so long an easy escape valve, is all but exhausted. Deforestation and erosion of overused lands are destroying the region's resource base—and future generations' prospects of livelihood—at a truly alarming rate. The rural poor, unable to find a piece of land with which to support themselves or sufficient work and wages on the export plantations, continue flooding into the capital cities. There they live in cardboard shacks, survive by their wits, and develop a taste for wheat bread and Coca-Cola. The government, which never cared whether these people were hungry when they were forgotten and isolated peasants, obliges by authorizing yet more wheat imports.

Continuing rural poverty, environmental destruction, rural-urban migration, and increasing import dependence are serious problems with important long-term economic and social consequences. Yet alarming as these problems may be, up to now they are not being adequately addressed by local governments wrapped up in shorter-term pressures of debt financing and export promotion, or even in stabilizing their own political power. For the moment area governments are most concerned with solvency and survival.

Furthermore, the problems of Central American agriculture are largely structural ones having to do with the distribution of land, wealth, services, and political power. These are explosive political issues that, given the rural oligarchs' continuing power in these societies, most are loath to touch. AID, still smarting from the fiasco of the Salvadoran land-reform program, is not in a hurry to burn its hands again. As explained above, its current policy focuses on economic stabilization and "structural adjustment"—measures that tend to concentrate income and are imposed even in the face of popular discontent— not on the redistributive measures so urgently needed.

The problems of Central American grain production are thus being largely ignored. Rather than addressing the needs of the poor peasant grain farmers, which would address the dual problems of rural poverty and stagnating grain production in one blow, AID has shifted its attention to the introduction of high-value export crops. Rather than seeking to protect the incomes of local grain producers, AID is supporting structural adjustment programs that will tear down the few protective measures and subsidies this sector does enjoy. If as a consequence of increased competition and neglect Central American grain production were to stagnate further—no problem, the United States will be more than happy to supply.

Much of the debate over the future of the Central American grain production has to do with the peasant sector's supposed inefficiency and high costs. AID officials argue that grain production will never bring these small farmers a decent income; it is better that they switch to other crops. They point to the United States' lower grain prices and higher yields to emphasize just how backward and inefficient the Central American producers are. AID economists speak of economic opportunity costs and the need to open the economy to international market forces. Meanwhile urban consumers, as well as cattle and poultry feeders, pressure their governments to ensure a constant supply of cheap grains and bread.

With U.S. grain prices having such an influence on the area and the U.S. farmer being proposed as a source of grain supply for Central America, it is important to understand something of the dynamics of grain production and prices in the United States. It is to that topic we now turn.

THE FOREIGN FACTOR IN U.S. FARMING

The food security of Central America is tied to the dynamics of U.S. agriculture. Central America's agricultural system is strongly influenced not only by U.S. food-aid and agricultural-development programs, but also by U.S. commodity trade. The United States is the region's main source of food imports and its main agroexport market.[8] Furthermore, as the world's main grain supplier, the United States has a decisive influence on international commodity markets.

Since World War II, agriculture in the United States has grown increasingly dependent on export production. Today, one-third of U.S. corn production and two-thirds of U.S. wheat is shipped abroad, and agricultural exports bring in over $25 billion a year. Only a small percentage of these exports goes to Central America, but the imperatives that drive U.S. exports greatly affect food production in the region.

Over the past few decades in particular, foreign markets have been the escape valve of U.S. agriculture, plagued throughout the century by surplus production and depressed prices. Caught up in a cost/price squeeze, individual U.S. farmers compensate for lower unit earnings by constantly striving to increase their productivity, thus contributing to surpluses and depressing prices even further.[9] Government-supported agricultural research, which has brought great advances in such fields as chemical pest control, mechanization, or genetic engineering, has been another factor behind the tremendous increase in U.S. agricultural productivity over the past fifty years. United States productive potential now far outstrips domestic U.S. demand.

Over the years the U.S. government has developed various mechanisms to attempt to support agricultural production and prices. The most basic of these, for this discussion, is the "loan rate," a predetermined low sale price that triggers U.S. price-support measures. It is called the loan rate because when prices fall to this predetermined level, the main measure taken by the U.S. government is to lend farmers money to enable them to hold off selling their crop until prices improve. In effect, when there is a surplus the loan rate determines the market price of U.S. commodities. The U.S. government also makes certain use of supply-management programs, especially those based on reducing acreage. These include paying farmers to put fragile land in conservation reserves and tying loan eligibility to leaving a certain number of acres idle.[10]

A supply-management focus predominated in the 1930s and 1940s but did not prevent substantial surpluses from accumulating in the wake of the Korean War. In the early 1950s this approach was abandoned in favor of a surplus-reduction strategy based on both PL 480 aid and exports. The main tool of the export thrust was lowering the loan rate to make U.S. exports more competitive. Foreign sales, stimulated not just by the low price but also by rising demand in both the Eastern bloc and developing countries, quickly began to rise.

United States agricultural exports registered a tremendous increase over the next three decades, particularly in the 1970s. From 1970 to 1982 they rose seven times over to reach a height of $42 billion. This largess was largely lost on U.S. farmers, however. Despite planting "fencerow to fencerow," as exhorted by administration officials, their earnings were limited by the same low prices that helped move these commodities abroad. In fact, average annual net farm income in 1974–80 stood at just half the level, in real terms, that it had been in 1942–54.[11] The main beneficiaries of this high-volume, low-price export push were agricultural supply industries and the large grain corporations, who earned their usual commission on each sale.

So low were farm incomes that the U.S. government began to give farmers "subsidy payments" to make up for the low loan rate price. Farm groups argued, however, that this "subsidy" went not so much to the farmer as to the grain corporations. Though they hurt farmers, low prices did not affect the corporations' earnings, but rather helped them maximize sales abroad. With fair producer prices, argued the farmers, no such subsidy would be needed.

In the early 1980s U.S. agricultural exports suddenly slumped, falling to $25 billion by 1986. Many debates were held on the reasons for this decline, and many solutions were proposed. Some economists pointed to the worldwide recession, Third World debt problems, and an overvalued U.S. dollar as explaining the sliding foreign sales, and they proposed measures such as debt relief. Others focused more on foreign competition, held to be either "fair" (in which case the U.S. farmers were guilty of inefficiency) or "unfair" (in which case the problem was the export subsidies used by other grain exporters to compete with U.S. sales). Ultimately it was the latter "free-market" interpretation, supported by the grain companies, that won out, and in the 1985 farm bill weak supply-management policies were combined with a further drastic lowering of the loan rate. Meanwhile the United States began to pressure its competitors to stop subsidizing their exports. In effect, a trade war had been declared.

This trade war has had drastic effects on both the U.S. budget and the U.S. agricultural economy. With farm prices so low, even below the cost of production, subsidy payments to farmers ballooned. When these were cut back, farmers' incomes dropped and many farm operations, already suffering from high interest rates and elevated production costs, went bankrupt. Millions of family farmers, through no fault of their own, suddenly lost their land and their livelihood. The fabric of rural America was unraveling, and export-driven policies were largely to blame.

Meanwhile surpluses, and depressed prices, remained. Despite the lowered loan rate and a more aggressive use of a whole array of export subsidy programs (EEP, GSM-102, and even PL 480), the hoped-for export revival in export earnings did not materialize.

Farm groups argue that this whole price drive is a mistaken approach. Agricultural competitors, as hungry for export markets as is the United States, will always struggle to match the U.S. price, no matter how low that might go. Strong-arm U.S. tactics to prohibit them from using subsidies are a losing battle. Meanwhile the earnings on even high-volume U.S. sales are undercut by low unit prices, and U.S. farmers are left living on government "subsidies" or losing their farms altogether. The farmers' movement advocates better-designed and more strenuous supply-management programs to bring prices back up to profitable levels and encourages negotiations with agricultural competitors for fair division of a then much more profitable market.[12]

Adjusting U.S. output to the total quantity really needed (for the domestic market, exports, aid programs, and reserves) would have other advantages as well. The all-out export drive of the past few decades resulted in damaging and wasteful overuse of the nation's land, water, and fuel as well as a high dependence on chemical fertilizers and pesticides. Overirrigation made groundwater levels drop in many regions. The farm belt has been rapidly losing its world-renowned topsoil, and erosion rates have never been worse.

Not only has the price-driven export push hurt U.S. farmers, strained the federal budget, and destroyed the nation's nonrenewable resources, it has also had a serious negative impact on the developing world. Grain-exporting countries like Argentina and Brazil have seen their export earnings undermined just when they most need them to help meet their debt payments. And grain producers throughout the developing world, not just in Central America, have seen their livelihoods undermined by competition from artificially low U.S. prices.

The developing world is an important market for U.S. agricultural products, in particular feed grains.[13] But those purchases must be made from a position of economic strength, which in most developing countries depends on a healthy, broad-based farm sector. Throughout the world, the best markets for U.S. agricultural exports are those with broad-based income growth, which itself depends on a healthy farm sector and diversified productive structures. As incomes rise, demand for grain-fed meat and wheat products also increase; and with overall economic strength, countries can then afford to import these products.[14]

Horning into poor countries' markets with cheap grains is another matter altogether. This competition, in the interest of short-term sales, can undermine the type of long-term development that would benefit both the United States and the developing world. Throwing poor Third World farmers out of business will bring neither growth nor social stability. Neither should U.S. exporters feel complacent about sales to poor countries motivated largely by these nations' loss of self-sufficiency and high rural-urban migration rates. The sharp reduction in developing countries' imports in the wake of the recent debt crisis shows just how fragile many of these economies, and thus U.S. markets, are.

The export lobby in the United States, however, seems to lack this long-term vision; nor does it often show a clear understanding of how the dynamics of economic development affect demand. In 1985 President Reagan's secretary of agriculture John Block explained the administration's blunt approach: "The push by some developing nations to become self-sufficient in food production may be reminiscent of a by-gone era. Those countries could save money by importing more of their food from the United States. Modern trade practices may mean that the world's major food producing nations, especially the United States, are the best source of food for some developing countries."[15]

Central American countries, like developing countries around the world, are being encouraged to make food-security decisions based on a short-term economic calculus that ignores the income and employment needs of their own people. Falling rural incomes, unemployment, and exaggerated rural-urban migration provide no basis for long-term growth and welfare.

Furthermore, Block's contention that the ideal of self-sufficiency belongs to a "by-gone era" implies that the developing world can continue to rely on the United States for its supplies. Even a cursory look at history shows the folly of that approach. What about the "world food crisis" of 1973–74, when massive Soviet purchases pushed the price of grain beyond the reach of many poor countries? What about Washington's repeated use of trade and aid embargoes against countries that have dared to step out of its geopolitical orbit? What about the more recent price rises brought on by the 1988 drought? The boom-and-bust cycles that characterize U.S. agriculture, and the even greater instability in world food trade and prices, make the abandonment of self-sufficiency a risky strategy.

THE ROLE OF FOOD AID

Food aid is intricately connected to the export-oriented U.S. farm policy we have been describing. PL 480 is not just a foreign-assistance program, it is also an export-promotion program set up and designed to aid U.S. agroexporters. As such, food aid can provide competition for recipient-country producers.

In the 1950s and early 1960s PL 480 loans were an important mechanism to help keep down U.S. surpluses, financing a third of more of total U.S. agricultural exports. With the tremendous surge in commercial U.S. exports, however, this surplus disposal function was largely superseded. Especially when export prices soared during the 1973–74 world food crisis, PL 480 program levels were cut back sharply. No longer did the United States have to give out soft loans to move its products when countries were lining up to buy them with cash. But soon Congress, emphasizing the program's other political, economic, and humanitarian objectives, decided to maintain PL 480 by mandating minimum tonnage levels. Since then PL 480 has represented a fairly steady 4–6 percent of the value of U.S. exports.

The reduced role of PL 480 in surplus disposal does not, however, mean that its role in supporting U.S. agricultural interests is over. It still helps boost U.S. exports that extra bit higher and, even more important, helps to penetrate and build future commercial markets. For USDA and the grain companies, the promotion of U.S. agriculture is still a central PL 480 objective. Indeed, in their recent efforts to revive U.S. commodity exports, these agricultural interests have been continually promoting the market-development role of this program. Market development is not just a side effect of PL 480, it is an integral part of program design.

In Central America, the political objectives of the U.S. food-aid program—the stabilization and pacification of the region—are paramount. If allocations were made on market-development grounds alone, these countries, except perhaps for Costa Rica, would certainly not figure on the list of candidates. Nevertheless, once introduced into the region, PL 480 does have an important impact on local agricultural markets and production. In particular, it is fomenting the region's import dependency on the United States.

Central American import dependency means not just more U.S. sales, but a food dependency that further strengthens the U.S. political and military control over this area. This import dependency can have very harmful consequences for the long-term development and political stability of the Central American region.

By using PL 480 in pursuit of immediate political and economic objectives in Central America, AID and USDA are ignoring other important program goals, in particular, those of supporting the local food production and the economic development of the recipient countries—approaches that in the long run might be more in the interests of both U.S. and Central American farmers. While supporting the Central American governments, U.S. food aid is undermining the already weak grain sectors of these countries. This it does in four distinct ways:

– By serving as a market-development tool.
– By encouraging a preexisting propensity to substitute local production with food imports.
– By lowering local food prices and production.
– By promoting, through conditionality, certain models of agricultural development and food distribution.

NEW MARKET FRONTIERS

A major goal of U.S. food-aid and credit-guarantee programs is to encourage recipient countries to rely on imports from the United States. PL 480's market-development function has been pursued mostly through channeling aid to countries that previously were not major importers, thereby introducing them to the United States as a source of supply. The program has proved an effective tool of market penetration. As P L 480's agribusiness lobby frequently points out, seven of the top ten commercial customers for U.S. agricultural commodities—including Japan, Taiwan, South Korea, and Egypt—were previously food-aid recipients.[16]

The food-aid program also represents a free government service designed to help grain-trading companies expand both their current and future sales. Title I sales generate the same profits for the big U.S. grain companies as does any other commercial export. The only difference is that the U.S. government immediately pays the bill.[17] From the point of view of the grain corporations, then, Title I creates immediate markets by having the U.S. government finance purchases that otherwise might not have been made. The recipient countries, meanwhile, come to depend on these foreign food supplies.

In Central America, the main goal of P L 480 is to give balance-of-payments and budgetary support to the region's U.S.-allied governments, especially the unstable Salvadoran regime. Yet this same aid fosters a long-term dependence on U.S. imports. Title I assistance and credit-guarantee programs keep Central American markets stocked with U.S. foods even when countries would not be able to afford them commercially.

Title I commodities are a major source of supply for Central American agroindustries. By encouraging the growth of poultry farms, wheat mills, and soap and vegetable-oil factories, P L 480 helps create a structural dependence on continued imports. When the food aid stops, these industries, needing the supplies to continue their level of operations, will pressure their governments to keep importing the commodities even on commercial terms.

In addition, the Title I sales process is intentionally set up to train local agroindustrialists in the art of importing from the United States.[18] For each Title I transaction, private Central American importers fly to the United States, where they are taken step by step through each phase of the sale: opening the bidding process, filling out the proper forms, arranging transport, and so forth. They also, of course, make their personal and professional contacts within U SDA and the private grain and shipping companies. This training mechanism not only helps build up Central American technical import capabilities, it also builds loyalty to U.S. suppliers as opposed to those from other countries.

The local currency generated from food-aid resales, especially those funds channeled into new Section 108 private-sector credit programs, also plays a part in market development. At least 5 percent of Section 108 funds are required to go into market-development activities such as consumer education efforts, trade fairs, or port building. Of course, the "self-help measures" stipulated by AID in food-aid agreements have long contained measures to promote an increased openness to trade with the United States. At times, recipients must even promise to allow the United States a "fair market share" of future imports of a certain commodity. In Central America, food-aid agreements have required recipient countries to build new storage facilities for imported grains.

U.S. food aid also shapes consumer tastes. Title I, as we discuss below, has price effects that help shift consumption patterns toward imported goods. Distributive programs do the job by giving foreign foods away free. Admittedly, low-income aid recipients will not be as good a market as those with more spending power; but these distributive programs are very large, covering up to a third of the entire Central American population. As soft-drink manufacturers well know, small purchases, multiplied by millions, quickly add up.

Under distributive food-aid programs, such items as powdered milk, lentils, and wheat flour are put directly into the hands of more than eight million Central American consumers, many of whom might not have tried these products otherwise.[19] The "nutritional education" that often accompanies these handouts teaches recipients how to prepare these food to make them acceptable to local tastes and needs. Most people in Central America do not have ovens; thus women are taught to use their wheat-flour rations to make pancakes; and *panqueques* are now a food that every Guatemalan City slum child seems to know and love. Besides getting used to eating foreign foods, recipients may also get the impression that these are somehow superior to their traditional diet.

Of all distributive programs, feeding schoolchildren probably has the most impact on changing consumer tastes and demand. These programs tend to be very large, to hit recipients at a formative age, and to cover the children of middle-class as well as poor families.[20] Schoolchildren are often fed imported foods such as nonfat dry milk, canned sardines, corn-soy-wheat mix, oatmeal, or processed cheese. When these children are adult consumers, many of them may be choosing Quaker Oats for breakfast and sardines for lunch.

Market development is an important part of the U.S. agricultural system's agroexport drive. Government support for market development through food aid and other subsidies has opened up Central America and other Third World regions to U.S. commodities. The tragedy lies in food aid's tendency to develop tastes and needs for imports that countries really cannot afford. On the day these aid programs end, food imports will suddenly require governments to dig deep into their dollar reserves.

ENCOURAGING IMPORT DEPENDENCY

For Central American governments and private-sector elites, U.S. food aid is very enticing. It offers the government immediate dollar and budgetary support on easy payment terms. The food-processing industries benefit by easier access to commodities of lower price and often higher quality than those available on the internal market. Without food aid and other U.S. export promotion schemes, it would be difficult for dollar-short governments to maintain such a high level of food imports.

Central American governments, chronically in deficit, in particular appreciate the budgetary support offered by Title I local-currency generations. Food aid as economic aid actually gives recipient governments a vested interest in maximizing assistance. Instead of calculating exactly how much food needs to be imported to cover agricultural shortfalls, government officials are often calculating how much budgetary support will be generated by each Title I transaction. Eagerness to get the local currency generated through aid resales often outweighs concern over possible adverse effects in the agricultural sector.

Ironically, since the resale funds are channeled largely to agricultural programs, the Ministry of Agriculture is left with a certain conflict of interest. Agricultural ministries are well aware that smaller and more carefully programmed food aid flows might be the best thing for local farmers, but these might also mean cuts in the ministry's budget because of lost local currency. In addition, these ministries are under heavy pressure from agroindustries that want them to open the door to the lower-priced U.S. market.

AID suffers similar vested interests. By focusing on food aid's role in giving additional economic support to U.S. allies—support, furthermore, that is easy to get through the U.S. Congress—close calculations of market need are often left aside. The sudden upward revision in the FY 1985 Title I request for

Guatemala, for example, was a response not to a sudden Guatemalan shortfall but rather to Congress's cutting back on ESF assistance for that country. By seeking to maximize aid flows, AID may end up allotting amounts of food aid that exceed real market needs.

Sometimes these programmed shipments are cut back, as was a FY 1986 donation of powdered milk to Costa Rica, but at other times they go through. AID is pushing a heaping food-aid platter at Central America. Washington AID officials have been known to refer jokingly to the problem of "stuffability." As the head of the Guatemala Food Security program described it, "If we ask for five, AID says, 'take ten, take ten.'" Area agricultural ministers have begun to express worry about high levels of Title I assistance in regional forums.

AID itself has acknowledged that it may be giving countries more food aid than they can absorb. In 1987 testimony before a congressional committee, AID official Thomas Reese reported that AID was investigating possible overprogramming of food aid. "This problem," he conceded, "may be especially critical in Latin and Central America. . . . commercial markets may not be able to absorb additional food without negative effects."[21] Yet one year later U.S. Ambassador Edwin Corr insisted on requesting a higher level of Title I aid for El Salvador than USDA officials in charge of calculating Salvador's internal market needs were prepared to recommend. The ambassador reportedly felt so strongly about the Salvadoran government's need for more aid that he sent a cable off to Washington without the customary USDA endorsement signatures.

In this case the politically motivated escalation in food-aid shipments to El Salvador apparently alarmed even some USDA officials. Normally, though, USDA has shared AID's lack of concern about overprogramming or disincentive effects. After all, the department's job is to promote U.S. agricultural exports.

Responding to concern that the U.S. food-aid program was negatively affecting agricultural production in the Third World, the U.S. Congress in 1977 passed the Bellmon Amendment. This legislation stipulates that no food aid be delivered until the USDA determines that the planned aid will not create disincentives for local prices and production and that the country has sufficient storage capacity and other infrastructure to handle the food.[22]

In Central America this legal obligation is being performed in a most

Food Security: A Regional Issue

Food imports compete with Central American production not only for domestic markets but also for regional ones. Although all Central American countries are now importing basic grains in addition to wheat, these nations also occasionally produce marketable surpluses of beans, corn, or rice. There is, however, virtually no regional trade in basic grains. To find buyers for their extra rice or beans, Central American countries have had to look as far as Africa, even though neighboring nations may be experiencing shortages in those very commodities.

Why don't Central American countries enjoying surpluses trade with those in the region with commodity deficits? Food aid is a major reason. If a country comes up short in basic grains, AID often suggests importing that commodity as food aid, and local governments, enticed by Title I's easy credit terms, accept. International market prices also play an important role. Central American producers simply cannot compete effectively with lower international prices (kept low in large part through developed country subsidies) and are often forced to sell their produce at a loss.

To protect and support the Central American countries' grain production, the Central American Grain Protocol of 1966 stipulated that any Central American Common Market country wishing to import must offer first-sale rights to other market members. Although this agreement was never fully operable, it is now being further undermined by cheap Title I food flooding into the region. Central American agricultural ministers are upset about this outside competition. In 1985, largely at the instigation of the Honduran minister of natural resources, the Central American Marketing and Price Stabilization Commission (CCMEP) addressed this problem and agreed to:

"Exhort the U.S. government that when a country from the area requests PL480 assistance to cover a deficit of a food product that is produced in Central America, that this be covered with the surplus production of the countries of this subregion, by which manner acquisition costs will be reduced by eliminating value added in marketing and transport."

"Recommend to the area countries that [PL480 imports] be effected only when emergency shortages affect the whole Central American region, in this way avoiding that these purchases become permanent; excepting those articles which because of their special characteristics cannot be produced locally."[23]

In 1987 commission rhetoric was even stronger. Members acknowledged that international prices are often lower than Central American prices, but they attributed high Central American production costs to the high prices of imported inputs and elevated interest rates and traced low international prices back to exporting-country subsidies. The danger, it was suggested, is that "a country can run the risk of dismantling its agricultural structure to substitute it with imports sold through what may be temporary dumping practices."

The discussion continued: "Donations that supposedly cover emergency situations [*situaciones emergentes*] can, nevertheless, have disincentive effects because they always affect producer prices. . . . it would be better that such assistance come in the form of other products such as machinery or inputs." CCMEP's final resolutions were for all food-aid imports (donations and con-
Continued

cessional sales) to be realized through the local marketing institutes, "to insure that this support . . . does not harm productive structures," and to orient these programs in support of local production.[24]

Just a few months later, the Regional Council for Agricultural Cooperation (CORECA) officially adopted a resolution questioning the benefits of food aid and requesting the Central American Nutrition Institute to help member countries study the possible negative effects of food aid on self-sufficiency, as well as its role in changing food-consumption habits.[25]

Although Central American agricul-

tural officials are increasingly recognizing that cheap food imports and food aid can undermine agricultural livelihoods and long-term food security and undercut cooperation among the Central American countries, other government interests often override these agricultural and regional concerns. In the short term it is indeed cheaper, and often easier, to import food from the United States than from a Central American neighbor. Encouraged by the U.S. government and multilateral banks, cheap food policies almost always win the day against policies that stress regional cooperation and regional food security.

perfunctory manner. Every time a new food-aid agreement is signed, USDA officials cable Washington reporting compliance with the amendment. Usually these determinations state that the planned aid will not significantly affect local agricultural production because the internal production of that commodity is insufficient (or in the case of wheat, nonexistent).

The USDA's Determination 13495 in December 1987 for importing into Guatemala $15 million in wheat and $3 million in vegetable oil simply states: "The shortfall in vegetable oil production to meet domestic demand during 1988 is estimated at 35–40,000 MT. The importation of vegetable oil considered under this program will not constitute a disincentive to oilseeds/vegetable oil production." Regarding wheat, the same determination explains that only 46,000 metric tons (MT) is produced locally in Guatemala and that the wheat requirements for the country were estimated to be 201,000 MT for 1988, and "consequently the wheat imports will not constitute a disincentive to wheat production." Determination 927 for El Salvador in January 1988 states: "Because of El Salvador's climate and terrain, conditions preclude wheat production. All wheat for processing and consumption is imported. Consequently, the importation of wheat considered will not disincentivate domestic production."

For Central America, at least, Bellmon amendment determinations contain no hard supply and demand data nor any serious analysis of price effects. The programming of food aid in dollars introduces an added element of uncertainty into this determination, since at the time the cables are sent exact tonnage levels still are not known. But even more seriously, substitution effects between different commodities (such as wheat substituting for rice or corn) are not acknowledged, thereby excusing wheat—the main component of U.S. food aid to Central America—altogether from consideration. This routine method of complying with the Bellmon amendment violates the intent of the law and ignores AID instructions on the matter. According to the AID food-aid handbook: "An analysis is needed of any substantial disincentive effect of supplying requested commodities . . . to the recipient country's domestic production. . . . If the Country Team has reason to conclude that distribution of PL 480 Title I commodities may have a substantial disincentive effect on domestic production of the *same or related* agricultural commodities in the importing country, the reasons should be fully explained and immediately reported to Washington." (Authors' emphasis.)[26]

WHAT ABOUT WHEAT?

More than two-thirds of the total volume of government-to-government food aid to Central America is in the form of wheat. (See table 3.) In the 1980s, Title I and Section 416 wheat deliveries to Central America have exploded. Ten years ago Costa Rica, El Salvador, Guatemala, and Honduras bought all their wheat on commercial terms from the United States or other suppliers. Today some 95 percent of the wheat imported by these four countries is covered by U.S. food-aid loans. Title I wheat sales to Central America not only are financing these countries' wheat imports, they are also helping to push wheat imports to higher levels than ever before.

Though of all the Central American countries only Guatemala produces any wheat, products such as bread, pasta, pastries, and pancakes are eaten throughout the region. The streets of San Salvador are lined with pizza parlors, and many Guatemalan restaurants routinely serve sliced bread instead of corn tortillas. Asked what was the typical local dish, a Honduran soldier in Tegucigalpa told us "chow mein noodles."

Despite annual USDA determinations assuring that all is well, there is evidence that the abundance of concessional wheat is creating important disincentive effects for locally produced basic grains, particularly corn and rice. Traditional patterns of consumption and production are being significantly affected, and the region is becoming dangerously dependent on U.S. goodwill for its continuing food supplies.

What Are Disincentive Effects?

Price disincentives occur when food imports increase local food supply above the level of effective demand. This causes prices to fall, undermining the earnings of local farmers. As a result, local farmers tend to produce less or shift to other crops.

If priced the same as locally produced commodities, food imports can lower prices by increasing overall supply. If the imports are priced below the local product, these imported commodities will take over the market share formerly filled by local suppliers. These disincentive effects usually occur within one product but also occur between products that are close substitutes, such as the basic grains (wheat, corn, and rice).

Central Americans have not always eaten wheat. It was not until the 1950s that wheat-flour products started to become common. Various factors—both economic and social—led the Central American populations to start consuming more wheat. One was USDA promotional programs as well as advertising by local (but frequently U.S.-owned) wheat milling companies. Another was rising income and urbanization spurred by several decades of industrial growth.

Studies from around Central America, confirming a worldwide trend, show that wheat consumption normally rises both with family income and with urbanization.[27] Wheat is what economists call a "positive good"; that is, as families get more income, they spend a greater proportion of their budget on wheat products. This contrasts with an "inferior good" such as corn, to which wealthier families direct a declining proportion of their income.

The substitution of wheat for other grains is also associated with urbanization. One study was able to isolate the influence of urbanization on Honduran wheat consumption: "Being in a large city, rather than in a rural area, means a person consumes daily 28 grams more of wheat, for the same per capita income and family size."[28] This difference might be partially explained by the greater convenience of mass-produced bread compared with traditionally prepared grain products; only processed corn products, such as cornflakes or ready-made tortillas, seem to have much acceptance on the urban market. Another factor is the urban population's high exposure to advertising and to U.S. life styles.

For all these reasons, wheat consumption in Central America steadily increased from 1950 to 1980. Wheat consumption has been rising steadily over the past four decades, even in the absence of government-to-government food aid. In Guatemala, for example, average per capita apparent consump-

TABLE 3

Government-to-Government Food Aid to Central America by Commodity,
FY 1979–87

Product	Thousands of Metric Tons	Millions of Dollars	Percentage of Total $
Wheat/wheat flour	2,269.2	$485.6	69.1
Vegetable oil	126.3	78.4	11.2
Corn/sorghum	539.1	64.2	9.1
Tallow	119.0	47.8	6.8
Rice	38.9	11.9	1.7
Soybeans/soy meal	32.2	7.1	1.0
Cornmeal	32.0	3.0	0.4
Nonfat dry milk	3.6	2.8	0.4
Beans	5.6	2.1	0.3
Total	3,166.0	$702.9	100.0

Source: PL 480 Title I sales agreement and U.S. Agricultural Attaché reports.

tion of wheat increased about 25 percent over this thirty-year period. In Honduras, per capita apparent consumption rose from forty-five grams in 1973 to fifty-eight in 1983.[29] According to the USDA, by 1980 wheat represented a significant part of the Central American diet—ranging from 6 percent of average caloric intake in Honduras to 11 percent in Costa Rica.[30] The significant level of wheat consumption in Costa Rica can probably be attributed to that country's higher per capita income, better income distribution, and higher degree of urbanization, compared with the other Central American countries.

When balance-of-payments problems and recession hit Central America in the early 1980s, wheat imports initially slumped, but they quickly recovered as Title I programs began to finance an ever increasing share of these imports. By 1984, Title I credits were covering the bulk of Central American wheat imports, and these purchases continued and even accelerated their upward climb. (See fig. 3)

Between 1982 and 1987, despite the continuing stagnation of the Central American economies, a continual erosion in average real incomes, and ongo-

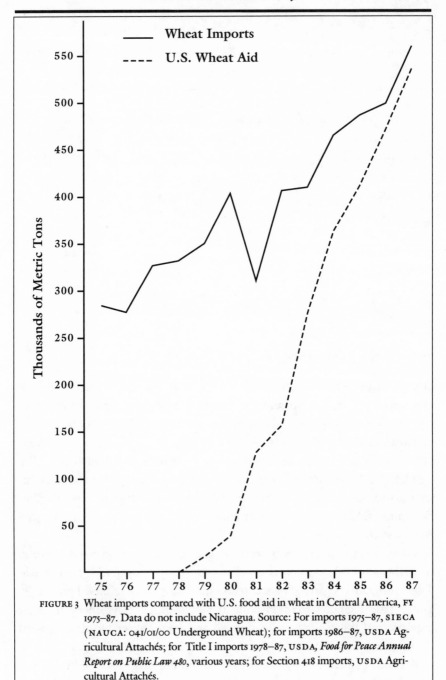

FIGURE 3 Wheat imports compared with U.S. food aid in wheat in Central America, FY
1975–87. Data do not include Nicaragua. Source: For imports 1975–87, SIECA
(NAUCA: 041/01/00 Underground Wheat); for imports 1986–87, USDA Agricultural Attachés; for Title I imports 1978–87, USDA, *Food for Peace Annual
Report on Public Law 480*, various years; for Section 418 imports, USDA Agricultural Attachés.

ing balance-of-payments problems, wheat imports to Central America rose some 37 percent, over three times as fast as population.[31] Two factors brought new impulsion to Central American wheat imports. The first was a sharp drop in international wheat prices as world surplus stocks increased and the United States revised its price-support policies.[32] The second factor was the encouragement given wheat imports under PL 480's super-soft financing terms. Wheat was suddenly cheaper on the international market, and Central American countries no longer needed cold cash to import it. They simply signed Title I agreements with AID that allowed them up to forty years to pay.

These factors in turn had an impact on Central American wheat consumption. Large quantities of wheat imported at favorable low prices caused internal wheat prices to fall. Wheat became relatively cheaper compared to corn or rice. As a result, consumers began to buy more wheat-based products. As an AID/USDA–contracted study of Honduran agricultural policy concluded:

> At the consumer level, one of the most pronounced trends in prices has been a decline in the price of wheat-flour relative to the retail price of most other basic foods. Regression analysis of the determinants of wheat demand indicates that this trend in prices has strongly influenced the change in consumer diets toward more use of wheat products. It seems likely that the pricing policy on wheat imports has encouraged the substitution, at the margin, of wheat products for corn and other traditional staples in the average diet.[33]

Another Honduras study showed the same results: "Wheat imports would have been about 22 percent lower in 1985 if wheat's domestic price had been maintained constant in real terms at the 1975 level."[34] The volume of wheat consumption per capita, which had represented 14 percent of that of corn and rice in 1975–77, rose to 22 percent by 1984–86.[35]

Most of the increased wheat consumption is concentrated in the cities. But the favorable price of wheat and its easy availability are starting to change consumption patterns in rural areas as well. This was noted by the U.S. agricultural attaché's 1987 report on the basic grains situation in Costa Rica: "Low-income people living in rural areas have begun to substitute pasta for rice for about two meals a week, as people find pasta more convenient to carry to remote areas and because pasta prices compare favorably to rice prices."[36]

For the four countries under study, between 1980 and 1985 the per capita availability of corn and rice markedly declined, while wheat, in contrast, held steady or else increased.[37] The increasing consumption of wheat in Central

America—fomented in part by U.S. food aid—may be bringing nutrition losses to poor families. An AID-contracted study in Honduras concluded that corn was about twice as cost effective as wheat in terms of nutritional value. Families that are switching to wheat as a daily food may be suffering substantial nutritional losses.[38]

The Honduras report also assessed the negative impact that lower wheat prices and increased imports were having on local corn prices and production. The study concluded that wheat imports were undermining the market price of corn for farmers, who as a result were cutting back on corn production. According to the model used in the study, the corn output growth rate might have been cut by more than half in recent years as a direct result of cheap wheat imports.

In Honduras we talked to Ramon Velásquez, director of the Institute of Social and Economic Investigation, about changing consumption patterns in Honduras. "Bread is having a profound impact on Honduras," he warned, "but so far nobody seems to be paying any attention to the deepening crisis." Velásquez suggests that the loss of income to corn farmers is promoting rural-urban migration: "It used to be that a peasant's security was intimately connected to his having his own *milpa* [cornfield]. But that is changing as bread is replacing corn as the main staple. It doesn't make any short-term sense to grow corn any longer as wheat prices drop relative to corn. Bread is proletarianizing Honduras as people give up the fight to produce their own food and seek income to buy bread. This pushes them to the cities, creating new urban problems."[39]

It is not clear to what degree PL 480 itself is responsible for these trends. Even without PL 480, low U.S. wheat prices would have encouraged rising imports and consumption. But in the absence of Title I food aid, the dollar-short Central American governments would undoubtedly have imported less.

A Catholic Relief Services evaluation of food aid in Honduras drew this conclusion:

> Without the benefit of a Title I program, with its high grant element and soft loan terms, the Honduran government would have felt the true foreign exchange costs of the country's increasing dependency on wheat imports. . . . Feeling the squeeze, it is not completely unreasonable to suggest that in the medium term, the Government might have started to invest more in the agricultural sector and restrict wheat imports as a move towards self-sufficiency. The fact that successive

Governments have not pursued this policy may well be because the Title I program virtually eliminated the pressure to do so.[40]

DIRECT DISINCENTIVES

Title I wheat imports, through substitution effects, clearly are capable of creating serious disincentive effects for local corn and rice farmers—a possibility irresponsibly ignored by U.S. program managers in Central America. Local production also faces the challenge of direct competition from foreign commodities, especially corn, brought in through both distributional and resale programs. The danger exists that, unless carefully managed, these aid imports could undermine local production of those basic foods.

In the short term, food imports into Central America are necessary. Local food production in Central America is simply not meeting demand, so governments must allow imports of those items not being produced in adequate supply (vegetable oil, soybeans, corn, rice, and dairy products). Imports would occur whether food aid existed or not, and indeed they must occur if Central American food prices are not to go through the roof. But at the same time, the import option—made even easier by generous food-aid terms— enables these governments to continue to avoid the reforms needed to address flagging internal production. And in some cases, by helping to increase the total volume of imports beyond what is strictly necessary, soft credit and donations also dampen local prices and production.

Central American countries are now importing corn regularly. Central America—where corn was first cultivated and where Mayan legend tells how God made man from corn dough—is no longer able to grow enough corn to satisfy demand. Corn is the traditional basic food of the Central American people, and for the region's large Indian population, it is of deep cultural and religious significance.

But corn is also a feed grain, and in the past two decades burgeoning poultry and cattle industries have consumed an ever greater share of national corn supplies. Today about half of all Costa Rican corn goes to feed animals, and in the other three countries feed uses absorb up to a fifth of national supplies. Generally white corn is used for human consumption and yellow corn for animal feed.

The production of yellow corn in Central America may soon become history if present trends continue. The import of cheap yellow corn—through either commercial or food-aid channels—is rendering production of feed grain a losing proposition for Central America's farmers. A 1984 AID study of the basic grains sector in El Salvador concluded that the level of corn imports from the United States was causing a "substantial decline in the production of yellow corn, which tends to be produced by small farmers."[41] In Costa Rica it is deliberate government policy to stop supporting production of both yellow corn and sorghum and to meet feed uses entirely through imports.[42]

Washington has promoted the rising level of food imports through Title I, Section 416, and Commodity Credit Corporation (CCC) credit guarantee programs. When countries find themselves coming up short in corn production, they can now easily complement domestic production with corn imported on favorable terms. In 1987 the Section 416 Sugar Quota program simply donated large quantities of yellow corn to Central American governments for resale to local agroindustries. The small farmers who produce most of the region's basic grains lose out whenever corn is imported from the United States. Corn imports mean downward pressure on prices and thus reduced production incentives. Easy access to cheap imported corn also encourages governments to pay less attention to the technical, credit, and marketing needs of small farmers.

But there are many sectors of society that benefit from cheap corn imports. What may be a disincentive for corn farmers is a plus for industrial corn consumers like the poultry industry. In recent years the import price has been as little as two-thirds the price of local production. Throughout Central America, the poultry industry has pressured governments to open the national ports to these cheap imports. The government, eager to keep down the price of popular consumer items like chicken and eggs, is usually willing to comply. In the case of Section 416 donations, the government itself realizes a substantial profit on these resales.

Unlike corn, which is produced mostly by peasant farmers, rice is produced mainly by larger commercial farms in Central America. Protected markets, government subsidies, and technical and infrastructure support have made rice production a profitable business—an oddity in the region's basic grains sector. But now cheap imports and the availability of foreign food aid and import financing are beginning to threaten rice farmers as well.

Costa Rica is the country where AID and other international financial institutions have had the most success in imposing structural adjustment on the agricultural sector, and it appears that rice production may be the first victim of these new austerity policies. Pressured by Title I self-help measures, the government has tightened credit to the rice growers and dropped farm subsidies for this sector. The reduced support for the rice growers has resulted in dramatic declines in production, conveniently being substituted for by low-priced Title I imports.[43]

Food aid is also covering much of the region's vegetable oil imports. Except for Honduras, Central American countries have never been able to cover their vegetable oil needs through local production. This shortfall in supply was aggravated in the 1980s by the sharp decline in cotton production, which produces cottonseed oil as a by-product. The resulting shortages have largely been filled by vegetable-oil imports covered by Title I and CCC programs. El Salvador, for example, now imports 90 percent of its vegetable oil through Title I.

Given the obvious oil shortage and assuming proper management, these oil imports cannot be said to constitute a serious disincentive for internal cotton production. As cotton production increases again, however, such large vegetable-oil imports may cause a tug-of-war to develop between the owners of the cotton gins and consumer demand for cheaper oil prices. Even as is, cheap oil imports may be inhibiting the potential development of other oil-supplying crops, such as soybeans, sesame, palm oil, and peanuts. Nor is the United States interested in supporting the efforts toward increasing internal oil supplies. Under the Bumpers amendment, AID is legally bound not to support efforts to produce any crop that might eventually compete with U.S. products on international markets.

DISTRIBUTIVE PROGRAMS ALSO CREATE DISINCENTIVES

Distributive food aid to Central America—those foods that are donated to the poor and needy—is not nearly as large as government-to-government food assistance. Title II distributive programs represent less than one-fifth of the value of total U.S. food assistance to Central America. The World Food Programme, AID, and participating NGOs (nongovernmental organizations) claim that these donations have no significant market effects. Each agency points out that the food items it distributes represent only a small percentage of total consumption of those products. In addition, program managers also claim that free rations, since they are directed to poor people without much market power, do not significantly affect market demand and prices.

Although considerably smaller than government-to-government aid programs, distributive food-aid programs still do have important market effects. Title I food aid largely substitutes for normal commercial imports, exceeding import needs only at the margin; distributive food aid, by contrast, is completely additional. Furthermore, Title I imports, at least in theory, are planned to meet real market needs, and a central government office oversees their import, whereas distributional food aid is simply brought in willy-nilly. Finally, these programs have important leakages that do affect food markets, especially on a local level.

Distributive food aid affects food markets in two ways: donated rations may be substituted for items usually consumed, leading to a reduction in family food purchases, or the rations may be resold at discount prices on the local market. In both cases distributive food aid can adversely affect the local food market. Disincentive effects are most noticeable when the donations include high-value items like dairy products that are produced locally in relatively small quantities.

The PL 480 program prohibits the sale of distributed food aid, except for special "monetization" programs designed to raise funds for the administering agencies. Beneficiaries themselves are strictly prohibited from reselling their rations, and each can or bag they are handed is marked "Not to be sold or exchanged." Nevertheless, the resale of donated food—by both beneficiaries and corrupt government workers—is common. One AID-contracted audit of Honduran programs reported: "Illicit sale of FFP [Food for Peace] commodities was detected in all ten markets visited by the audit team."[44]

Most distribution agencies cut from program rolls any beneficiaries caught selling their rations, but given how widespread resales are, some project managers prefer to look the other way. In fact a few agency workers told us that they consider it normal and justifiable that beneficiaries sell some of their rations, either to get cash or because they do not like the food. In these cases workers may just advise them to refrain from selling their rations near the distribution centers, to avoid congestion and because it would look bad for the program.

The illicit sale of donated food aid is also an institutional occurrence especially common in government programs. Food is siphoned off on both national and local levels. In Guatemala the long-rumored corruption of the National Reconstruction Committee was confirmed in February 1987 when the government's national accounting office suddenly discovered $800,000 worth of WFP food missing. In El Salvador, a government inspector we interviewed reported finding entire fifty-pound sacks of powdered milk inside cheese factories, still unopened, indicating that they had been sold from government or NGO warehouses before ever being divided up among the intended beneficiaries. We obtained a copy of an FAO consultant's report on the cheese sector that confirmed this practice as well as the negative effect it was having on local production. Those who were attempting to make quality cheese based on fresh milk, complained the report, were being driven out of business.[45]

In Central America it is now quite common to find donated food aid being used in restaurants and by food processors such as ice-cream manufacturers. In Honduras we were told of a case where the local ice-cream company sent its trucks around to all the feeding centers to collect the powdered milk just hours after each commodity delivery. And even the fanciest restaurants in Guatemala City serve dishes made with surplus Section 416 yellow cheese.

When we asked organizations like CARE (Cooperative for American Relief Everywhere) or WFP about possible disincentive effects created by their programs, they always pointed out that the amounts of food they bring in represent only a small percentage of local production. This is true, but since these programs are often concentrated in certain geographical areas, such as the Guatemalan highlands or drought-stricken southern Honduras, the impact on local markets might still be significant. Furthermore, given the multiplicity of programs currently selling and handing out food aid, the question of food aid's share of overall consumption is more properly addressed at a cumulative level.

Unfortunately, national-level monitoring of food-aid programs occurs rarely in Central America; governments would do well to institute such monitoring. El Salvador the government office in charge of regulating basic grains imports recently did a study of the milk sector. It found that imports of powdered milk represented a full third of national supplies. Of these imports, food aid accounted for over 95 percent (61 percent through three distributive programs and 35 percent through a Section 206 emergency government resale program). The study concluded: "The low acquisition cost of non-fat industrial-use milk stimulates its use as an ingredient in the production of fresh cheeses, increasing demand and also stimulating the use of some humanitarian aid milk for this same end. Logically, this creates a disincentive for national production. . . . mechanisms should be created to supply the market without arriving at saturation, which is when non-fat milk begins to be channeled to undesired uses."[46]

Resale of powdered-milk donations is also a serious problem in Guatemala. One local magazine recently reported that milk donations increased nearly tenfold between 1983 and 1986, and that up to 80 percent of these donations were sold on the black market for half the price local producers charged for their fresh milk. These donations were reported to be an important factor in the drying up of investment in the dairy sector, with the number of Holstein herds declining from ninety to just five.[47]

Only the more organized Costa Rican milk producers have been able to protect themselves from the competition presented by these cut-rate sales of donated powdered milk. Under intense pressure from the local dairy sector, the Costa Rican National Production Council declared in 1987 that national self-sufficiency in milk was being threatened by U.S. food aid and subsidized sales. Shortly afterward, the government turned down the remaining three-quarters of a Section 416 powdered-milk donation.[48]

Central America's agricultural ministries have been caught unawares by the rapid increase in food donations over the past decade. No office even tabulates, much less regulates, these imports. Nor is it likely that anyone will soon start to do so. One problem is that the whole world of food-distribution programs has up to now been relegated to the ministries of health, the social welfare office, or at best the planning ministry, and in all three cases the focus is not on agricultural effects but on the developmental and charitable uses of this food. Food donations are seen not as part of a food system but simply as a social welfare activity best supervised by social workers and nutritionists.

Any attempt at monitoring food aid will also run up against the network of political interests that depend on food aid for patronage schemes, budgetary support, and financial gain. As one food security expert we interviewed in El Salvador quipped, "The government's new food-aid policy—if ever approved—is doomed to be ineffective. Too many interests like the food-aid scene just how it is. You see, for some there is purpose in the disorder."

In San Salvador, government employees in charge of regulating agricultural imports acknowledged to us that their office has no systematic control over food-aid deals. Food-aid programs, they complained, "respond largely to ad hoc political decisions. Half the time we find out that some minister has signed a food-aid agreement only when we see him in the newspaper receiving the shipment at the dock."

Special problems can occur when recipient institutions decide to "monetize" (resell) food commodities. In these cases the market effect is the same as that of a commercial import, but the government's import regulation office may not have any say in the sale. For example, in 1987 CONADES (National Commission to Aid the Displaced) decided to sell a large donation of Italian pasta. CONADES had previously made similar sales (mostly of rice) to pad its operating budget. In the instance of the pasta, however, no one had apparently realized that the amount CONADES planned to sell represented more than half of the local wheat millers' yearly sales. When they found out—from the newspapers—the sale was quickly halted, but the problem remained of what to do with all the pasta, which CONADES did not really need. The millers suggested that CONADES donate it to the armed forces, but the head of CONADES's planning office told us that "even if we give it to the army, a lot of it will still probably find its way onto the market."

SUMMARY

The paradox of an agriculturally rich region such as Central America lacking food security can be blamed largely on this region's dual agricultural system. While the area's large plantations supply the U.S. market with coffee, bananas, sugar, and beef, most of the local population, lacking sufficient land or income, is malnourished. National food production has been relegated to the impoverished peasant sector and thus left largely bereft of government support. Peasant land pressures are destroying the area's resource base. Grain production is falling behind demand, and food imports are on the rise.

In recent years it has been cheaper for the Central American countries to import grain from the United States than to rely on their own production. This price difference reflects not just the neglect of local grain production, but also recent changes in U.S. farm policy that form part of an intense export drive. In the middle of a trade war with its agricultural competitors, the United States has cut its prices to the lowest levels ever. Not only has this strategy hurt U.S. farmers, it is undermining the livelihoods of Central American farmers.

Cheap U.S. grain prices encourage Central American countries to turn to the import option instead of undertaking the reforms needed to boost their own grain production and to attack rural poverty. Food-aid programs, designed largely to help U.S. agroexporters penetrate new foreign markets and to underwrite U.S. foreign policy, further promote this escape. Central America is now financing the bulk of its agricultural commodity imports through food-aid programs as local agriculture continues to stagnate.

To the extent that U.S. food aid encourages government food imports beyond what they might otherwise be—and there is evidence that this has occurred—it also creates disincentives for local grain production. Allocated largely on strategic grounds, in order to give maximum economic support to area governments, food aid to Central America at times is even exceeding local market needs and thereby undercutting the prices, and the production, of local grains. The region's agroindustrialists, eager for access to the cheaper U.S. market, have also been pushing toward maximum use of these programs. USDA and AID are not adequately implementing congressionally imposed guidelines to protect local producers against these disincentives.

Food aid also serves to shape local demand toward foreign foods, especially wheat, and thereby fosters a long-term import dependence that further threatens this region's food security. The growing reliance on imported food is not in response to price effects alone. U.S. food-aid programs also come with a hidden agenda that is being used to shape Central America's agricultural economy according to a questionable and self-interested U.S. development philosophy. It is to this topic that we turn in the following chapter.

4

Food Aid's Reform Diet

*The PL 480 [Title I] program is designed to subject
us to food dependency and to implement what are
clearly political/economic objectives—yet it has
been presented in our country as an "assistance
program."*

Letter from a coalition of *campesino*
associations to Costa Rica's
president, Oscar Arias Sánchez
3 September 1987

WHEN GOVERNMENT officials shake hands on food-aid agreements, they
often get more than cheap food. They accept an entire philosophy of agricultural development. In this chapter we focus on the agricultural development
policies that accompany U.S. food aid. Through policy dialogues, self-help
measures, and local-currency projects, AID is using U.S. food aid to help
reorient the agricultural structure of Central America.

Trying to understand the logic of policymakers in Washington is a major
pastime in Central America. Decisions on Capitol Hill reverberate with a
vengeance up and down the isthmus. Only ten years ago, AID was champion-
ing government-owned stabilization institutes and regional food-security
projects. Although promoting U.S. trade and investment in the Third World
has always been part of AID's mission, the agency has also at times backed
broader and less self-interested development goals. In the 1960s and 1970s,
AID put more of its budget behind development projects that promoted local
food production and distribution. It funded agricultural development banks,

grain-stabilization institutes, and cooperative-formation institutions for peasant farmers.

Typical of this basic-needs-oriented approach to development was AID's *Agricultural Development Policy Paper*, published in 1978, which called for a "broadly participatory, employment-oriented agricultural production strategy." It defined two main objectives of AID's development assistance: increase recipient countries' capacity to expand and distribute food supplies to alleviate hunger and malnutrition, and increase the participation of poor people in the process and benefits of development. The 1978 policy paper concluded that the neglect of the local food-production sector was a key cause of poverty, hunger, and underdevelopment in the Third World. It warned that "net foodgrain deficits in developing countries [would] become much worse by 1985" if this neglect persisted. The AID report advised that poor countries not rely on the surplus production of other nations: "Although it is conceivable that surplus grain from other countries would be sufficient to meet this demand, substantially increased imports would cause an immense financial drain for both the developing countries and the developed countries, which would undoubtedly be called upon to finance much of the transfer. Even if these deficits were eliminated by food transfers, serious undernutrition would persist because of the distribution problem."[1]

In the 1960s and early 1970s AID sponsored many government infrastructure projects (both social and physical) in Central America, backed new agroexports (such as cotton and sugar), and lent its support to industrialization efforts conducted under the umbrella of the Central American Common Market. The agency pointed to the ensuing rapid growth as proof of its success. For the continuing problems of poverty and malnutrition, in the mid–1970s AID proposed a complementary "basic needs" approach that involved support for population control and targeted nutritional, educational, and health programs.

All seemed well, but in the late 1970s AID's bubble suddenly burst. In Central America and throughout the Third World, debt ballooned, income-substituting industries collapsed, and growth halted. At that time AID, along with other foreign financial institutions like the Interamerican Development Bank, began looking for a new economic-growth model it could stand behind.

The failure of the internally oriented model, which relied heavily on state protection and subsidies, was blamed largely on inefficient government intervention; as we explained in chapter 2, the new goal was to get the state out of the economy and let the free market do its work. With investment drying up and economies grinding to a halt, AID began talking less about helping the "poorest of the poor" and more about promoting the private sector. With countries no longer able to pay their foreign debts, AID abandoned internal-market-oriented policies for a new focus on exports. The Foreign Assistance Act of 1973 and Public Law 480 still contain language about meeting the basic needs of the poor and supporting projects that produce a stable food supply. These days, however, AID is largely ignoring these developmental guidelines or is reinterpreting them according to its born-again faith in marketplace justice and neoliberal economics.

At first glance it seems that food aid would have no place in a neoliberal development strategy. Food aid, after all, represents government intervention in the marketplace and contravenes all the principles of free-market and free-enterprise development. Despite this apparent contradiction, U.S. food aid has become a key player in the drive to restructure Central American agriculture along neoliberal lines, as part of larger structural-adjustment policies. Through food-aid negotiations and "policy dialogues" with the recipient governments, a series of policy reforms and development projects are being set in place by AID.

Agricultural-sector policies are an important component of structural-adjustment programs, and Title I is a useful means of leverage in shaping agricultural policy. " PL 480 has a meaningful role to play as a vehicle for policy dialogue," states Judith Gilmore, Food for Peace's division chief for Latin America, "particularly as Latin American countries progress from stabilization to economic development, where agriculture can serve as an engine of growth."[2]

UNCLE SAM INTERVENES

Privatization and agroexport promotion are two leading elements in AID's agricultural development strategy in Central America.[3] Both elements are drawn from a commitment to free-market policies, based on an economic vision in which unfettered market forces are the final arbiter. If Central American farmers cannot produce corn or beans more cheaply than their counterparts in the industrialized world, then they should switch crops or move to the city. Countries should produce the commodities in which they currently have comparative advantage—even if this means they become dependent on foreign producers for their food staples. Maximum participation in world markets is preferred to protectionist measures that seek to buffer internal production from the influence of international prices. For Central America today, this means an all-out export push, concentrating on export-platform assembly industries and specialty fruits and vegetables.

Privatization is the second thrust of current AID policies in the region. Government intervention through price subsidies and protectionism is said to distort the market and contribute to inefficient production and government deficits. Price liberalization and devaluation, along with increased involvement for the private sector, are offered as solutions. Chief target of the privatization assault is what is often called the "benefactor state." Thus AID seeks both to reduce state involvement in the agricultural economy and to boost private agrobusiness participation in the production and marketing of the new export crops.

FOOD SECURITY UNDER ATTACK

Neoliberal economic strategy, leveraged by economic aid and food-aid packages, is shaking the structure of Central American food production and distribution systems. Part of the attack has centered on subsidized credit and the market interventions of the grain-stabilization institutes. The private sector, meanwhile, is receiving generous support and assistance. As part of its food-aid program, AID is:

- Channeling Title I local currency into private-sector financial institutions with the stipulation that the funds be lent out at market rates, a requirement that excludes many small grain farmers unable to qualify for commercial loans.
- Specifying that government-to-government food aid be sold directly to private-sector companies rather than passing through stabilization institutes.
- Insisting that agricultural marketing institutes operate without losses, forcing the termination of subsidized guaranteed prices for grain farmers.
- Pressuring governments to privatize parts of the marketing institutes and food-distribution networks.
- Lobbying against protectionist policies designed to promote regional and national self-sufficiency.

The degree to which AID insists that governments conform to the agency's new neoliberal development principles depends on the varying levels of political crisis in each country and the extent of the local government's role in the national economy. It is in Costa Rica that this strategy is being most clearly played out, but major elements can also be seen in Honduras, Guatemala, and El Salvador.

COSTA RICA: *CAMPESINO* FARMERS FIGHT FOR SURVIVAL

In Costa Rica, efforts to privatize the national grain-stabilization institute and to impose the economics of comparative advantage have sparked controversy and conflict. *Campesino* associations have blocked highways, occupied government buildings, and marched to San José to protest the new policies.[4] The reforms stipulated by AID and other international lenders not only have spawned turmoil in the streets but have also brought havoc to the Ministry of Agriculture, which has seen the passing of six ministers in as many years. Restructuring has moved ahead rapidly in Costa Rica. The consequent social costs and disruption in rural areas are among the first signs that instead of stabilizing the politics and economy of Central American nations, AID may actually be sowing the seeds of social turmoil and economic dislocation.

Costa Rica is the Central American country with the highest standard of living, the most government involvement in the economy, and the highest level of public services. It has also had the most extensive and effective government market-intervention policies. In the 1970s Costa Rica was considered something of a model for the growth-with-equity school of development. But late in the decade weakening export markets, rising import costs, and heavy debt payments—the same factors affecting nations throughout the Third World—caused much of that to crumble. By 1981 Costa Rica was forced to suspend payments on its foreign debt, an action akin to declaring bankruptcy.

Costa Rica was bailed out, but at the usual price: an imposed program of structural adjustment and austerity. As a condition of their financial support, AID, the World Bank, and the International Monetary Fund (IMF) have insisted on a shake-up in the country's economic policies: reduced government spending, reform of the financial sector, and devaluation. In this effort they received the support of an influential sector of the country's own power structure, which also favors free-market economic policies. The agricultural and food sectors have been affected in particular by four of these reforms: a curtailment of credit and price-support programs for grain producers; the privatization of components of the national stabilization institute; smaller budgets for government agencies that provide technical and land-distribution services for the nation's small farmers; and the increased promotion of non-traditional agroexports.

Food-aid programs have become another form of pressure to set the structural-adjustment program in place. A 1986 AID–Costa Rica "Action Plan" states, "We will also attempt to enhance the use of PL 480 in the policy dialogue particularly concerning agricultural prices and GOCR credit policy which constrains productivity in this sector." The same year the USDA *Food for Peace Annual Report* showcased the U.S. food-aid program in Costa Rica as a success story of how food aid could be used to promote policy reform.[5]

A main target of structural adjustment has been the National Production Council (CNP), which has been promoting basic grains production and stabilizing internal prices and supplies for the past three decades. CNP has traditionally handled all foreign agricultural commodity trade and also intervenes heavily—more than any other marketing institute in the region—in the local basic grains market. By the mid–1980s, CNP was purchasing up to 80 percent of all basic grains production at forty locations around the country.

Through import controls and price support programs, the CNP kept producer prices higher than international levels; in some cases, especially for rice, the CNP has compensated for these high prices by subsidizing a cheaper consumer sale price out of its budget. CNP grains have also been channeled directly to needy families through a variety of government-sponsored family welfare and feeding programs.[6]

The CNP has had some serious problems in its operations. There were allegations of corruption and inefficiency. Whereas its targeted subsidy and food distribution programs worked fairly well, across-the-board consumer subsidies proved to be a strain on the government budget.[7] The council also took occasional losses on exports. The country did sometimes produce grain surpluses, especially of rice. But having bought up those grains at the higher internal price, CNP then found itself having to export them at a loss.

In the early 1980s, when large amounts of economic assistance began flowing into Costa Rica, AID took a look at the bottom line of CNP's annual budget and saw a large deficit. In CNP and other government ministries concerned with the agricultural sector, AID saw policies and programs that violated the principles of comparative advantage and free-market competition. Together with the IMF and the World Bank, AID set out to adjust the country's agricultural sector in line with its neoliberal vision.

Since 1982, when Costa Rica first began receiving Title I food aid, AID has been using the program's "self-help" conditions to chip away at CNP. It has done this by insisting that Costa Rica remove subsidies and protective trade barriers for agricultural production even if this means an end to self-sufficiency in basic grains. The assault on what AID sees as an inefficient and economically unsound food system has included the following self-help measures: CNP must align prices for basic grains and vegetables to match world market prices, CNP should operate without incurring any deficits, and consumer subsidies for grains should be eliminated.[8]

In its program strategy for Costa Rica, AID has stated that it will use local currency to "assist in restructuring the economy from an emphasis on public-sector investment and import substitution to one which looks more to the private sector and exports to achieve long-term growth. . . . Maximizing the involvement of the private sector is central to the strategy because . . . the private sector is the only sound alternative for providing jobs and generating foreign exchange."[9]

Through food-aid sales agreements and other conditions, AID has forced sharp reductions in the credit formerly available to small farmers. CNP's budget has been dramatically cut. Its role in the rice and sorghum markets has been privatized. In addition, AID has imposed a far-reaching monetary reform that has undermined the role of the Central Bank while giving private banks easier access to local currency and foreign-exchange lines of credit. As a result, the small farmers who produce most of the country's corn and beans have been effectively excluded from credit opportunities.[10] Farmers are also suffering from such problems as the soaring prices of imported fertilizer and chemicals, which have risen as a result of currency devaluation and price liberalization. With basic grains production no longer profitable, acreage devoted to grains has been sharply curtailed. The resulting shortfalls in annual harvests are now being covered by U.S. food aid and commercial sales. A recent U.S. Agricultural Attaché report describes the situation as follows:

> In market year 1986/87, Costa Rican production of rice, corn, and sorghum is estimated to be down. Further drops in the production of all three commodities are projected for MY 1987/88 due to lack of financing. The National Production Council has moved out of rice purchases and will disengage itself from sorghum purchases in January 1988 in order to avoid losses in domestic acquisition and exports of these grains. A private and public sector organization, the Oficina de

Arroz (Rice Office), has been established to manage the rice situation in Costa Rica, but will not be involved in buying rice from domestic producers. Large imports of corn and rice are projected for MY 1987/88, as production of these crops falls short of consumption levels.[11]

In 1988 further prompting by international donors led the government of Costa Rica to adopt an agricultural zoning program, under which government support would be circumscribed to nineteen priority crops grown in certain zones. As the 1988 Agricultural Attaché report describes it: "Those who do not adhere to the priorities in terms of product and/or location will presumably be left to fend for themselves." The priority list did include rice, beans, and white corn, but it excluded both sorghum and yellow corn. The clear intention is that Costa Rica give up producing its own feed grains and import these from the United States. Corn and sorghum production has already fallen sharply off: acreage planted in corn declined from 75,000 hectares in 1987 to an estimated 55,000 hectacres in 1988 and 1989, and sorghum acreage plummeted from 16,000 to just 5,000 over the same period.[12]

This open abandonment of support for basic grains production contrasts sharply with the strong support AID is giving to promoting export production. The ruling Costa Rican National Liberation party, which has incorporated this free-market development philosophy into its own platform, calls the new farm policy "Agricultura de Cambio" (Agriculture of Change).[13] The new policy is to promote nontraditional export crops such as pineapple, flowers, ornamental plants, and vegetables, as well as the development of agroindustries such as an orange-juice concentrate plant. Whereas credit and subsidies are being reduced for basic grains, agroexport production now enjoys an array of attractive tax incentives, investment benefits, technical-assistance programs, production subsidies, and marketing-assistance projects.

Some within the government, such as the president of the Central Bank, have strongly backed these free-market policies and have openly advocated the dissolution of the peasant sector because of its purported backwardness and inefficiency. Opposition is being offered by more moderate members of the government, however, who think it is important to protect rural livelihoods, internal food production, and self-sufficiency.[14] Costa Rican peasant and rice farmers are also mounting a stiff resistance to changes they believe not only are unwise but are also undermining their way of life.

FARMERS CALL FOR AN END TO FOOD AID

Basic grains farmers throughout Central America are facing many of the same problems as those in Costa Rica, but Costa Rican peasants have been the first to publicly demand the suspension of the PL 480 agreements with their government. According to a broad coalition of rural associations, U.S. food aid "has been the instrument and the opening that has been used to progressively smash the production of grains (yellow corn and rice) and then to proceed to justify massive imports of those grains."[15]

There are several factors that might explain the comparatively strong and vocal opposition to food aid and aid-imposed farm policy in Costa Rica. Costa Rica has traditionally been the Central American country with the most enlightened social policies and the strongest support for small-farm agriculture. The Costa Rican peasantry is better educated and organized than those in the other countries, more technified, and well integrated into national credit and marketing systems. The democratic tradition of this country (compared with the extreme repression employed in other countries) has also left its people better organized and less afraid to speak up for their rights. At the same time, structural adjustment has gone much further in this country than in its neighbors, and the contrast between Costa Rica's new neoliberal policies and its former social-democratic ones is strong.

Throughout the 1980s, small farmers and landless peasants have become increasingly militant in their opposition to the agricultural policies of the Costa Rican government. Lack of response to their complaints, and repressive measures used by the civil guard, have only served to broaden their movement and heighten their militancy. More recently larger rice farmers, also feeling the pinch of the new adjustment policies, also joined the opposition.

Costa Rican farmers are demanding that the "Agriculture of Change" thrust be modified. They suggest a more balanced agriculture program that aims for food self-sufficiency and protects the interests of basic-grain farmers, and at the same time helps small farmers diversify their production. A broad national coalition called the National Union of the Agrarian Sector (UNSA) offers an alternative vision of agricultural development for Costa Rica. Although Costa Rica's agricultural sector does differ from those of other Central American countries in several ways (such as the history of a strong stabilization institute), most of the proposals offered by UNSA could just as well apply to the rest of the region.

Costa Rican peasant organizations reject the notion that basic grains farmers are hopelessly backward and deserve to fade away as an agrarian sector. They claim that the reason they are not more productive is that they have insufficient access to credit and technical assistance. Furthermore, the Costa Rican peasants point out that although their output per labor unit is low, their output per land unit is in fact frequently higher than that of the large export plantations. They say that if the government is interested in making the agrarian sector more efficient it should redistribute uncultivated land to land-less and land-poor *campesinos* and take steps to ensure that the large estates and plantations are farmed more intensively.[16]

Furthermore, Costa Rican grain farmers charge that U.S. commodity imports—through both commercial and food-aid channels—represent unfair competition, since these sales are subsidized by the U.S. government. UNSA calls for the immediate suspension of all agreements with AID, to be followed by the renegotiation of the terms and objectives of the agreements relating to agriculture.

The small farmers propose that all the resources generated by food-aid sales should go entirely to the National Production Council. With this revenue, CNP would be better able to support local food production and to help small farmers diversify and technify their production. *Campesino* growers recognize that there have been waste and corruption associated with CNP policies. They complain that most CNP subsidies have benefited the large rice growers and feed industries, not the corn, bean, and sorghum farmers who have been most severely affected by the AID-sponsored restructuring.[17] But rather than eliminate the National Production Council, they propose that it be reformed.

José Picado, representative of the Permanent Council of Workers, sees the privatization of CNP as part of "the dismantling of the state" sponsored by foreign agencies like AID. In this process, certain of the attributes that have distinguished Costa Rica from other Central American countries—a healthy small farm sector and effective government social services—are being lost. In their collective letter to President Oscar Arias in September 1987, *campesino* organizations argued that the government should play a role in boosting national food production rather than adopting policies that destroy national food security. "For economic and social reasons, and for reasons of sovereignty and independence, Costa Rica should be self-sufficient in food production," the farmers wrote to the president.

In the name of economic growth, AID is using food aid to help establish a new economic order in Costa Rican agriculture. In the process, at least some Costa Rican farmers say it may be undermining the prosperity and political stability long enjoyed by this armyless nation. Antonio Capela, who heads the Association of Basic Grains Producers in Costa Rica, told us that "agriculture has long been the foundation of social peace in Costa Rica. The U.S. government probably doesn't realize that its aid programs are destroying the economy and peace of Costa Rica."

RESTRUCTURING THROUGHOUT THE REGION

Restructuring adjustments in the agricultural sector are most evident in Costa Rica owing to the substantially larger role the state plays in that agricultural system. For example, whereas in Costa Rica the CNP has historically purchased the bulk of the country's production, the Honduran marketing institute has a much weaker role, and the Guatemalan and Salvadoran institutes have long been largely inoperable. Nonetheless, many of the same restructuring forces seen in Costa Rica are also at work in other Central American countries.

After Costa Rica, Honduras is the Central American country with the most organized peasantry and the most state support for small-farm agriculture. The country underwent a limited land reform in the 1970s; it has a strong rural cooperative movement; and the Honduran Agricultural Marketing Institute (IHMA), set up in 1978, buys up about a fifth of total grain production, which it markets through a network of state-run outlets. IHMA is also in charge of handling all wheat imports, including those financed through PL 480 Title I.

Honduras is also the Central American country with the longest involvement in U.S. government-to-government food-aid programs. A recipient of Title I since 1974, in the 1970s the country also signed on for a series of Title I/III agreements, under which Title I payments would be forgiven if the country agreed to undertake certain agricultural-sector reforms, largely centering on cooperative development and small-farmer irrigation schemes.[18] AID was also instrumental in establishing IHMA and encouraging government regulation of the basic grains market. As part of a 1979 Title I agreement, for example, the Honduran government assured AID that it would "continue with plans for developing an adequate grain storage and price stabilization program." But in the era of Reaganomics, AID began moving to reduce the government's role in the Honduran food system.

During the 1980s, Title I "self-help" measures for Honduras began to stress the need for privatization and free-market economics. The 1984 Title I agreement stated that the government should "proceed with the divestiture of agricultural sector organizations which can more effectively operate in the private sector." Concerning the role of the IHMA, AID called for the "increased role of the private sector in the marketing of grains," the sale of some of the institute's grain storage facilities, and the adoption of policies that allow for the "free-market determination of basic grains."

AID has commissioned several studies by U.S. consultants that propose the creation of a private commodities trading system, much like the one that exists in the United States.[19] The agency even flew IHMA officials to Ecuador to see an AID-sponsored commodity market at work. IHMA officials fear that AID is out to dismantle their institution altogether. Few would disagree that IHMA needs reform, given its large deficit, inefficiency, and waste. But as a food security consultant for the European Economic Community (EEC) pointed out to us: "Perhaps the Honduran state has not been such a success in managing the basic grains market, but a commodities market would be even riskier. Maybe it could work where there is a highly technified agriculture with large producers and developed markets, but this isn't the case in Honduras."

Both AID and the private sector acknowledge the dangers—including the loss of livelihood for Honduran grain farmers, rural unrest, and increasing rural-urban migration—that the complete liberalization of the agricultural sector could bring. But step by step AID is starting to insist that the free market be given free rein in Honduran agriculture. In recent years, the relative neglect of basic grains production is making itself felt; the country has been importing substantial amounts of corn, as well as smaller amounts of both rice and beans.

After Costa Rica, Guatemala is the Central American country most deeply involved in structural adjustment. In recent years the *quetzal* was sharply devalued, interest rates increased, and state expenditures were held down. The adjustment program has affected basic grains production in various ways: an even smaller role for the grain-marketing institute, decreased credit for small basic grains farmers, and substantially higher input prices. Foreign-funded programs to promote nontraditional exports and to improve rural infrastructure are also encouraging small farmers to diversify production away from corn and beans to other crops. Government efforts to maintain and promote grain production, for their part, have been centered mostly on the distribution of subsidized fertilizer since 1986. Devaluation has doubled or tripled the prices of the imported fertilizers that nearly all Guatemalan peasant farmers use, but internal grain prices have not risen enough to make up the difference. The result, in the words of one local agricultural expert, is that "in strictly financial terms, raising corn is currently a losing proposition."

Besides the increase in input prices, perhaps the biggest change in agricultural policy over recent years has been the weakening of INDECA, the Guatemalan grain marketing institute. Long limited by budgetary constraints, low storage capacity, inefficiency, and corruption, INDECA purchases only a small proportion of internal grains production and has consequently been unable either to effectively guarantee producer prices or to stabilize the market.[20] In recent years its funding levels have fallen even further, except when the Monetary Council grants it the financing to make an emergency import. Unable to afford internal grain purchases, the institute's share of grain purchases fell from a high of 17 percent in 1975–76 to 7 percent in 1981–82 to less than 1 percent currently. In 1987 INDECA corn purchases on the local market were an insignificant 58,000 *quintales* (1 qn. = 100 lbs.).[21] The institute has ended up renting out much of its warehouse space to private businesses; there has also been some talk of privatization.[22]

At least one reason for INDECA's operating deficits in the 1980s was food requisitions made by the Guatemalan army. From 1982 to 1986 the army, as part of its Assistance Plan for Conflict Areas (PAAC), issued special decrees that permitted it to use several million dollars worth of grains stored by INDECA.[23] INDECA has also been called upon by the army to assist in constructing development poles by placing small grain silos in such strategic areas as the Ixil Triangle and in Playa Grande. Such a role has continued into the Cerezo administration as part of the Multi-sectoral Plan for the Ixil Triangle.

INDECA's market regulation function, meanwhile, has been reduced largely to authorizing occasional imports of wheat, corn, beans, and vegetable oil—some handled by INDECA itself and some handled by the private sector. These imports, by making up internal shortages, help hold food prices down. Given the difference between U.S. and internal market prices and the absence of effective price control mechanisms, they can also mean windfall profits for the importer. Indeed, the low U.S. price appeared to be a major factor behind the poultry feeders' successful 1987 campaign to have INDECA declare an internal shortage—even though the institute at first had determined market supplies to be adequate—and authorize yellow-corn imports.[24]

AID's main demand regarding INDECA is its stipulation, contained in all Title I sales agreements 1985, that all U.S. food aid, "to the extent possible," be channeled directly to the private sector instead of being imported by INDECA. The effect is to deprive INDECA of the control over food supplies it would need to strengthen its abilities to successfully regulate Guatemala's grain markets.

Basic grains producers have been hurt by the absence of effective market regulation.[25] Without access to adequate storage facilities, at harvest time they are forced to sell their crops to intermediaries at low prices. Guatemala grain farmers have also suffered from the lack of credit for basic grains production. Between 1984 and 1987, public-sector credit for basic grains production dropped by almost half. In addition, Title I sales agreements have required the agricultural development bank BANDESA to lend its funds "at the maximum interest rate allowed by the monetary board . . . in order to avoid subsidized credit."

El Salvador, because of its civil war and strong U.S. economic support, cannot really be included in this discussion of agricultural readjustment measures. Basic grains production, badly hit by the war, is currently supported mostly through fertilizer imports. The government also maintains guaranteed producer prices, but just as in Guatemala, the ability of the local marketing institute to buy enough grains to influence those prices is virtually nil. AID largely ignores and excludes the grain-stabilization institute, concentrating its resources instead on promoting both new and traditional agroexports.

Vigorous and expensive U.S. government support for its domestic farm sector explains to a large degree the success of U.S. agriculture. Extensive government intervention has characterized U.S. farming for most of this century. Although this intervention has made the United States the world's most productive agricultural economy, the U.S. government is undermining agricultural development in Central America and other parts of the Third World by insisting that local governments dismantle government support and protection for their own agricultural producers.

Citing the need for budget cutting and praising the virtues of an unregulated private sector, AID is using food-aid agreements to push government out of the farm sector. This practice seems rather hypocritical considering Washington's own close involvement with the domestic farm economy. As agricultural analyst Richard Gilmore has pointed out: "Government remains the first and last link in the agricultural chain. Grain does not move from field to market through the magic of Adam Smith's 'invisible hand.' Instead, government is a principal in all phases of the grain trade from its origination on the farm to final delivery. No group in the agricultural chain, including the largest grain merchants, could prosper without some government assistance."[26]

AGROEXPORT FEVER

Coupled with AID's push for the privatization of the farm sector is a renewed interest in promoting exports. Agroexports are of course nothing new in Central America, having been the motor of these economies since colonial days. Indeed, these countries' extreme dependence on exports has been blamed for many of their woes: glaring inequalities in income and wealth, an atrophied internal market, and sudden fluctuations in national income and growth in tandem with market fortunes.[27] In the late 1970s and early 1980s, falling terms of trade and the weakening of export markets were important factors in these countries' growing indebtedness.

Today the need to meet ballooning debt repayments, in addition to regular import needs, has added new urgency to the push for more exports. Area governments share AID's concern with generating more dollars to pay their debts, knowing that failure to meet repayments would mean an immediate drying up of access to further import credits and loans, without which these import-dependent economies would grind to a halt. But it is AID and the international banks, as representatives of the creditor countries, that are the real forces behind the renewed export drive.

Today's export push in Central America involves both export platform industries and new agricultural crops such as flowers, ornamental plants, pineapple, snow peas, broccoli, miniature vegetables, macadamia nuts, and other specialty fruits and vegetables, especially those that cannot be widely cultivated in the United States during the winter. Some of these involve minimal processing, such as freezing. One AID regional proposal notes: "The strategy for growth in Central America depends heavily on increasing nontraditional agricultural and agribusiness exports."

Throughout Central America, both PL 480 food-aid programs are being used to support this new agroexport push. Title I local currency is going into increased credit for agribusiness investors, technical assistance, marketing projects, the construction of fumigation chambers and processing plants, and government incentives and subsidies for the new crops. An increasing amount of Title I local currency is being specifically earmarked as credit for private-sector agribusiness investment under the new Section 108 provisions of PL 480 (discussed in chap. 2). In its food-aid agreement with Costa Rica, AID advises that self-help measures be undertaken in recognition of "the need to increase domestic production and export of nontraditional agribusiness products to increase Costa Rica's foreign exchange earnings."

Title II food donations are also being used to support the development of nontraditionals, through food-for-work programs that supply small farmers and colonizers with food rations in return for their taking a risk on the new crops. In Guatemala, for example, CARE rations supported a colonization program centered on cardamom production. The WFP uses Title II food aid in agricultural diversification projects in nearly every country.

The new nontraditional crops are heralded not just as new sources of foreign exchange, but also as a solution for the rural poverty that plagues this region. In contrast to the traditional export crops of coffee, cotton, bananas, and sugar, the production of many of these new vegetables, fruits, and flowers lends itself to small-scale, labor-intensive production. Furthermore, they bring much better returns to peasant farmers than the traditional corn and beans. Time and time again, we heard USDA and AID officials argue that it would make better economic sense for Central American farmers to produce export-quality vegetables than to continue producing basic grains. Anthony Cauterucci, AID mission director in Honduras, stated this approach clearly: "We are looking at moving subsistence-oriented agriculture toward high commercial value agriculture and linking *campesinos* to the export process."[28]

There is widespread recognition in Central America that economic development must entail increased and diversified exports and that a solution must be found to the serious problems of rural poverty and growing land pressures. AID's strong new focus on nontraditional agroexports, however, strikes many observers as dangerously unbalanced. The agency shows a blithe disregard both of the serious risks involved and of the social side of its profit-oriented economic calculations.

In Central America, AID is promoting nontraditional agroexports almost to the complete exclusion of basic grains production, even though grain production still absorbs the energies and provides the income of most of the region's farmers. In reviewing a list of AID's "Agriculture, Nutrition, and Rural Development" projects for the region, we could not find even one bilateral program whose title mentioned basic grains. Farmers that are engaged in grain production are simply being neglected.

Furthermore, AID pursues this one-sided export strategy with the help of Title I food-aid programs that by law are supposed to be used to promote "local food production"—for example, by encouraging land to be used for food rather than nonfood crops. In Honduras, a study of AID's Title I program noted that only 0.5 percent of Title I local currency was allocated for the specific purpose of promoting the production of basic grains.[29] In every country, both Title I self-help measures and local currency are being earmarked not for basic grains but for nontraditionals. But miniature vegetables, broccoli, pineapple, and snow peas are not foods eaten by Central Americans. Since many of these export items will be grown on lands currently dedicated to basic grains, in the absence of a dramatic increase in basic grains productivity, a wholesale switch to the new nontraditionals will lower local grain supplies. As an AID-contracted evaluation of Guatemala's PL 480 program warned, "The Strategy's encouragement of production of nontraditional fruits and vegetables for export among small farmers previously limited to growing staples, may reduce per capita food availability as cropping patterns change."[30]

There exists an unwritten assumption that the projected success of the nontraditional agroexport production not only will spark widespread economic development but will eventually enable the region to pay for its ever increasing food imports. Yet this development scenario seems both unrealistic and risky. For example, a recent study by the EEC-sponsored Central America Food Security Program (CADESCA) calculates that if current trends continue the isthmus will be importing $1.1 billion a year in basic grains by the year 2000. If the region is to cover this import bill with new export production, it will have to export not only this same value in nontraditional fruits and vegetables, but also enough to cover the high costs of agricultural inputs, such as fertilizer and chemicals, needed to pay for this expanded production.[31]

There are few guarantees that the U.S. market, where most of the region's nontraditional exports are sold, will absorb this amount of fruits and vegetables, especially given fierce competition from other suppliers. Not just the Central American countries, but developing nations around the world, are attempting to break into developed countries' specialty markets. Depending on imports to meet national food needs is a risky strategy. Neither export earnings nor world food supplies and prices are so stable as to ensure food import capacities into the future. Come another world food shortage like that experienced in 1973 and 1974, or a U.S. recession, these countries could suddenly find themselves unable to purchase enough food to feed their populations.

More problematic even than the wisdom of abandoning self-sufficiency is whether the new agroexports do indeed represent a solution to the problems of rural poverty in Central America. There is no doubt that these new crops are more profitable than basic grains production. However, their wholesale introduction raises serious distributional questions as well as a strong factor of risk.

Only a few peasant farmers—for example, those who are literate, live near a road, and have enough collateral to qualify for credit—are able to break into the new agriculture. Nontraditional agroexport production, as small farmers are quick to point out, requires significantly higher investment (seed, fertilizers, pesticides, irrigation) and technical know-how than traditional basic grains farming. As intensive specialty farming takes off, land values will rise and poorer and more marginal farmers will likely be squeezed off their holdings, adding a new group of landless farmers to those who will be competing for the new jobs provided. A continued concentration on agroexport production, in the absence of previous income redistribution measures, will likely lead to an even more unequal distribution of income and the further marginalization of an important, and already disadvantaged, social sector.

It is also necessary to see how the increased income generated by the new crops will be distributed. A recent study by PREALC (Regional Employment Program for Latin America and the Caribbean), the United Nations' regional employment research program, concluded that export crops, with the exception of cattle raising, generate a greater number of jobs per land unit than does basic grains production. However, "given the current concentration of land holdings dedicated to these crops and the character of the production processes, a strengthening of these activities would benefit a limited number of producers and permanent workers, leading to a greater overall concentration of income distribution. . . . Past experience has shown that a high percent of [export crop] profits go to consumption and luxury expenditures. That is, the so called 'comparative advantage,' when national income is distributed, could go to luxury consumption and not to the strengthening of investment and economic growth. Income distribution and redistribution measures thus arise as key elements for economic efficiency to be effectively realized."[32]

Some farmers will benefit more than others, but the ones that will benefit the most are the packing, processing, and marketing firms, many of them foreign owned. Marketing the new nontraditionals is a very complicated matter; timely transportation of these perishable items is the key. Indeed, many fruits and flowers are currently rushed to the United States by plane. Only commercial-level farmers and agribusiness investors generally have access to this kind of capital and technical expertise.[33] Indeed, so complicated is the marketing of these new crops that this phase is normally handled by specialized companies that contract out with small producers for their crop. Under this arrangement it is the producer that bears the burden of risk (since his sale price is normally tied to current market price) and the intermediary who realizes most of the profit.

An issue of concern is whether foreign exchange generated through the new crops will actually be used for imports of goods and services that improve the food consumption and nutritional situation of the poor.[34] Yet with most of the foreign exchange being earned by large multinational firms, this seems highly unlikely. In Costa Rica, for example, it is Del Monte that dominates the nontraditional export scene. In 1988 Del Monte subsidiaries exported $116.8 million worth of bananas, pineapples, papayas, mangoes, lemons, and squash—equal to almost 9 percent of the country's total exports.[35]

Relying on nontraditionals can be very risky for small Central American farmers. Most of the region's grain producers raise corn both for their own consumption needs and for sale. That way, even in a bad year they can hope to at least cover their own family's food needs. Furthermore, basic grains have low input costs and a year-round market, with undemanding quality standards, that can absorb small amounts at a time. It is easy enough for any Central American producer to take his grains to the nearest town plaza for sale. Nontraditionals, however, are much more difficult both to grow and to market. The input costs of these crops are very high (snow pea production requires thirteen times the investment for corn, according to one Guatemalan study). The crops must be grown to specification, be ready on certain dates, and also meet rigorous quality standards. If, after they have made the heavy investment required to raise their crop, local farmers' production is for any reason rejected, they have no way to store that product and almost no alternative sale outlets. Nor can their families live for the rest of the year on roses and broccoli.

Export markets themselves are notoriously fickle, as exporters of traditional products such as coffee, cotton, and sugar already well know. Oversupply (caused, for example, by a boom year in some far-off competitor) can suddenly cause the bottom to drop out of even the most profitable market. The recent world glut of cardamom, a spice consumed almost exclusively in the Far East, left Central American producers holding unsalable supplies.[36] In the fast-moving world of specialty vegetables and plants, where production time may be just a few months and competition is fierce, these booms and slumps occur not over years, but even over weeks.

Another problem is shifts in import policies in recipient countries. When the U.S. market began to be deluged with cut flowers from Central America, U.S. growers demanded and got protection from this foreign competition, again leaving Central American growers in the lurch. In discussing the subject of nontraditional exports with area farmers and economists, there was particular concern about dependence on a market propped up by the Caribbean Basin Initiative (CBI), a U.S. trade and investment promotion program that will expire in the mid–1990s.

AID's suggestion that Central America specialize in growing specialty fruits and vegetables and rely on imports for its basic grains needs has serious drawbacks. One is that this formula ignores the large social weight of the Central American peasantry, offering only a partial solution to the enormous problems of rural poverty and unemployment. Efforts to intensify production per land unit should not be pursued to the exclusion of efforts to distribute land resources more equally. Nor should local grain production be dismantled until after a real alternative is found for all the region's grain producers. The sharp policy shifts now being introduced will only increase rural poverty and rural-urban migration.

SUMMARY

From Washington, the proposed restructuring of Central America's agrarian sector seems like basic economic sense. In a world of perfectly free markets and equal access to resources, the economics of comparative advantage and unregulated private enterprise might be appropriate. But no country of the world, and certainly not those of Central America, matches that idealistic description. In fact, for many Central Americans, U.S. aid and U.S.-sponsored restructuring seem like nothing more than refried colonialism.

Dismantling what little protection exists for the Central American basic grains sector could have very serious social consequences for these countries. Unprotected peasant farmers simply cannot compete against the heavily subsidized, highly technical U.S. farm sector, especially when cheap U.S. farm exports are being supported by concessional food-aid programs. Given the high cost of Central American grain production and the current low price for U.S. grains, the result of free market policies would be that cheaper imports would replace locally produced grains. For the U.S. farm economy, this would mean increased exports, but for the Central American grain farmers it would spell ruin.

Central American peasant farmers are already among the poorest and most malnourished people in their countries. A further deterioration of income and living standards would likely push even more of them off the farm and into the already overcrowded cities. But with the industrial sector now in collapse and the government cutting back on its own spending and investment, there simply would not be enough paid employment for those leaving the land. Even now, most of the peasants pushed out of grain farming are ending up as more empty bellies in the region's teeming urban slums.

The alternative model of agricultural development being proposed by AID—the intensive cultivation of specialty fruits and vegetables—offers little real hope of resolving the very serious social problems of rural poverty and unemployment. In Central America, AID development policies supported by food aid are not a solution the region's serious problems of food security, poverty, and malnutrition. Although there is the obligatory mention of "growth with equity" in AID's strategy documents, the current focus in agricultural policy is on boosting exports and private-sector participation and reducing the government's role in the economy, with little attention paid to how these changes will affect the lot of the poor majority.

Economic policy reforms and export promotion are not bad in themselves, but given the highly unequal structure of land and wealth in Central America and the historic neglect of these countries' peasant and grains-producing sector, they cannot be posed as the ultimate or only solution to the region's poverty and political instability. Other problems must also be addressed—in particular, the lack of access of the rural poor to adequate land as well as to appropriate technology, education, credit, and marketing facilities.

Food aid is being used to help push Central American governments toward restructuring their agriculture in accordance with the imperatives of comparative advantage and the free market. But this approach, as one close observer commented, means throwing the Central American peasantry to the wolves. Such solutions doom most peasant producers to further marginalization and take from them what little food security they now have. In the long run these proposals are likely to increase rural poverty and boost the flow of people to the region's already overcrowded cities. In addition, by making these nations more dependent on food imports, they threaten them with greater instability and risk.

Instead of being used to tear down the food-production and distribution system of Central America, U.S. food and development assistance might better be spent helping governments promote more profitable and more productive basic grains farming. As AID states, there does need to be a better correlation between market costs and pricing. But this should first be done on a national and regional level, not an international one. While local agriculture is being built up, protectionist barriers against cheap imports should remain in place—if not on economic grounds, then in accord with social and political reality. Local-currency funds, as Costa Rican farmers have suggested, could be directed back into government institutions that support and protect small farmers. Producer prices should be held high enough to support expanded basic grains production. As in the United States, there could also be targeted government programs (like food stamps) that would ensure that all people have access to affordable staple foods.

5

Food for People

*The problem we have is that foreign organizations
keep dumping food on us, like tons of powdered milk
that we have to give away. We spend all our time
trying to distribute the food so that we don't really
have time to do the social action work we were originally set up to do.*

Staff official for national CARITAS
Guatemala, May 1988

UNTIL THIS POINT, we have concentrated on the economic, foreign-policy, and agricultural issues of government-to-government resale food aid. Distributive food assistance, though much smaller in both value and tonnage, also deserves close attention. It is the most visible part of Washington's food-aid program and directly affects the lives of millions of poor Central Americans. Distributive food aid is channeled through private and government agencies for donation directly to hungry, poor, and malnourished people. Most of it comes through Title II of PL 480, with a smaller amount channeled through the Section 416 program.

As established by law, the principal objectives of distributive U.S. food aid are:
- To meet famine or other urgent or extraordinary relief requirements.
- To combat malnutrition, especially in children.
- To promote economic and community development in friendly developing countries.
- To distribute food to needy persons and to nonprofit school-lunch and preschool-feeding programs.[1]

The combination of humanitarian and development objectives seems a fitting way to distribute U.S. farm surplus. But there is often more image than substance to distributive food programs. The projects may look good on paper, but in our project visits we frequently found disaster.

We began our investigation of distributive food programs by trying to determine if the stated objectives were being met. Was this food aid meeting the need for emergency relief? Was it combating malnutrition? Did it promote economic and community development? Were needy people and children actually benefiting from the food donations? Was the food aid being used for ulterior political, religious, or military ends? In this and the following two chapters, we describe what we found in answer to those questions.

THE FOOD-AID FLOOD

Distributive food-aid projects have existed in the Central American region since the 1950s. In the early years, Title II food went mostly to maternal/child or school-feeding programs. But with the political/economic crisis of the 1980s, both donors and programs have multiplied. Today, wherever one goes in Central America, one is likely to see some church, NGO (nongovernmental organization), or government agency passing out food. Food-distribution programs have come to pervade the social landscape of the region. According to AID, already in 1983 more than 5 million Central Americans, a quarter of the region's population, were receiving some sort of food aid.[2] For 1985 some sources were putting the figure as high as 8.2 million, representing 35 percent of the region's population.[3] In El Salvador, AID and WFP figures for 1987 show 37 percent of the population receiving distributive food aid, and calculations for Guatemala put the share in that same year at 29 percent.[4]

United States food assistance to Central America has ballooned as a direct result of the region's political and military turmoil. AID's Title II food aid to this region—including the part it channeled through the World Food Programme (WFP)—jumped from $5.5 million in 1979 to nearly $60 million annually in the late 1980s.[5]

Like Title I assistance, Title II food has also been concentrated on U.S. regional allies. Three countries—El Salvador, Guatemala, and Honduras—receive 99 percent of all Title II assistance allocated to the seven countries of the region. The share of regional Title II food going to El Salvador jumped from one-fifth in 1980 to over half in 1987, whereas Nicaragua, also suffering the effects of war, was eliminated altogether. Most of the increased flow of Title II food has been through the World Food Programme.

Distributive food aid is of three main types: supplementary feeding, food-for-work (FFW), and emergency relief.

– Supplementary-feeding programs target those whose future development will be most affected by malnutrition: young children and pregnant and lactating women, along with their babies. Primary schools, child-care centers, and health clinics sponsor most supplementary-feeding programs.

– Food-for-work programs, which are becoming increasingly common in Central America, give food in full or partial payment for public works and community-development projects. Sometimes food is given as an incentive for participating in educational programs. Food-for-work is the preferred distribution method of the World Food Programme and is also common in AID programs.

– Emergency relief programs are for disasters and crises. In Central America, victims of earthquakes, floods, drought, and hurricanes have all received emergency food aid. In the 1980s, however, most emergency relief has gone to refugees and the internally displaced—the victims of the man-made disasters (wars and repression) that ravage the region.

WHO IS IN THE FOOD LINE?

From the grain silos of the Midwest to the bellies of hungry Central Americans, U.S. food aid follows a complicated path, passing through several layers of donors and administrators before ever reaching the final beneficiary. The multiple actors involved in food-aid distribution make it difficult not only to trace the flow of food aid from original source to final use, but also to ensure program accountability.

The U.S. government's role in food distribution is limited to that of donor. Its main job is simply to supply the food and ship it to each country's port of entry. U.S. government agencies have never developed the capacity to administer complicated and time-consuming food-distribution programs within every recipient country. AID relies on others—foreign governments, the WFP, and NGOs—to perform these tasks. (See fig. 4.)

In Central America, the traditional bilateral U.S. program is accompanied by donations from the United Nations World Food Programme (itself largely supplied by the United States), the European Economic Community (EEC),

---

Title II

Title II is the distributive component of PL 480. Administered by AID, this program donates U.S. food to nongovernmental organizations (NGOs), the World Food Programme, and foreign governments. These agencies use the food in a variety of supplementary-feeding, food-for-work, and emergency relief projects.

In Central America the countries receiving Title II assistance are Honduras, El Salvador, and Guatemala. Some Title II food goes directly to the government of El Salvador. Most, however, is delivered to selected NGOs (mainly CARE and Catholic Relief Services) and to the World Food Programme. These "cooperating sponsors" receive the food free but must pay internal transport, storage, and distribution costs themselves. At times they can get financial support for their related costs from the local government or from beneficiary contributions. These NGO sponsors do not operate the food projects themselves, however, but rather hand the food on to local private and government agencies that manage the final distribution.

Almost all the food donated under Title II consists of surplus stocks acquired by the Commodity Credit Corporation (CCC) under U.S. farm price support programs. Each year Congress appropriates funds to purchase the CCC commodities to be distributed under the Title II program. The U.S. government also pays for these products' processing, enriching, packing, labeling, handling, and transport to foreign ports of entry. The program distributes about twenty-five commodities, including wheat, wheat flour, corn, rice, vegetable oil, nonfat dry milk, lentils, and also specially prepared supplementary foods such as soy-fortified grains and soy-milk blends. Currently, 75 percent of nonemergency Title II food must be processed commodities—a measure designed to benefit U.S. food-processing firms. Worldwide, Title II represents about a third of total U.S. food assistance. In Central America, in recent years it has made up about 20 percent of the value of total U.S. food aid.

Canada, and West Germany.[6] The donated food is channeled through a maze of government agencies and NGOs, which then redistribute it to thousands of churches and neighborhood organizations.

The World Food Programme directs most of its food to government ministries, which in turn hand out food allotments through a wide assortment of public-sector programs.[7] WFP food is also distributed by NGOs that have UN contracts to sponsor refugee programs. Bilateral U.S. aid, in contrast, is distributed mostly through NGOs. Only in El Salvador does Title II food, under an emergency program, go directly to government institutions.

Congress has mandated that most distributive food aid be administered by nongovernmental organizations. Experience has shown Congress that direct reliance on foreign governments opens the door to corruption and politicization. In 1975, in the wake of the food-aid abuses experienced during the

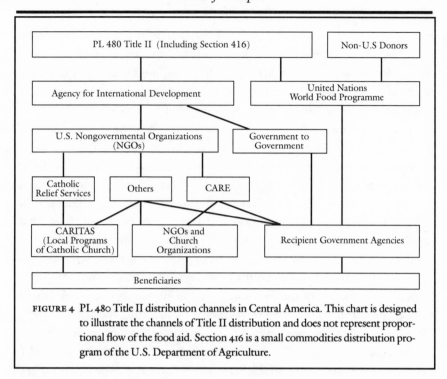

FIGURE 4 PL 480 Title II distribution channels in Central America. This chart is designed to illustrate the channels of Title II distribution and does not represent proportional flow of the food aid. Section 416 is a small commodities distribution program of the U.S. Department of Agriculture.

Vietnam War, the International Development and Food Assistance Act required that two-thirds of the specified minimum donation level be channeled through WFP or voluntary agencies. For 1988 the minimum WFP and private organization share stood at 75 percent of all U.S. distributive food—leaving just a quarter eligible to go directly to foreign governments. The intent of Congress is that AID should rely on the considerable technical expertise and nonpolitical focus of such multilateral institutions as WFP and the UN High Commission for Refugees and of such U.S. NGOs as Catholic Relief Services (CRS) and CARE. The organizations, both multilateral and private, that channel Title II food to local recipients are called "cooperating sponsors."

CARE and CRS have traditionally handled the vast majority of the distributive food channeled through private organizations. In the past several years, however, AID has also entered into contracts with such NGOs as Church World Service, the Salvadoran Mission Warehouse, Salvadoran Evangelical Aid and Development Committee (CESAD), World Share, and World Vision.

Cooperating sponsors rarely distribute directly to recipients. Their main responsibilities are logistics, financial support, and monitoring. Actual distribution of food to beneficiaries is relegated to a vast network of NGOs, churches, and government agencies that contract with cooperating sponsors. At this level—where one is dealing with literally hundreds of government offices and local organizations—instances of petty corruption, politicization, and religious evangelism associated with distributive food aid are very nearly the norm. In Central America, approximately half of the food channeled through AID's cooperating sponsors actually ends up in the hands of government institutions. These range from health and education ministries to military-controlled reconstruction and development organizations.

AID's relations with cooperating sponsors are ambiguous. Though the U.S. government supplies the food and often finances the organizations' development projects, these private organizations are considered to be independent. In fact, there is little AID oversight or evaluation. AID input is usually limited to tracing commodity flows rather than conducting any deeper analysis or evaluation of the food-aid programs of these sponsors. Although there exists a large volume of AID regulations concerning the distribution of Title II food, AID does not always ensure that these regulations are enforced. At the same time, AID in Central America has sometimes pressured its NGO partners, particularly CRS in El Salvador, to undertake questionable and politicized projects.

CATHOLIC RELIEF SERVICES: A PROFILE

Catholic Relief Services is the humanitarian assistance branch of the U.S. Catholic Conference. Founded in 1943, this relief and development agency has long been an important channel for distributing U.S. food around the world. CRS, in turn, depends heavily on the U.S. government for its foreign-aid resources; AID food and funding currently represent some 75 percent of its budget.[8]

CRS has distributed Title II food in Guatemala, Honduras, and El Salvador for some twenty-five years.[9] The agency's role is to pass the food on to its local Catholic church counterpart agency, known as CARITAS, for use in church-run distribution programs. These are mostly maternal/child oriented, but in Guatemala and Honduras some parishes have also sponsored local community-development activities using food-for-work.

As a rule, the CRS-CARITAS programs are more humanitarian than development-oriented. Usually managed by local church committees, including untrained volunteers and religious, these programs tend to have poorly defined goals and weak management, targeting, and control procedures.[10] Most of these church programs simply aim to get food into the hands of the needy, without a clear idea of what these handouts are supposed to accomplish in terms of nutrition, income, or health. Despite the CRS practice of asking project beneficiaries to make a small contribution toward transport and administration costs, these projects also tend to suffer chronic funding problems that further impede effective program management. Largely owing to these management and funding problems, CRS is now in the process of closing down its Honduran program.[11]

The close church link is both a strength and a weakness of CRS programs. Church personnel tend to be more dedicated and honest than many government employees running comparable projects. However, they sometimes do not adequately separate their religious and aid activities. Not infrequently, church personnel use the food distributions to remind participants to attend mass or participate in other church activities.

The strong link with the local Catholic church—which in Guatemala and El Salvador has suffered fierce government repression—also makes the CRS offices in Central America hesitant about working too closely with the area's governments or getting involved in AID's more openly political projects. In El Salvador, in particular, CRS channels EEC food to an independent Catholic church program for the displaced. This program has refused offers of increased AID support on the grounds of the political strings attached.

CARE: A PROFILE

The largest private cooperating sponsor in U.S food-aid programs, both worldwide and in Central America, is the Cooperative for American Relief Everywhere (CARE). Founded in 1945 to channel U.S. relief aid to war-devastated Europe, CARE distributed surplus U.S. military rations for its first year and a half. Later, other items were added to the CARE package, and beginning in 1954 CARE became the major distributor of PL 480 Title II food.[12] CARE expanded into an international relief, food distribution, and development agency, with associate members around the world.

Like CRS, CARE is largely dependent on government food and funding for its programs. Private contributions and revenue account for less than 10 percent of the U.S. CARE's total support and revenue. Although CARE reports that contributions from foreign governments and foreign associates are increasing, U.S. CARE continues to depend on AID for virtually all its food donations and for the bulk of its development programs.[13]

In Central America, CARE moves twice the volume of food as does CRS, the next largest NGO food program. Having shut down both its Nicaraguan and Panamanian programs in the early 1980s, CARE currently sponsors Title II food programs only in Guatemala and Honduras. These two programs, however, are expanding rapidly; from 1980 to 1986 the volume of CARE commodities going to Guatemala and Honduras more than doubled.[14]

For both its food-distribution and development projects, CARE's preferred mode of operation is to work with and through local governments. CARE says it channels food through local government agencies to build local institutional capacities and as a means of achieving sustainable development. In Guatemala CARE food distributions support a nationwide maternal/child health program run out of state health clinics, a reforestation program involving the National Forestry Institute and the Peace Corps, and a major urban slum renewal program managed by the Guatemala City mayor's office. In Honduras, CARE food goes to maternal/child health programs run by the Ministry of Health, an urban food-for-work project, and the National Social Welfare Committee, as well as to the national school-feeding program.[15] The government agencies themselves run the programs, with CARE providing mostly supervision and backup support along with some training and technical assistance.

A smaller portion of CARE food goes to a variety of privately run feeding programs, orphanages, and day-care centers, including many run by church groups. Like its other programs, these food distribution projects are for the most part included in the joint CARE-government programming. The larger of these private groups, such as World Vision, Save the Children, and Christian Children's Fund, pass some of these donations on to other community groups and churches. Since most Catholic-run food programs are supplied by CRS, it is mostly Protestant or evangelical organizations that receive Title II commodities from CARE. In Guatemala, some of the most prominent evangelical groups, like El Verbo and AMG International, hand out CARE-supplied food.[16]

CARE, in line with its role as a professional development agency, has a much stronger development focus and better monitoring of its food programs than does CRS. Its Title II maternal/child health programs in Guatemala and

Honduras have in recent years received AID enhancement grants to help improve project implementation through tighter supervision and more complementary nutritional education and health efforts. CARE–Honduras food programs also receive ESF local currencies. CARE has used FFW in both reforestation and potable water projects and is now using it in urban renewal in Guatemala.

In its Central American operations, CARE has not shown the same strong concern with political independence and neutrality as has CRS. This is probably due to three factors: CARE's dependence on U.S. government food, freight subsidies, and grants;[17] its tradition of working with local governments, and its lack of an independent and local base like that enjoyed by CRS.[18] Among the more controversial of CARE's Central American projects have been its FY 1983 relief program for Nicaraguan Miskito refugees in Honduras, many of whom were contras and contra supporters,[19] and its 1979–84 food-for-work colonization project and ongoing development projects in the conflictive and military-controlled Playa Grande region in Guatemala.[20] CARE's current food-for-work program in the Guatemala City slums also has strong political overtones. One of the specific goals of this program is to help stem urban unrest in order to stabilize the Vinicio Cerezo government.[21]

NO FREE LUNCH

Distributive food is not free, either for the donor or for the recipient country. In the United States, tax revenue pays the $700 million annual bill for the purchase and transport of Title II food.[22] Within each recipient country, transport, storage, and administration represent additional costs. In Central America, in-country food-program costs have been estimated at one-third of the value of the Title II commodities being distributed.[23] This tab is covered by a combination of NGO, government, and beneficiary resources.

Food-program logistics—which require transporting bulky, perishable items to distribution sites around the country—are overwhelming. Even after the food finally arrives at each distribution site, project workers must deal with the tasks of unloading, storage, protection against theft, repackaging, weighing, beneficiary selection and control, and distribution. In recent years AID has also begun to require that educational or health activities be incorporated into distribution programs. To be carried out effectively, these complementary activities require substantial human and material resources of their own.

Section 416

Section 416 of the Agricultural Trade Act of 1949 is a U.S. government food donation program not covered by PL 480 authorizations. Section 416 was established as a mechanism to dispose of surplus Commodity Credit Corporation (CCC) dairy products by donating them to needy people at home and overseas. Section 416 was considered not so much a foreign aid program as a humanitarian way of reducing CCC stocks.

In 1966 the foreign donations authority was removed from Section 416, but in 1982, in response to increasingly burdensome dairy stocks, powdered milk donations abroad were restored. In 1984 and 1985 Section 416 was expanded to cover a much wider variety of CCC-held foods, including wheat, sorghum, corn, and rice, and in addition, a minimum tonnage level was established for this program.[24] These donations are to complement, not replace, ongoing PL 480 Title II programs.

Section 416 is a relatively uncontrolled and thus easily politicized program. Since the CCC covers all costs (including international transport), Congress does not have to appropriate special funds for Section 416 and has consequently imposed few restrictions on program management beyond the Bellmon amendment, which guards against disincentive effects of U.S. food aid.[25] Allocations are particularly loose. Practically any private or foreign government agency can apply to the local AID mission for Section 416 food. AID writes up the donation agreements, largely first come, first served, with final approval dependent on the Food Aid Subcommittee of the Development Coordinating Committee. Monetization is allowed case by case.[26] In addition, the specific commodities available fluctuate widely from year to year, creating major problems for program planning. Currently, major cutbacks are occurring owing to the 1988 drought.

In Central America, AID has enjoyed a free hand to use the program to increase its overall level of assistance to the "friendly" countries in the region. In fiscal years 1986 and 1987, the share of 416 donations going to the tiny Central American region exceeded 8 percent of the world total.[27] Section 416 has been channeled through the WFP for El Salvador, Panama, Honduras, Guatemala, and Costa Rica. Small bilateral shipments have gone directly to the Panamanian and Costa Rican governments; both donations experienced management problems. In Panama some of a 1983 Section 416 powdered milk donation was later found abandoned and partially spoiled in a "First Lady" warehouse.[28] In Costa Rica a large powdered milk shipment planned for FY 1986 was sharply cut back after local protests over possible disincentive effects.

Guatemala has been by far the largest recipient of Section 416 in Central America. More than twenty NGOs and Guatemalan government agencies, including many fundamentalist Christian groups, received Section 416 powdered milk in an ad hoc 1984–85 distribution to assist victims of the army counterinsurgency campaign.[29] More recently, a large amount of Section 416 food, including powdered milk, butter oil, and processed cheese, has been distributed through the new NGO World Share for a questionable and poorly managed urban food-for-work program.

Food-aid programs commonly rely on volunteer labor, or else teachers, health workers, and religious may take on food-distribution tasks in addition to their normal jobs. Not having paid project personnel saves on costs but virtually ensures a poorly managed program. At the same time, social-service workers are distracted from their primary tasks of education, health care, and spiritual assistance.

Although the food distributed to beneficiaries is officially "free," programs involve costs for them as well. Recipients, especially in CRS-CARITAS programs, are often required to pay a small fee to help cover the program's overall administrative and transport costs. Often they must travel long distances to the distribution site, stand in line for hours to get their rations, and then face the problem and expense of transporting often bulky commodities back home. Especially for isolated rural villagers, these expenses can be large, at times approximating the market value of the food itself—one more reason beneficiaries so often choose to sell their rations.

MONETIZATION: THE NEW WAVE

In recent years financing problems have become more acute for food program sponsors. Stricter AID requirements and controls have increased NGO administration and personnel costs at the same time that their income from private contributions has stagnated. Local government support, never very reliable, has in the 1980s been curtailed even further owing to budgetary cutbacks.

AID financial support for food program management has traditionally been limited. No direct AID development assistance goes to food-aid operating costs. CARE programs in Guatemala and Honduras were both recently given one-time program enhancement grants, but these do not cover ordinary operating costs; rather, they are directed toward complementary activities. At most, AID authorizes local governments to use their aid-generated local currencies for these purposes.[30] Thus the Honduran government channels ESF currencies to CARE, and in El Salvador both ESF and Title I funds are used to finance various government displaced-persons programs. These approaches are not widespread, however, and also are viewed with some disquiet by the NGOs, who fear that increased dependence on government funding not only will bring frustrating bureaucratic delays but may also reduce their independence and autonomy. Thus many NGOs are turning to a new fundraising mechanism: the resale (or monetization) of donated foods. Monetization is attractive to NGOs because, with the commodities already in hand, it is a fairly quick and simple matter to sell them locally for cash.

In the past, NGO resale of donated U.S. commodities was discouraged on the grounds that the food had been donated specifically for free distribution to the poor. In addition, resale of donated food could open the door to charges of dumping. But as the WFP and other donors began making increasing use of this mechanism and NGO funding problems became more acute, the U.S. Congress reconsidered its position.[31] In the Food Security Act of 1985, Congress responded to NGO pressure by mandating that at least 5 percent of the worldwide value of U.S. commodity donations be available to NGOs for monetization. In 1987 this minimum monetization level was raised to 10 percent.[32]

CARE, a monetization supporter, has already made use of this process in its Central American programs, selling rice to the Guatemalan grain-stabilization institute to raise funds for an urban food-for-work project.[33] World Share soon followed suit, with the sale of wheat to local Guatemalan millers.

Despite the new trend toward monetization, however, not all NGO and AID staff members are convinced that this is an appropriate financing route. One concern, especially if monetization is used to support general development activities, is that this alternative still does not reduce NGO dependence on U.S. government resources for these organizations' supposedly "private" programs. The main worry, however, is that uncontrolled resales could cause market disruptions, harming local food producers and shopkeepers. Though individual amounts sold might be low, once various agencies get into the act the total market effect could be significant. As an internal CRS report noted, "Every addition to supply has a depressive impact on prices. The impact might be too small for the monetizer to notice, but it will not go unnoticed by farmers who are competing with low-priced imports."[34]

COMBATING MALNUTRITION

Despite the expense and effort put into U.S. food-aid programs in Central America, and despite the harmful side effects and the lack of evidence that these programs do significantly improve the nutrition of their beneficiaries, CARE and CRS have been distributing food aid in Central America for roughly three decades. Though the widespread assumption is that their programs must have done some good, these agencies cannot actually show any concrete nutritional results for their efforts. Indeed, many of the project personnel we interviewed had their doubts as to the nutritional effectiveness of their programs. Commonly, they told us that in their own opinion nutritional impact had been "nil," "nonexistent," or "minimal."

Nor were we able to locate any methodologically sound evaluations showing that CARE or CRS programs had been effective in alleviating malnutrition in the region. Most evaluations of Central American food-aid programs, lacking appropriate methodology including baseline data, rely on impressionistic evidence as to the impact of these programs. They then claim positive results, but with no hard evidence to back up these assertions. Indeed, in all our travels and interviews, we were able to find only two attempts to do a statistical analysis on the nutritional effects of ongoing Central American food-distribution programs, both with vague and disappointing results.

A private 1984 study of a child-feeding program in Guatemala found no significant improvement in nutritional status, in part because most of the children in the program were not malnourished to begin with.[35] An AID-contracted evaluation in 1987 of the Title II maternal/child health program in Honduras (which AID itself has criticized for poor methodology) showed "some impact" on a woman's success in childbearing and the height (though not the weight) of her children. The report noted, however, that "this impact was not of the magnitude that one would expect after almost 30 years of food distribution."[36]

Worldwide, the findings on the nutritional effects of food-distribution programs are also surprisingly weak and inconclusive. Some studies report significant nutritional improvement, but many others find limited or even negative impact.[37] Two major factors explain these mixed reports. The first is the real methodological difficulty involved in measuring nutritional effects and attributing them to food supplements as opposed to some other cause. The second is the great variability in the design and execution of different supplementary feeding schemes. There is little doubt that well-run programs can show positive nutritional effects (though their cost-benefit ratio is another matter altogether). The poor results reported from around the world, then, suggest the existence of a great many ineffective programs.

The limited nutritional impact of supplementary food distributions has been traced to five main factors:

– Many beneficiaries are not malnourished to begin with. This is especially true of school-feeding programs.[38]

- Food aid is a unidimensional solution to a complex problem. Malnutrition can be due as much to poor health and sanitary conditions (leading, for example, to recurrent diarrhea) as to an inadequate diet.
- The intended beneficiaries often share their food rations—calculated to meet their individual caloric needs—with other family members.
- Food aid is frequently sold or fed to domestic animals.
- Food aid often substitutes for, rather than supplements, usual food consumption. Families save money on their food bill, but total food intake may remain about the same.

The first four items can all be partially remedied through program redesign: for example, better targeting, combining food distribution with nutritional education, calculating rations for families and not just for selected individuals, and distributing only food adapted to local needs and tastes. But the substitution problem is more intractable. The whole idea of supplementary feeding is to provide enough additional food to bring the beneficiary's diet up to adequate nutritional levels. In practice, however, additionality is extremely difficult to ensure. Even on-site feeding of prepared foods, such as in school-lunch programs, does not guarantee that intake will be increased much beyond usual levels. Knowing that their children will be fed at school, financially strapped mothers may simply give them less food at home.

Resale and substituting donated for purchased food are both ways for families to turn their rations into extra income. Though these practices limit nutritional impact, the resource transfer is still of economic benefit to the family, which sees an increase in its total income equal to the value of the food rations. The main effect of many food-aid programs, therefore, is basically an increase in total family income.

If the main effect is on income, one must ask if food-aid programs—with all their expense and administrative complexity—are the best way to achieve this increase. If the goal is simply to help poor families, without pretending any direct effects on their nutritional status, other income-generating job or credit programs might well be more suitable.

REACHING THE NEEDIEST

Most food-aid beneficiaries are poor, especially by U.S. standards, and helping the poor is almost always one of the stated intentions of the donations. These circumstances do not necessarily mean, however, that food aid is an appropriate solution for poverty. For starters, the number of people that can feasibly be covered by these programs is often far less than the total sum of people in need. Well over half of all Central American children suffer some degree of malnutrition,[39] yet maternal/child food programs rarely reach more than a quarter of the target population. In 1983 the beneficiary population as a percentage of the maternal/infant population stood at 15 percent in Honduras, 16 percent in El Salvador, 20 percent in Guatemala, and 34 percent in Costa Rica.[40] This low coverage would not be so serious a problem with adequate targeting to ensure the food gets to those who really need it most. Yet with the exception of emergency food relief, food-aid programs do not usually reach the poorest of the poor. Commonly, food-aid programs concentrate their services in the most geographically accessible areas of the country or those where an institutional infrastructure, such as a church or public-health center network, already exists.[41]

Advocates of distributive food aid argue that these programs, especially food-for-work, are self-targeting. This means that they automatically go to the poorer and hungrier because no one else is willing to go through the inconvenience that being a food-aid beneficiary entails. To some extent this is true, but there are many exceptions to this rule. School-feeding programs are the most obvious.

School-feeding programs cover only those relatively privileged children who do attend school, and they usually include all the children in those schools regardless of their nutritional and economic status. Furthermore, schools in Central America tend to be concentrated in cities and other accessible areas. For these reasons, school feeding usually does not reach the most disadvantaged children, at the same time that it includes many children of middle-class families.

Nutritionally, the most vulnerable groups are pregnant and lactating mothers and children between six months and three years of age. Almost all Central American maternal/child programs, however, accept children up to five or even seven years of age. School feeding, of course, bypasses the younger children altogether.

Many programs select beneficiaries not on the basis of physical growth retardation, a fairly objective measure, but by subjective estimations of poverty and need. This encourages recipients to play "poor me" or to badger program workers to let them in. Another route can be friendship or political influence. One woman waiting in a food line told us about pulling down her skirt on the street to show a nun a festering wound from an operation and thereby convince the sister to put her on a distribution list. Another had nudged her way into the same program with a letter of recommendation from the mayor's sister, and still another by helping the nuns in their home for the elderly. All agreed that the dirtier and more disheveled one looked, the better one's chances of being accepted.

Beneficiary selection is frequently loose and rife with corruption. For example, a recent CARE evaluation of six hundred maternal/child programs run by government health posts in Guatemala found 30 percent registering commodity shortages, 54 percent with questionable management of funds, 48 percent with an outdated beneficiary list, and 25 percent distributing food to unauthorized beneficiaries. Though CARE has subsequently tightened up this program, these types of problems are endemic to nearly all food programs, especially those run by government personnel. Community promoters in charge of food distribution commonly reward their friends and members of the same political party. Donations handled by government assistance agencies often turn up on the shelves of local shopkeepers. Beneficiary lists are frequently inflated, and leftover food is handed out to members of the sponsoring institution. Perhaps because it is seen as something of a free good, food aid seems to attract and nourish corruption and greed.

LET THEM DRINK MILK

Food-aid programs hand out what foreign donors want to give away, not what the poor and hungry necessarily need or want. In the 1980s the world food-aid basket became more varied as donor-country surpluses expanded from cereals to include more items such as lentils, sugar, and milk. Still, it remains donor-country surpluses and marketing priorities, not recipient needs, that largely determine the ration mix. Waiting in a food line in Guatemala City, one mother wistfully remarked, "I do hope that this time they give us some real food and not just all that other stuff. I need corn to make my tortillas." Her haul that day, from both U.S. and other foreign donors: powdered milk, lentils, wheat flour, canned chicken curry, and baby formula.[42]

Title II aid consists mostly of wheat flour, bulgur wheat, dried peas, yellow corn, vegetable oil, nonfat dry milk, rice, and several special blends prepared with soy, dry milk, and wheat.[43] Though these foods may not always be the most appropriate, neither are they as strange to Central Americans as some others. Section 416, centered on surplus commodities held by the CCC, in 1987 was distributing dry milk, butter oil, and seven-pound cans of processed yellow cheese. The next year, as dairy supplies dried up, it switched to wheat and powdered milk. The World Food Programme, with its multiple donors, offers a wide variety of products including wheat flour, yellow corn, beans, vegetable oil, powdered milk, soups, and canned meat and fish. Although the greater range of its commodity basket might seem to make it easier to provide food packages acceptable to local tastes, in Central America WFP distributions have included such exotic items as canned curried chicken and European cheeses. Besides these official donations, some NGOs and churches also distribute whatever private donors dump on them, from jars of baby food to laxatives and diet drinks.

Nearly all these foods, with the exception of rice and possibly wheat, encounter acceptability problems in Central America, where the diet of the poor is based on corn, black or red beans, and sometimes rice. Corn is the staple of the Central American diet, but the corn distributed under Title II is yellow, whereas the local population is more accustomed to white corn. Aid recipients in El Salvador and Guatemala complained to us that U.S. yellow corn does not have the best consistency for making tortillas. Neither are the Central American poor used to drinking milk, and many report that the powdered milk distributed under Title II gives them diarrhea. Some U.S. vegetable oils, and especially butter oil, have a different taste and consistency than the cooking oils Central Americans are accustomed to, and many rural inhabitants have traditionally used not oil but lard. Beans are rarely of the variety eaten in the country, and for many wheat is mostly a luxury food consumed in small amounts or on special occasions.

Processed cheese, distributed in Guatemala under the Section 416 World Share program, is outright disliked. A 1985 Congressional Research Service report concluded, "Cheese has very limited potential for increased use in Africa and Central America. Traditionally, the introduction and assimilation of fermented food products into the food supply occurs slowly, if at all." The report also pointed to "the storage, refrigeration, and handling requirement of cheese" as another limiting factor.[44] Nevertheless, large quantities of processed cheese went to a Section 416 program in Guatemala the following year. Not surprisingly, most of the recipients of this cheese, who certainly did not own refrigerators, immediately sold it to restaurants, stores, or passing middle- and upper-class motorists who already had a taste for this U.S. food.

The World Share case is an extreme example, owing to the inappropriate nature of the products being distributed. Most of the food donated through other programs does appear to be eaten by recipient families. But resale, especially of the foods less well liked, does occur. These resales, though frowned upon by donors, often make good economic sense for program beneficiaries, allowing them to trade products they may not need or want, or products they are hard pressed to transport home, for cash to buy daily necessities. Salvadoran displaced persons told us they sold their yellow corn rations to local chicken feeders, then used the money to buy the white corn they preferred.

Sadly, these foods are often resold for a fraction of their real value. In Guatemala City, U.S. powdered milk sells on the street for just twenty cents a pound and processed cheese for eighty cents—less than half the price of these same products in the stores. One widow in a food-for-work program, trying to support herself and four children, calculated her take for a full week's work as forty pounds of yellow corn and just $5.20 from the resale of milk, cheese, and oil—not nearly enough to support a family of five.

But even stranger things happen to food aid. Powdered milk is commonly used to fatten domestic livestock—with excellent results, we were told. One vocational high school in Guatemala City uses donated powdered milk in its pig-feeding project. In the Guatemalan highlands town of Nebaj, we heard of people feeding canned curried chicken to their chickens. Others eat the curried chicken themselves, but only after washing off the sauce.

NUTRITIONAL EDUCATION

Food-aid officials recognize that the food being handed out is often not eaten by the intended beneficiaries but is fed to animals or sold. But since donors and project staff can often do little to change the ration mix, they try to change the tastes and attitudes of the recipients instead. Under the guise of "nutritional education"—what would ideally be programs to teach recipients how their nutritional needs could best be met using local resources and how basic sanitation and health practices could protect them from disease and diarrhea—food-aid personnel too often simply teach recipients how to prepare the new and foreign foods.

AID officially requires that nutritional education accompany supplementary feeding programs. In its regulation handbook, AID states that in maternal/child health food projects "a nutritional educational component (which might also include elements of health and/or family planning) should be considered essential. . . . The lack of such a program would give rise to consideration for discontinuing support."[45]

It is thought, and rightly so, that poor people in underdeveloped countries could benefit from basic nutritional education. At least part of the incidence of malnutrition is due to lack of knowledge about appropriate breast-feeding and weaning practices, what constitutes a balanced diet, the care of children with diarrhea, and the most cost-effective way to feed a family. But in practice much of the nutritional education taking place in Central America resembles the suggested recipes displayed on the back of commercial food packages showing new and tasty ways to use more of that item.

Nutritional-education classes are often no more than impromptu lectures on why recipients should be eating the rations so generously being given to them. Other times cooking classes are held to show recipients how to prepare the foreign food. As a staff member of the U.S.-based World Share explained, "The people aren't used to eating the food we give them, so we have classes to tell them how to prepare it." So before being given their allotment of processed cheese, powdered milk, and wheat flour, World Share recipients listen to a project staff member tell them how to make pancakes, a white sauce, "cheese whiz" (using a blender), and cheese tacos.[46] Most often the suggested recipes include only those items being distributed. But in one food-aid training session we visited, Guatemalan government nutritionists were being taught to advise WFP food-aid recipients—supposedly the poorest of the poor—to dress up their canned sardines with imported olive oil, an expensive product normally purchased only by the upper class.[47]

Many food-aid agencies justify their distribution of foreign foods precisely on the grounds that these foods do not form part of the poor person's normal diet. Being additional, food aid presumably will not undermine local market demand for traditional grains (and will also be more traceable if illicitly sold). Some program managers also argue that these foreign foods, especially high-protein products such as nonfat dry milk or soy-based powders, are somehow better, or more healthful, than the local diet. This assumption is both ethnocentric and inaccurate. The traditional Central American grain-based diet, consumed in adequate proportions and supplemented by local fruits and vegetables, contains a full complement of proteins and other nutrients and is perfectly capable of supporting normal growth and development. Most malnutrition in the area is the result of an overall lack of caloric intake, not a lack of protein per se.[48]

Milk, the great food-program favorite, has special dangers and disadvantages. Many Central Americans lack the enzyme needed to digest milk.[49] Throughout the region, mothers complain that powdered milk gives their children diarrhea. The distribution of powdered milk can also encourage increased bottle feeding of infants and small children—an extremely dangerous practice in the poor sanitary conditions under which most Central American families live. Illiterate mothers often do not mix the milk in the right proportion or sterilize the bottles. Often they have no access to clean water or adequately constructed latrines, and the floors of their homes are made of dirt. The bottles almost inevitably become contaminated, and the children end up with diarrhea and disease. "One good bout of diarrhea," in the words of one local doctor, "can quickly undo whatever nutritional benefit might have been gained through months of feeding."[50]

Food aid, particularly from private donors, often comes packaged with foreign-language instructions. One wonders, for example, what recipients think of Slim Fast, "the natural way to lose weight," when they take it back to their homes.[51] One church program we visited was giving out Belgian infant-feeding formula to any mother who reported an infant at home. Not only was the milk past its expiration date, but all the instructions on each can were in Arabic.[52]

Though some foreign food is sold to get money to buy other items, most of it is usually eaten. In a short time this free food can change dietary habits, especially those of children. Youngsters throughout Central America are growing up on a largely foreign diet of wheat flour, vegetable oil, and powdered milk. These imported foods are often high-value products and therefore not a cost-effective way for poor families to meet their nutritional needs. In Honduras, for example, it has been calculated that "corn is about twice as effective as wheat as a source of nutrition, measured in terms of the lempira cost of a calorie and a gram of protein obtained from each product."[53] As long as they are free, families will be able to satisfy their taste for these new foods. In the long run, though, there is no free lunch. Poor Central Americans will have expensive food tastes, and these countries will be dependent on imported foods they can ill afford.

Changing consumption patterns and the often ineffective nature of supplementary feeding programs are not the only reasons for growing disillusionment with those programs. Traditional food handouts—especially maternal/child programs—are also notorious for building psychological dependency. These open-ended programs, by failing to attack the roots of the problems they seek to alleviate, provide temporary benefits that last only as long as the programs.

At first many agencies saw food aid as a way to provide immediate help, show results quickly, and thereby gain credibility. But once agencies started distributing food aid they often found it hard to stop. Shutting down projects not only leaves needy beneficiaries in the lurch but is also likely to be met with protest. "Maternal/child feeding is the worse thing that ever happened to this community," complained one priest in Guatemala, "but now I can't get out of it. My parishioners would be in an uproar if I ever stopped the food."

Recipient individuals—and governments—soon come to depend on food aid without ever exploring the structural causes of poverty and malnutrition. Food-aid recipients come to see these handouts as their right and their price for participating in all programs. We were informed by many NGOs that the first question they are now being asked when working in new communities is, What will you give us?

Food aid teaches poor families to look to "charity," not their own capabilities, to meet their day-to-day needs. Instead of looking toward concrete long-term solutions for their problems, people come to focus only on what they can get free. As described by a social worker for the AID-financed Salvadoran National Commission to Aid the Displaced (CONADES): "The idea is just 'gimmie, gimmie, gimmie,' even if they don't really need the commodity being distributed. They see a line for something, they get in it. Some of the displaced even have hoards of clothes and stuff that they never use. They ask for food aid even though they don't like the foods being given out."[54]

Many families, meanwhile, practically make their living by going from program to program, collecting a supplementary ration at each. The dispersion of food-aid organizations and their poor coordination make this possible. One woman in Guatemala City was enrolled in five programs. We met others who traveled from one end of the city to the other to take advantage of food-aid projects. In El Salvador, one nun recounted to us the scene that occurred when an army civic-action program turned up in her village to distribute U.S. food aid at the same time that a private program was handing out food. "The people didn't know what to do. They were running back and forth across the square like crazy, all trying to keep their place in two lines simultaneously."

Another Salvadoran social worker described handing out food in San Salvador several days after the 1986 earthquake: "These people were in no danger of starving. Things had already pretty much settled down by the time our truck arrived. Yet they all just scrambled to get the food, even pushing and shoving. It was very sad to see, all these people acting wild, acting just like animals." Others described to us similar scenes that occurred following the 1976 earthquake in Guatemala.

Handing out food and then trying to convince the population to eat it can have unexpected and unintended side effects. Drawing on their experiences in Guatemala, two development workers observed that nutrition programs based on free foreign food convince many mothers that their children can be healthy only if they eat the foods given away in the program. "Instead of teaching a woman how she can feed her child well using things the family has produced or purchased locally, this approach takes away the family's dignity and, in effect, says that they are not capable of feeding their children adequately without outside help."[55] Many poor Guatemalans reportedly consider the government's maternal/child feeding program (open only to pregnant and lactating women and children under six) as an incentive to keep having children. As one rural promoter described local attitudes, "If one has another baby, then one gets more food."

EMERGENCY RELIEF

Hurricanes, earthquakes, floods, and drought inflict themselves on the Central American isthmus with disproportional frequency. Since the 1960s the United States and other foreign donors have been responding to these disasters with shipments of emergency food relief. In the 1970s both Guatemala and Nicaragua were hit by major earthquakes, and Honduras suffered a hurricane followed by drought. Many NGOs and churches that initially entered with emergency relief programs stayed on after these crises to run supplementary feeding and development projects.

Natural disasters continue to plague Central America, and their victims continue to be assisted. In the 1980s, however, most emergency relief programs are directed to the victims of the civil wars and political violence that beset the region.

Emergency food relief, though often disparaged by those enthusiastic about using food aid as a development resource, is one of the best and most logical uses of these donations. When people's normal access to food is interrupted by sudden disaster, threatening them with starvation and want, food assistance is an appropriate and appreciated response. Refugees and displaced persons throughout the region can attest to the value of having foreign agencies provide food and other basic needs in times of desperation. In Central America, however, the positive nature of emergency food relief is being undermined by many inappropriate programs and by the increasing politicization of emergency food aid.

Most disaster-assistance experts agree that emergency aid, to truly be of use in relief and reconstruction efforts, must meet a basic series of conditions.[56] Any food supplied must be:

– Appropriate to the need created by the disaster: Food aid would be appropriate only for disasters where food supplies are lost (drought or flood) or where a population's income or access to food has been cut off (refugees and the internally displaced).
– Appropriate to the time frame of the disruption: Food aid should arrive immediately after the disaster and not be extended beyond the time it is really needed.
– Appropriate to local customs and traditions: Where possible, food aid should conform to local dietary customs.
– Not disruptive to existing coping mechanisms: Food-aid programs should not undermine local leadership and self-help efforts.
– Not disruptive to local markets: Food aid has to be carefully managed to avoid creating disincentives for local farm production, and should, in fact, be bought on the local market when possible.

Emergency assistance must be managed with great care if it is not to create unwanted side effects. In Central America that care has often been lacking. After a hurricane or an earthquake strikes, a large amount of relief aid from a variety of private and public sources flows into the affected area. Because of inefficient and often unconcerned governments, there is usually no control over the kind and amount of food aid that comes rushing into the stricken area.

Relief efforts following the 1976 earthquake in Guatemala offer a classic example of the problems caused by unneeded and inappropriate food aid. Although harvests were not affected by the earthquake, foreign food aid flooded into the Guatemala highlands, seriously depressing prices for local farmers.[57] The careless distribution of food aid also affected deep-rooted social structures. Leadership in Indian communities was often reduced to a test of who could get more food aid for the village. As several development workers later denounced:

> The relief programs following the earthquake have strongly affected how local people have chosen their leaders. Instead of looking to honest, hard-working leaders with good judgment, the people have often followed the men who were able to secure for their followers the largest amount of goods. These men, all too often, are those who are deceitful, who have painted the conditions in their villages as black as possible, who fibbed about what help they had already received, and who didn't mind cheating when filling out forms.[58]

The guidelines for effective and appropriate emergency food relief continue to be violated in the 1980s, especially in programs for victims of the region's violence. Increasingly, army-linked national emergency commissions, known as CONE in Guatemala and COPEN in Honduras, coordinate aid to disaster areas. Emergency food-aid programs in Guatemala, El Salvador, and Honduras are often more political than humanitarian in nature.

The internal displaced, since they are generally not afforded the same guarantees and protection as those who have fled their country of origin, are particularly susceptible to political pressures. Whereas Guatemalan refugees living in Mexico and Salvadorans in Honduras have a certain status and protection as international refugees, those displaced people remaining in their own countries remain subject to many of the same political pressures that forced them to flee their homes in the first place. As described in chapter 7, emergency food for the displaced population is generally routed through the hands of the local government and army.

FOOD FOR IMAGE

Among the many types of foreign assistance, food aid has the most psychological and symbolic weight. Foreign donors make certain that those who eat this food do not forget where it came from. Title II food comes packaged with the red, white, and blue emblem of AID, with the inscription "Furnished by the people of the United States of America," and cooperating sponsors are requested to make sure, through additional publicity, that beneficiaries know it was the United States that sent it. This requirement is not taken lightly; in 1983 CARE and CRS programs in Honduras were censured for failing to provide sufficient publicity.[59]

Not just the U.S. government, but the churches, NGOs, local government agencies, and food-aid committees who hand out the food also try to cash in on these programs' goodwill value.

The government social welfare agency, almost always headed up by the first lady, typically is deeply involved in food distribution. Local mayors and officials frequently use food aid to win support for their political parties. Armies use food donations in civic-action programs designed to build up their image. For NGOs, food aid offers easy access to otherwise hostile or suspicious communities. Local development committees often welcome food aid as a way to bolster their own position in the community.

The Catholic church's charitable programs (usually administered by the diocesan CARITAS organizations) have long been based on foreign food donations. While AID prohibits the use of food aid for evangelism, food-aid programs have clearly helped the Catholic church maintain its hold on poor congregations. The food is a way to attract people to religious services and other church activities and to manifest religious workers' concern for the poor. The easy food-aid route has contributed to the conservative and paternalistic nature of most CARITAS programs. For many volunteers and clergy involved in CARITAS, Christian charity translates into lining up parishioners in food lines. Not uncommonly, the nuns handing out the food use the opportunity to encourage attendance at Sunday mass.

Bags of U.S. food aid have been a common sight in the warehouses of the local Catholic church for decades now. Lately they are also turning up in the evangelical churches that are mushrooming in Central America. Much of this food the evangelical groups have acquired from their own private sources. Organizations like the Christian Broadcasting Network (CBN), Knights of Malta, Larry Jones's Ministries International, and Gospel Crusade solicit donations from U.S. industries and then distribute these foods—including such inappropriate items as canned baby food and diet foods—to their missions abroad.

A substantial portion, however, also comes from U.S. government sources. In both Guatemala and Honduras, CARE food goes to a wide assortment of pentecostal and fundamentalist missions. In El Salvador, the Salvadoran Evangelical Committee for Relief and Development (CESAD) has distributed AID-supplied Title II food to displaced persons organized into local committees with the help of evangelical pastors.[60]

In Guatemala, AID has channeled part of two different Section 416 donations to evangelical churches and other private agencies. The distribution lists for these powdered milk shipments, the first destined largely for the victims of the army violence of 1982–83 and the second an ad hoc distribution occurring in 1987, gives some indication of the huge proliferation of evangelical groups in this country. AID's choices included such pentecostal organizations as Youth with a Mission, ASIDE (Evangelical Indigenous Association), Facts of Faith, Prince of Peace church, Latin American Missionary Challenge, and FUNDAPI (a branch of the El Verbo church).[61]

It is accepted in Central America that religious organizations—both Catholic and evangelical—are an important channel for U.S. food aid. AID has long considered churches an efficient vehicle for distributing food to the needy abroad. While there is an undeniable logic to this argument, especially given the corruption so often seen in the social programs run by government agencies, the close link between U.S. food aid and religion in Central America does raise some important church/state issues. Specifically, one might ask just who is supporting whose agenda. If both the U.S. government and the religious program sponsor agree on common humanitarian and development goals, with the religious motivation for the churches' involvement remaining largely in the background, then there is no problem with this approach. But to the extent that these religious organizations use taxpayer-funded food aid for proselytizing and to support their particular religious or ideological agendas, then these programs are certainly not an appropriate use of U.S. government funds.

Given the evangelical groups' active proselytizing and their often aggressively anticommunist stance, their growing access to U.S. government food donations gives particular grounds for concern. In a region as poor as Central America, especially with large population sectors uprooted and dependent on others for sustenance, food aid can be a potent resource in evangelistic and political campaigns.

NO COORDINATION

The Central American food-aid scene is nothing if not complex. Indeed, just sorting out who is giving food to whom is a major headache. A wide range of donors channel their food to both government and private agencies, which either operate distribution programs themselves or hand the food over to others. Often one agency will receive food from several sources. The kinds and amounts of foods distributed, and beneficiary selection criteria, vary widely between programs. Up to now there has been almost no coordination between different donors and distributing agencies. Often one agency does not even know what another is doing.

Programs are rarely guided by, or incorporated into, the host government's development plans.[62] Indeed, the Central American governments do not seem to have any food-aid planning criteria, except to encourage more agencies and more food to pour in. Guatemala's Christian Democratic government, for example, aims to "maximize donations of [food] aid until we can become self-sufficient."[63]

One reason governments make little attempt to incorporate food-aid resources into larger development efforts, or to critically assess their effect, is decreasing social-service and development budgets. Food assistance is sometimes the only program the Central American governments can really point to when it comes to describing their commitment to such concepts as "equity," "spreading the benefits of growth," "employment generation," and "participation." Since the goal in these cases is largely political image, a serious cost-benefit analysis is never undertaken, nor are alternative approaches to the same problems considered.

At present the only two agencies in a position to actively guide and shape the Central American food scene would be the World Food Programme, the largest distributing agency in the region, and AID, which is the original source of at least 80 percent of all the food aid to Guatemala, El Salvador, and Honduras. In 1984 ROCAP, the regional AID office, did donate $5.6 million to the Central American Nutritional Institute (INCAP) to finance technical studies on food-aid program design and to help set up national coordination offices. With AID encouragement, most Central American governments are now finally trying to define official food-aid policies and guidelines.[64]

The national coordinating commissions being proposed, however, are fragile bureaucratic constructions that have so far proved helpless against the entrenched power of those ministries that currently control the various aid flows. El Salvador's policy, for example, was at last word still bogged down in jockeying over which ministry will head the proposed oversight commission. One UN food-security expert we interviewed doubted that the coordinating commission would ever become effective, because too many illicit interests are served through the present anarchic setup. Not even the INCAP-run research projects have been able to really get off the ground, once again owing to the rivalry and thinly disguised political agendas of the government agencies involved.

The private distribution agencies, for their part, are understandably leery of government bureaucracy and political manipulation and not keen to subject themselves to local government coordination. In a free-for-all, each agency at least keeps its own independence. Currently, those that wish to work with the government do so, and those that do not can usually operate fairly independently. Coordination among donors, meanwhile, is hampered by the organizations' different political and development agendas. One positive development, nevertheless, is a worldwide computerized donation recording system now being started up by WFP.

AID has in recent years tightened its guidelines in order to maximize the development and nutritional impact of food-distribution programs. But in Central America, at least, agency missions have not been strict about enforcing those revised regulations. Although most NGO directors recognize the weakness of their programs, few seem ready to take firm action to remedy their problems without outside pressure. "Food aid is a freebie that nobody wants to give up," observed Honduran CRS director Patrick Ahern, "yet no-one wants to put a lot of resources into food aid to make it work."[65]

In Central America, AID's political agenda often seems to outweigh development concerns. Rather than working to shape up existing programs, AID has approved increased levels of U.S. food aid and invited inexperienced NGOs such as CESAD and World Share to come in and set up shop. The functions of food aid in supporting local governments, in feeding evangelical fervor, and in softening the image of the U.S. regional role could all be viewed as strong pluses in the opinion of foreign-policy strategists. From this political perspective, it would matter little how efficiently these programs are run or how effective they are in combating poverty and malnutrition. At least in some quarters, the goal simply seems to be to reach more and more beneficiaries with food parcels reading "Furnished by the people of the United States of America."

SUMMARY

Throughout the region, from cloud-covered highland villages to the teeming shantytowns of the capital cities, needy people wait in long lines for free food rations. Schoolchildren eagerly await their soy cookies, and mothers depend on food aid to help make ends meet. For the Central American poor, free food is a welcome addition to the family's total resources for survival.

That distributive food aid is meant to assist hungry and destitute people makes it a difficult foreign-aid program to judge. Perhaps that is why the U.S. Congress is willing time after time to approve increased allocations for the PL 480 assistance. It is a serious mistake, however, to assume that handing free food to needy people constitutes an adequate or even an apt solution to the problems of hunger and poverty. The cost and effectiveness of distributive food aid needs to be evaluated.

These programs are not cheap. First the U.S. taxpayer pays for the food and its transport to Central America. There NGOs and local governments fund internal transport, storage, and distribution costs. Large amounts of valuable human resources—including the time and energy of trained professionals such as nurses, teachers, and social workers—go into the complex tasks of commodity management and distribution. Beneficiaries also spend their own time and resources in traveling to distribution sites, waiting in line, and transporting the food back to their homes. Not only are these programs costly, they can also have serious side effects. One of the most important is food aid's impact on consumption patterns by changing tastes from locally grown products to high-priced foreign foods.

The nutritional benefits of supplementary food programs, meanwhile, are far from clear. There is no hard proof that the dozens of programs being run in Central America, and around the world, have any significant nutritional impact. Related to the problem of limited nutritional effect is the issue of targeting. Few programs select beneficiaries on the objective basis of nutritional need. As a result, millions of dollars of food resources end up in the stomachs of those who were not malnourished to begin with. Indeed, most development experts regard food programs, unless very carefully managed and targeted, as an expensive and roundabout way to boost total family income.

The problems described above are familiar to most food-aid directors. Indeed, in our interviews we found that project personnel themselves, after seeing firsthand the weaknesses and effects of food-aid programs, were often their own strongest critics. Yet once involved in these programs, sponsoring agencies find it almost impossible to get out. They fear such a termination would provoke ire amoung beneficiaries and leave now-dependent families in the lurch. One Catholic church program in a Guatemala City shantytown, for example, debated closing its food-for-work program. Though every balance of pro and con factors came up negative, the group wavered for months before finally getting up the political will to close down the program.[66]

In contrast to the muddled nutritional and income goals of supplementary feeding programs, food aid for disaster victims does seem an appropriate and necessary response. But in these programs, we found the problems of poor administration and political manipulation to be even worse than usual.

Various factors contribute to the shoddy state of Central American food programs. First is the lack of adequate funding for program administration and trained personnel. Second is the large share of food aid that, after being passed from agency to agency, ends up being distributed by corrupt and inefficient government offices. Third is the entry of new and inexperienced NGOs, often with political and religious objectives, onto the Central American food-aid scene. Finally, there is the lack of coordination of this food-aid free-for-all. AID is starting to push in that direction, but its efforts are complicated by its own political interests and the political agendas of cooperating NGOs and government agencies.

AID's interest in coordination reflects not just a response to the proliferation of Central American programs, but also a larger rethinking of the appropriate role of U.S. food aid in situations of underdevelopment. The use of food aid to alleviate hunger is rapidly shifting to a focus on food-aid programs that support permanent development efforts. The following chapter will explore just what food for development means and what effect this new direction is having on the Central American people.

1, 2. Civic-action program in a Salvadoran village in 1988.

3. Catholic church feeding program with U.S.-donated food in Guatemala.

4. Selling U.S.-donated food on the streets of Guatemala City.

5. Selling bread, an ever-increasing staple food in Central America.

6. Preparing to plant corn, a traditional staple in Central American diets.

7. Mother and daughter shucking corn in Guatemala.

8. Mexican worker hauling sacks of onions in a UN storage facility in Comitan, Chiapas, Mexico, 1988. Photograph by David Maung, used by permission.

9. Internal refugees captured in
the mountains near Nebay receiving food from the
Guatemalan army at the Nebay
army base in El Quiché province. Photograph by Derrill
Bazzy, used by permission.

6

Food for Development

The innovative link-up of food aid with national development assistance programs has been of enormous help in removing the image food aid sometimes has of being aid of the second choice, good only for surplus disposal and valid only for welfare and emergency relief.

SALAHUDDIN AHMED
deputy director of World Food
Program, speaking to Latin American
Representatives, March 1987

WHEN FOOD aid was first included in the U.S. foreign-aid program, it was viewed mainly as a surplus-disposal and marketing mechanism. Later humanitarian and relief concerns became more closely integrated into the program, and distributive food aid was posited as an essential tool in the fight against world hunger. Today there is an emerging view of food aid as not just a nutritional supplement but a valuable and effective development resource in its own right. Advocates of this new approach say food aid can both ease hunger and spur development.[1]

AID's stress on food aid for development emerged about ten years ago.[2] Under the current development emphasis, food programs are required to show concrete, objective goals and effects, if not on nutritional levels, then in such areas as school attendance, increased use of health clinics, or the construction of infrastructure.

The current development emphasis of food aid was prompted by several factors. One was the growing recognition by international agencies in the

125

1960s and 1970s that world hunger was not a problem that could be solved simply through the endless handout of surplus food. Agencies began to cast about for programs that would avoid this "bottomless pit" effect, and if unable to show concrete nutritional impact, could at least show results on income, education, or health levels. Many donor organizations also wanted to create programs that avoided long-term beneficiary dependency. Key in promoting the new concept of food for development was the World Food Programme (WFP), a long-term champion of food-for-work (FFW) programs.[3] Other donors soon followed suit in looking for new ways to increase the developmental impact of their aid. Another influence in the move to food for development was the criticism that academic and development theorists made of surplus disposal and handout approaches.[4]

Recognition of the extensive costs related to food aid has also made program planners anxious to produce more tangible results per metric ton of food. Title II aid, we should remember, is purchased out of funds appropriated each year by Congress. As U.S. budgetary concerns have come to the fore, U.S. taxpayers and Congress are demanding concrete results from food-aid programs and increasingly insist on proper program management and accountability.[5]

The new development emphasis, though only partially implemented, is already having a significant effect on food aid to Central America. In particular, AID does not see the rationale for continuing open-ended welfare programs directed to the aged, the institutionalized, and others unable to fend for themselves. Where political conditions permit, these are being slowly phased out. A recent Guatemala evaluation, however, recommended maintaining relief programs in Guatemala to maintain political stability.[6] With the traditional "humanitarian" focus of food aid now taking a backseat, local CRS-CARITAS programs are under pressure to redesign their systems.[7] Food programs are encouraged to focus on social sectors young and healthy enough to be considered significant "human resources" and to combine their handouts with educational activities. Supplementary feeding is no longer justified only for its calorie impact but is seen as a way to lure mothers to health centers and children to school.

The most striking change in Central American food aid, however, is the enormous increase in food-for-work. Food-for-work programs, almost unknown in the region ten to fifteen years ago, are increasingly popular. A

1983–84 study of food programs in Central America identified twenty-one food-for-work projects out of a total of sixty-five.[8] Today, as both displaced persons and maternal/child programs move to the use of food-for-work, the share of FFW is undoubtedly much higher. Throughout Central America, poor people are being paid in food to build roads, community centers, and irrigation systems. Governments depend on FFW to implement colonization and resettlement projects for landless and displaced peasants and to promote the production of nontraditional export crops.

The changing orientation in food aid has had a far-reaching effect in Central America. Food aid can no longer be judged on nutritional or health grounds alone. The alternative goals of each program, be they infrastructure creation, employment generation, or increasing social organization, must also be considered. The potential beneficiaries of the programs are widened from those at nutritional risk to almost anyone, malnourished or not, who can be enticed with food to undertake new activities. In assessing this aspect of food aid in Central America, however, we found that, while glowing pronouncements as to the advantages of food-for-development are abundant, hard evidence on those positive results is seriously lacking. And our own interviews and project visits pointed up several serious problems rarely covered in internal NGO and WFP evaluations.

FOOD AS AN INCENTIVE

Supplementary feeding programs were originally designed to alleviate hunger and malnutrition directly by providing extra calories to vulnerable population groups such as pregnant and lactating women, toddlers, and school-age children. Today these programs are being used not just to supply more calories, but also to give the target groups incentives for adopting new behaviors that in the long run will indirectly affect their nutritional status. Maternal/child programs serve to draw mothers and children to local health centers, where they are to receive basic nutritional education, health, and vaccination services and where the children's growth can be monitored to detect low-grade malnutrition. School feeding is used to increase attendance and to improve students' concentration and learning capacity.

If food is to be distributed anyway, tying it to educational and health activities is not a bad idea. Indeed, nutritional education, growth monitoring, child vaccination, vitamin A supplementation, and other primary health activities have proved to be cost-effective ways of attacking the problem of malnutrition and its complex interactions with infection and disease. Studies from around the world have shown that a prime determinant of malnutrition in small children is the mother's level of education. The extension of supplementary feeding programs into the areas of nutritional education and health care is in many respects a positive move, implying a certain recognition of the complex causes for widespread malnutrition.

Our research in Central America, however, led us to ask some basic questions about these programs. First, are the educational and health activities really happening? If not, then why not? Second, on a more philosophical level, are food-distribution programs appropriate vehicles for these types of activities?

AID guidelines now require all maternal/child feeding programs to include an educational component.[9] In Central America, nearly every food project proposal at least pays lip service to nutritional and health education. From our project visits and interviews, however, we found these claims about the educational components of Central American food-aid programs to be greatly exaggerated. Only in the exceptional case, such as CARE programs that had received special AID "outreach grants," did maternal/child programs actually include the type of educational component required in the *AID Handbook* and described in project reports.

Many projects we visited, especially those run by church groups, had no educational or health component at all. At most the beneficiaries received "talks" on the preparation and use of the commodities being distributed. The lack of a nutritional-education component in projects, and the poor design and implementation of most of few educational efforts that do exist, have also been pointed out in several program and country evaluations. Lack of funding and a reliance on volunteer labor are mentioned as important constraints.[10]

In Honduras, we asked a consultant for Title II projects about the development aspects of food distribution. In her own experience, she said, "There is no nutrition or health education associated with the maternal/child health or school-feeding programs in Honduras. Absolutely none." Shortly before the interview, she had come across a chart listing CARE food projects around the world with a description of associated programs. According to this consultant, "All the projects listed education, hygiene, and health programs that accompanied CARE's food distribution. But it was a real joke. It was more like what they hope to do or think they should do rather than what is being done."[11]

One explanation for the distribution agencies' poor record in implementing education and health activities is the lack of complementary funding and trained personnel. Unless special funding, personnel, and materials are dedicated to health and educational activities, they will be done poorly or not at all. Training of local-level project workers is the key. Participants in a 1987 WFP evaluation mission to Guatemala reported that some distribution centers were religiously weighing and measuring each child—as required by program designers—but then writing all the children's measurements down on just one sheet of paper, without ever using this information to chart the individual children's growth. The mothers, meanwhile, were simply informed of the child's current weight with no further explanation of what the figure meant.[12] In both El Salvador and Guatemala, mothers told us they thought their children were being weighed to check that the mothers were giving the food rations to their children and not selling them.

Another problem is confusion over what nutritional education is and what it is supposed to achieve. The rationale behind nutritional education is that one of the causes of malnutrition is lack of knowledge. Many mothers simply are not aware of the nutritional needs of their children, especially toddlers in the weaning phase, nor do they know what nutrients are provided by different foods. It has been proved that a better understanding of these needs, and the most cost-effective way to meet them, can bring nutritional improvement even with no change in family income. Yet in Central America nutritional education is often taken to mean simply teaching beneficiaries to prepare and use the foreign foods being distributed. Thus two very different activities are going under the same "nutritional education" title.

Besides the formidable problems of implementation, the use of food as a lure brings us to a more fundamental question: Given the importance of education and preventive health care in reducing malnutrition and promoting development, is food aid the most appropriate and cost-effective vehicle for these activities?

Maternal/child feeding programs apparently do attract women to clinics and community centers. But attendance for food will last only as long as the food does. And attendance alone does not increase understanding. Indeed, the more fundamental and pervasive danger appears to be that the focus on food will distract both beneficiaries and program workers from their primary tasks. One health worker in Guatemala put the problem this way: "The food does serve to attract people to the health center, but this force is not then utilized. They just come in to get the food, and that's it." In many community centers, schools, and clinics, teachers and health workers are kept busy handling the logistics of food transport, unloading, repackaging, distribution, and perhaps preparation. Program directors can then point to the number of people who come in to get the food. Yet health workers, teachers, and other social service workers have been distracted from their primary tasks of health care, education, and provision of services.[13] And often these same health clinics lack basic supplies and medicines, and the schools have neither benches nor blackboards.

It is commonly assumed that school feeding helps increase attendance, and possibly concentration and learning, yet the evidence about its real impact is mixed.[14] One problem is the many determinants behind school attendance. Central American parents often do not send their children to school because they need them to work, because they cannot afford uniforms and books, or because there is no school within walking distance. School feeding simply cannot counterbalance all these constraints; furthermore, its effectiveness in doing so depends on such factors as the size of the ration.[15] School feeding must be recognized as an only partial and perhaps ineffective solution for the much larger problems of poverty, employment, and inadequate social services. Given its popularity, school feeding too easily slides into being the main focus of government and aid efforts. Before Central American educational problems can be solved, the region also needs improved schools, better training and salary levels for teachers, and increased employment and wage levels so that parents are not forced to put their children to work.

The most basic critique of food as a lure, however, would be the argument made by community development workers: that educational and health programs will be effective only if the participants are well motivated and understand the need for different nutrition and health practices on their own terms. The danger is that food aid may be shifting the population's motives for participating in health and educational programs from these activities' intrinsic benefits to the food itself. Popular education and grass-roots approaches are slower methods and must be carefully adapted to the needs and cultural context of each community.

FOOD-FOR-WORK

One step beyond the use of food aid as an education and health incentive is using food to induce participation in infrastructure and job-training programs, by the food-for-work approach. As described in the *AID Handbook*, "The goal of food-for-work projects is the achievement of needed agriculture/economic, and community improvements by providing commodities to support the labor of unemployed and underemployed local workers."[16] In these programs the nutritional goal has been largely superseded by a focus on the activities being promoted via payment in food.

In Central America and around the world, interest in food-for-work has swelled dramatically in recent years. Deficit-ridden governments have discovered food-for-work as a relatively inexpensive way to provide infrastructure and social services as well as extra employment. As the *Food for Peace Annual Report* put it, "Donations also directly help countries feed their labor force. Developing nations often pay their workers in U.S.-supplied food for their labor on schools, roads, sanitation systems, and agricultural projects."[17]

Project directors like the idea of a food program that leads to concrete physical changes and measurable results, and they hope that by requiring beneficiaries to do something in exchange for food they can avoid the paternalism and dependency that characterize more traditional programs. Furthermore, since these projects are usually group efforts, the programs are thought to foster popular participation and organization.

FFW is also held to have certain favorable effects on income distribution and family spending patterns. For one thing, these programs are to a large extent self-targeting to the poorest and unemployed; the low status of payment in kind keeps away all but the really needy. Related to the status factor, as well as to lower female wage-employment rates, is the high participation of women in these programs. Project directors in Central America, believing women are more likely than men to dedicate their earnings to feeding their families, see high female participation as a major plus for FFW. Finally, it is thought that wages paid in kind are more likely to increase family food consumption than would cash wages, which are more likely to be squandered on alcohol or luxury items. With this rationale, the German government runs food-for-work programs in Guatemala and Honduras that, even having the cash to cover wages costs, choose to spend these funds on food with which to compensate the workers.

The linking of food distribution with work, though at first glance a good idea, nevertheless poses some very complicated issues. Food-for-work only partially escapes the problems of traditional handouts, while introducing difficulties of its own. Since the food lasts only as long as there is work to be done, food-for-work programs tend to be much shorter term than other food-distribution programs. The usual pattern is for a large number of communities each to participate for the few months it takes to complete an infrastructure project. Short-term programs help avoid the problem of creating long-term beneficiary dependency, but of course they practically eliminate the possibility of improving the nutritional status of the participating community. In the worst of both worlds, sometimes strict time limits (say six months) are put on FFW resettlement and agricultural projects that (especially in the absence of careful technical and material support) do not become self-sufficient before the cutoff date.[18]

Where food-for-work projects are ongoing (frequently the case for those directed to the nutritionally vulnerable, slum dwellers, or the displaced), they tend to degenerate into make-work projects such as sweeping the streets. One development worker complained to us that the communities he worked with deliberately built poor-quality roads so that they could receive food to repair and rebuild them the following year.

Providing employment for the poor and unemployed is a major objective of FFW projects. Yet in Central America, like anywhere else, people would rather work for money than food—especially food they have no voice in choosing and are not accustomed to eating. As the amount of work expected increases, leaving workers unable to hold regular outside jobs, so does the problematic nature of a food wage. Families obviously have other needs (e.g., shoes, clothing, medicines, and bus fare) for which they need a cash income. In addition, the volumes of certain types of foods given become more and more difficult to consume. Even a U.S. family would find it difficult to eat twenty-eight pounds of processed cheese a month (the amount being distributed in the Guatemala City World Share program). Resale in these programs is exceedingly common. "This is double exploitation," quipped one local journalist, "First they make them work to get the food; then they have to work to sell it."

Despite the hopes of many program planners, payment in food does not necessarily lead to more food consumption. Even if they do not sell the food, food-for-work beneficiaries may simply reduce their normal food purchases. Simply put, each family has its own budget priorities, which continue to guide resource allocation despite the best intentions of food-program directors. To give payment in food in hopes of changing family consumption patterns not only is paternalistic, it is simply not very effective.

Payment in food can also be a violation of workers' rights. The International Labour Office (ILO) conventions, as well as most national legal codes, stipulate that all workers must be paid for their labor and must receive their pay in money, not goods. The only exceptions are those situations that escape the normal definition of "employment." Such a case would be self-help projects of direct benefit to the workers themselves, such as building their own houses or improving their own land. Self-help projects, paid in food, can be organized on a voluntary basis without being considered forced or unpaid labor. All other work is to be paid in cash.[19]

For public works FFW projects, where workers build roads, schools, bridges, or other social infrastructure not necessarily of direct benefit to themselves, the ILO has adopted a compromise formula. Half the wage can be paid in food, but half must be in money. This is the formula also inserted in AID's food-aid handbook and the one that the World Food Programme, ILO's sister UN agency, is also supposed to abide by.[20]

In Central America, however, this formula is not always respected. FFW project managers were always careful to refer to the FFW rations as an "incentive" for community improvement rather than a "wage." Yet in several cases we found FFW workers building and maintaining public services—activities falling outside the definition of what would strictly be self-help measures—and being paid only in food. In both Guatemala and El Salvador, road building in particular has been a central focus of FFW projects. Building short stretches of a local-access road or paving a street might conceivable be considered self-help, but the projects we saw were often going far beyond that—indeed were often linked to military penetration—and would thus enter the category of public works. The use of FFW as full payment for this work implies a serious lack of oversight on the part of both AID and the WFP.

An FFW project run by the Guatemalan City mayor's office with Section 416 food supplied by the NGO World Share is especially scandalous. This has slum dwellers picking up trash along the city's freeway and traveling to middle-class neighborhoods to spruce up the parks. Some work full time cleaning the city's slaughterhouses and vegetable markets, in areas of the city far away from their shantytown homes. Other groups of workers reforest the hills above the city and clean up illegal garbage dumps. Prison inmates work inside the city's prison farm, with the food going to their family members on the outside.[21]

This program clearly involves public works activities that would normally be done by paid municipal or government employees. Indeed, immediately before the 1987 Christmas season we interviewed workers—literally in tears—who had just been told that they were being laid off for the holidays because the food to pay them was going to arrive behind schedule. The importance of their work for the city services department was made clear when we later discovered that paid city workers were substituted for the FFW laborers until the next food shipment arrived some six weeks later.[22]

Through the use of FFW, city governments and road departments are able to stretch their budgets because they are getting the roads built and the streets cleaned with minimum cash outlay. Furthermore, since FFW workers are considered "volunteers," they are usually not entitled to vacations or health benefits or severance pay. When two workers in the CARE–Guatemala City slum-improvement project were buried in a landslide, for example, their families did not receive any city assistance or indemnity.

Governments can also save on costs by using donated food to supplement the pay of regular public workers. Indeed, this is the idea behind the fifty–fifty wage/food rule: expand employment and infrastructure creation by using donated food to lower wage costs on these projects. In Central America, two examples would be the Salvadoran FEDECREDITO project, which had displaced persons building roads for a combination of cash and food payments, and the food payments given to boost the salaries of Honduran literacy teachers.[23]

Besides the use of FFW in public works and services, where the main advantage for the worker is the food wage paid, FFW in Central America is also used in a variety of self-help programs of direct benefit to the project participants. WFP supports community development and small-farmer projects in every country, as well as rural resettlement and colonization programs in Costa Rica, Guatemala, and El Salvador. FFW forestry projects are run by CARE in Guatemala and the WFP in Honduras. The Guatemala City CARE program is putting drainage systems, pavements, and retaining walls into previously neglected slum areas. CARITAS has worked in small-scale social service provision. Several projects are oriented toward training people in productive skills. Here the focus is not so much on the food wage itself as on the benefits these programs are supposed to bring to poor rural and urban communities. And undoubtedly, well-designed FFW projects, especially those complemented with material inputs, may raise incomes and contribute to overall welfare.

One of the strongest arguments for FFW is indeed its effectiveness in creating infrastructure. The offer of food gets many more people involved in community development activities than would participate as unpaid volunteers, enabling more projects to be undertaken. And in Central America, cash to pay formal wages is often just not available.

FFW not only mobilizes labor but can even help mobilize material support. Local community leaders are sometimes able to win pledges of material resources for development projects by convincing donors that local labor, lined up with offers of food-for-work, is ready to cover project labor needs. If the focus of the program is the infrastructure itself, FFW is definitely one way to get things rolling.

Yet the use of FFW in social infrastructure, agricultural, and training programs, while eagerly embraced by both project directors and local governments, does bring certain problems. One is the issue of effectiveness. The type of labor employed—untrained and poorly nourished and often including women, children, and the aged—translates into low productivity and poor-quality results. Often no real provision is made for future maintenance; and having been paid with food to build something, it is unlikely that local townspeople will keep it in repair for free.[24]

A second question is cost. To achieve quality results, projects need complementary material inputs and, again because of the type of labor employed, substantial administrative and technical oversight. Though project directors save on wages, the administrative costs of FFW projects—at least those reasonably well run—are often higher than in normal development projects. Often these extra costs and administrative needs are not taken into account. As a consequence, FFW participants end up doing road repair, community cleanups and other nonpriority projects that require a minimum of additional inputs. In the shantytowns of Guatemala City, for example, armies of women from the World Share program are out every week busily sweeping the unpaved streets. Rural communities often turn to road repair, community cleanups, or chopping down weeds in the cemetery because these jobs do not require tools beyond a few shovels or machetes.

Another question is the effect F F W has on family incomes and on income distribution. Though workers in F F W projects do tend to be the poorest in their communities, the infrastructure they help create often disproportionately benefits the better-off. Studies of F F W from around the world show that the physical results of F F W projects, just as with most public service and infrastructure projects, are distributed unevenly. Roads mainly serve those with marketable produce and with vehicles; they offer little to *campesinos* who are often too poor even to take the bus. Land improvements mostly benefit those with land; and schools benefit only those families who can afford to send their children.

Finally, there is the underlying problem with the whole question of self-help: why poor people should have to build their own infrastructure and social services while the government supplies these to wealthier neighborhoods as a matter of course. Inhabitants of rich neighborhoods, after all, are not expected to pave the streets in front of their homes or to dig the trenches for their water and sewage systems.

Those who support self-help point out that Central America governments, for both political and economic reasons, are simply not providing needed services to poor communities. The choice, they say, is not between F F W and something better, but between F F W and nothing. What these F F W proponents fail to do, however, is to accept the necessity and the possibility for change. Instead of pressuring the government to serve all citizens equally, self-help proponents accept the status quo in the interest of some immediate improvement. Though perhaps more realistic, the self-help approach still seems to us somewhat unjust and exploitative. In essence, F F W projects are helping to lift the burden of providing for the public welfare off the government's shoulders and placing it on the poor.

FOOD-FOR-WORK: A FRAMEWORK FOR DEVELOPMENT?

Food-for-work requires beneficiaries to participate in educational and work activities in exchange for food. The focus of this aid has switched from providing more calories and proteins to producing tangible results in terms of increased educational levels, improved health practices, greater agricultural productivity, and more miles of roads built. But do these "tangible results" really provide the needed framework for development? Community-development experts stress the great importance of grass-roots participation in the design and implementation of programs. By focusing on the quick motivational fix of food, F F W proponents are glossing over the important questions of organization and consciousness that in the long run may be essential components of the development effort.

Food-for-work proponents, by pointing to the large numbers of people participating in their projects and their popularity in poor neighborhoods around the world, argue that their programs do have positive organizational effects. Yet these claims are largely based on supposition. Indeed, our own review of F F W in Central America has led us to believe these programs can have serious negative effects on internal community organization and politics. If the goal is long-term development, F F W should be up for a serious review.

One argument for F F W is that it leaves beneficiaries with more dignity and independence than do traditional handout programs. Even nutritionally oriented maternal/child and relief programs are increasingly adopting the food-for-work method in order to avoid paternalism and dependence.[25] But too often the activities being proposed are poorly designed make-work projects, unsuccessful in disguising these programs' fundamentally charitable—and top-down—nature.

In the eyes of many F F W participants, being forced to work for their rations did not make them feel more dignified, it made them feel exploited and even ridiculous. Most urban food-for-work participants are women, not just because they have more free time, but because many men considered it beneath their dignity to work on these highly public projects. One group of women cleaning up a garbage dump in Guatemala City told us that men from their community sometimes sat on a nearby hill and made fun of them as they worked. Cleaners in a Guatemala City market complained, "Here the mayor gets this food for free and then he makes us work to get it. That food was given to help poor people, not just to help him."

F F W is a fundamentally paternalistic and undemocratic approach to development. The bottom line is that whoever controls the food controls beneficiary activity. Donors and aid agencies have paid insufficient attention to this basic reality. Though many projects claim it is the the "community itself" that decides what projects it wishes to undertake, they rarely say exactly who it is in that community whose opinion they ask. It is still often the priest, the government promoter, or the local military official who, food in hand, decides what activities will be undertaken. Often, project managers decide on activities that are not a priority for the whole community. Volunteer labor, for all its problems, at least acts as a barometer of community interest. With FFW, however, the aid recipients will show up to work on any project, no matter how poorly conceived or unnecessary.

In Guatemala City, we observed one FFW gang busily sweeping dirt streets in the middle of a windstorm. "It's a total farce," said a neighborhood church worker. "The rest of the population is now throwing their garbage out on the streets expecting these other women to sweep it up. As far as the workers themselves are concerned, they don't even have to be holding a broom. All they have to do is is make sweeping motions with their arms four hours every week, and then go get in line for their food." In another case a local priest, to increase project labor requirements for a reforestation project, simply decided that the beneficiaries would all hand carry water up the mountain to water the trees.

Though the paternalistic nature of FFW is unfortunate, an even more serious problem of this approach is its influence on beneficiary motivation. Payment in food tends to shift the rationale for work in self-help and community projects away from the intrinsic benefits of the project itself to the reward of the food. Participation is high while the food lasts but falls off once supplies end, which partially explains the chronic problems with maintenance of FFW infrastructure projects. Once accustomed to food-for-work, local residents are likely to refuse to participate in any future development activity unless it is also paid in food. If this effect is true, and our experience leads us to believe it is, the spreading use of FFW throughout the Central American region should give great cause for concern. Food-for-work may actually be teaching behaviors extremely destructive for long-term development in the region. An agricultural extension worker in the Guatemalan highlands told us that some of the local farmers had refused to try new farming and conservation practices— despite offers of seeds, inputs, and technical assistance—because he had not offered food. In other cases, people who previously were participating happily in volunteer community self-betterment activities, upon hearing of other food-for-work projects, suddenly started feeling cheated and demanded that the promoting agency supply them with food.

A growing reliance on FFW also means that many communities will under- take no projects unless they can line up food in support. This dependency syndrome is pervasive in southern Honduras, which has been the target of dozens of food-for-work projects. A development consultant working on a Title II enhancement contract told us of a survey to find out what Honduran communities considered to be their main problems and how they thought these problems could best be solved. Among communities less accustomed to food-for-work projects, people said that better community organization and more training were needed to solve their problems. But in the southern department of Choluteca, "the people told us that '*hacer solicitudes*' (make more aid applications) was what they needed to do."

SOCIAL DISORGANIZATION

Closely associated with the paternalistic structure of food aid is the way distributive food programs undermine community organizations and popular efforts toward social change and development. Not only does FFW destroy other than self-interested rationales for project participation, it can also undercut grass-roots organizing and decision making by creating unrepresentative power structures and sowing dissension within a community. "Food aid is not just a pound of beans," explained a sociologist working in El Salvador's shantytowns. "It's a pound of beans that generates sympathy to those who distribute it and gives them credibility in the eyes of the community. Food aid is power."

Most distributive food-aid programs work through existing local groups. This is held to strengthen these local organizations and their role in the community. In the words of one AID-contracted evaluation of an urban FFW project in Guatemala:

> Because the proposed construction responded to community needs, it was possible to treat the food as an incentive, calling it a "collaboration" instead of regular wages. CARE and the Municipality agreed to work through community committees who would mobilize workers and play other important roles in getting the work done. This community development method . . . created the possibility of institutionalizing community committees as a more permanent feature of the barrios. . . . The Mission's priority goal of strengthening democratic institutions is well served by the Urban FFW project . . . communities are learning that, through democratic organization, they can successfully seek their rights from the government.[26]

These local committees are not involved in establishing overall program priorities, however, but are put in charge only of the day-to-day tasks of beneficiary selection, keeping track of work hours, and weighing and distributing food. The committees end up doing much of the mundane work involved in running the program without having much say in overall program direction and design. The tasks of supervising FFW work hours and food distribution do, however, give these local leaders a certain measure of control over how this resource will ultimately be divided among program beneficiaries. Often these people are in a position of being able to choose who gets into the program or to write down extra hours for a friend or relative. With food resources to distribute, an individual or neighborhood group can more easily gain influence and power among the poor.

At least one theorist has suggested that food aid lends itself to politicking more than other forms of aid. The high political value of distributional aid, he argues, "derives from the fact that it can be used to reward individuals and is therefore a more delicate tool than is financial aid with which a government can normally only reward communities by locating new capital assets in their area. For this reason, food-for-work participants (and indeed beneficiaries of supplementary feeding) may be selected on partisan or ethnic grounds."[27]

Food-aid power often goes not to real community leaders but to directorates established by churches, government, or NGOs. Government agencies in particular often select committees and communities associated with the ruling political party. Other times, preexisting community directorates may be considered too disorganized, inexperienced, or controversial to manage the food-aid program; or government agencies may wish, for political purposes, to create new local committees of their own. In a tour of marginal neighborhoods in San Salvador organized for us by the independent Committee of Marginal Communities, competition from government-backed committees was one of the most common complaints we heard. The effect of these new committees, of course, is to undermine the power and credibility of the existing organizations.

Within local organizations, a sudden infusion of food aid can have an extremely divisive and destabilizing effect. Abruptly, committee members have access to a resource that can be used as leverage for political power and personal gain. Although this sudden power and prestige seems to last only as long as the food, it can be a heady experience for as long as it continues—in fact, often too heady. Over and over again, we were told of committee members who were taking food on the sly, signing up their family members, or putting down extra FFW hours for their friends and political supporters. Leaders compete among themselves for control of the food resources, for they soon realize their local political future may rely on who has the contacts and the wiles to line up the most food for their community or their individual political supporters.

The case of one Guatemalan slum neighborhood illustrates some of the dangers involved. Doña Carmen (not her real name) was expelled by her neighbors from the local pro-development committee in early 1988 after her husband reportedly charged neighbors an inflated price for his services in an electrification project and she had been caught fudging the time sheets on a World Share food-for-work project. Not one to be stopped so easily, Doña Carmen went to the CARE Guatemala City office, still pretending to represent the community, and convinced them to give her the participant inscription sheets for a potable water project the community had been negotiating for some time. These sheets, reported local sources, she filled with the names of her friends and supporters, telling them that if they voted for her in the next community election they would be assured a place in the project. She won the election and gained control over the FFW project. Other committee members were reluctant to complain to CARE for fear that, unwilling to get involved in neighborhood wrangles, the agency would cancel the whole project and move elsewhere.

POLITICAL PATRONAGE

Another little-examined aspect of food-for-work is its use for political patronage. Though any type of aid program can be used by individuals and institutions to foster their own power, in the past the practice of directing distributional food aid mostly to vulnerable population groups made these programs harder to use for political ends. Usually these programs were managed by the relatively apolitical health or education ministries, or at most by the first lady's social welfare institute. With food-for-work, however, the picture changes dramatically. By expanding the range of agencies distributing the food from those oriented toward nutrition and health to any government department looking to mobilize labor, FFW opens the door to political manipulation of the food aid by local government officials. Throughout the region, public-sector offices ranging from agricultural extension agencies to municipal garbage departments are now striving to get food assigned for their activities. Any government document that argues the need for "integrating food aid into larger development efforts" is almost certainly proposing the adoption of food-for-work.

Political parties and politicized government agencies, once they get control of food aid, often use this resource to buy votes and reward the party faithful. The Christian Democratic party in El Salvador is notorious for using food-for-work and other aid projects to induce displaced persons and residents of poor shantytowns to attend government rallies. Those who participate in party politics get the aid, while those who decline to wave the party flag risk being cut off. Inhabitants of one San Salvadoran shantytown, for example, recounted their refusal to board buses sent to take them to a political rally. The next week the social worker that had been attending their neighborhood was withdrawn, and since then they have received no government aid.[28]

A Salvadoran sociologist working for an urban development program outlined the patronage process this way:

> Food-aid programs come with a political connotation. It is given to cause a good impression in the poor communities and to foster a protective image of the government toward the population. In El Salvador, food aid serves both the war strategy and the political strategy. Government agencies that distribute food aid attempt to win support for the governing party, and food aid forms an important part of a plan to build grassroots support for the party in power.
>
> The plan works by channeling food aid through a government agency like DIDECO or through the city governments, especially those controlled by the Christian Democrats. The mayor or local directorate enjoy more resources to distribute. On a local level, the goal is to make the population who receive food feel like they are members of the party. Food aid comes as a prize for the faithful. It's a hook, a lasso that ties people to the party, and with food aid programs the local committees of Christian Democrats show the people that they can get things done and get things given to them.

In Guatemala, the use of food aid in political patronage is not so advanced, but cases do still occur. Alvaro Arzu, mayor of Guatemala City and a current presidential candidate, is using CARE and World Share–supplied work programs to polish his own image and that of the city. Urban food-for-work teams clean the city markets, sweep the streets, clear vacant lots of garbage, and build infrastructure in slum areas. The mayor frequently runs advertisements on television showing the great progress being made. Interestingly, the director of World Share in Guatemala, Janet Irogoyen, is the mayor's cousin. The CARE Title II component has even broader political goals. It was explicitly designed to stabilize the Christian Democratic government installed in 1986. The project paper for CARE's FFW program in Guatemala City explained the food-aid stabilization strategy this way:

> The new government is instituting a set of economic reform measures intended to strengthen the economy, bring inflation under control and result in more equitable access to resources. However, for the short-term, the reform measures are expected to cause further price increases in basic necessities and reduced employment opportunities for unskilled laborers in the service and industrial sectors. The Government of Guatemala has expressed concern that the successful implementation of the reforms might be jeopardized if the austerity measures provoke a violent response, particularly from the urban poor. Thus the government is seeking ways to alleviate some of the negative effects that the reform measures are likely to have temporarily on this segment of the population. An urban FFW program is one of the means proposed.[29]

Not just government offices, but also religious groups are making use of the mobilizing potential of food-for-work. A 1985 Costa Rica evaluation noted the problem of the Catholic church's using an FFW project for church construction and repair, and in Guatemala we saw several examples of this same problem.[30] World Share food has been used both in church building and in "moral education" and catechism classes. In another case, a priest in one shantytown we visited argued for continuing a problematic and time-consuming FFW program because "it puts a thousand people in our hand." Finally, one colorful priest in Guatemala—Father Tiziano Sofia—has been using FFW to construct what some local journalists jokingly call a "personal jungle empire," an enormous complex of parochial buildings situated in the army "development pole" of Ixcán, Playa Grande. Father Tiziano has literally dozens of people employed in what he likes to call his jobs "training program," indistinguishable from normal manual labor except that workers are paid in a combination of cash and food.[31]

SUMMARY

At first glance, the switch from traditional supplementation programs to food for development seems a positive change. Using food as an incentive rather than a supplement allows program goals to be widened from difficult-to-achieve nutritional improvement to any activity beneficiaries can be organized to undertake. Children can be vaccinated, mothers educated, new crops planted, and needed social services installed—all through the motivating power of food. The idea of having food aid serve as a productive resource is appealing, especially when one compares these dynamic programs with the meager results of decades of handouts.

But food as a motivating tool also has its dangers, particularly in the context of unresponsive governments and unjust social structures. There is a serious flaw with this approach, having to do with the concept of what "development" means and what the development process requires. Nutritional and health education is needed. But if mothers are simply sitting through the classes to get their rations, one wonders how much they are really going to learn. With all the focus on food, health-education efforts are often reduced to a sideshow.

Community-based development depends on local initiative and capabilities, yet food aid is by nature a top-down program that breeds dependent attitudes. Making participants work for their food rations does little to overcome beneficiary dependency, because it is still others that control the food and thus the project. Furthermore, in the absence of complementary funding, these projects are often little more than make-work exercises. Grass-roots organizations rely on a sense of unity and common purpose, whereas food aid distorts a community's reasons for participation, often placing residents in competition with each other for access to limited food resources.

When used in public-works projects, the food-for-work approach is frequently exploitative of workers' rights to a fair money wage. Care must be taken to ensure these are indeed self-help projects that provide truly needed social services and productive improvements to the beneficiaries, and that these projects benefit all participants more or less equally. Otherwise the poorest end up laboring on projects that contribute mostly to improve the position of the relatively better-off. Even if these are true self-help projects, however, one conceptual problem remains and should be noted: the food-for-work approach shifts the burden of providing social services from the government onto the poor themselves.

Food-for-work programs, even more than supplementary feeding programs, also manipulate program participants for political and religious ends. Food is no longer just given away, it is consciously used to shape attitudes and behavior. The question is, of course, who controls the agenda and for what ends. The wide range of institutions now jumping on the food-for-work bandwagon thus gives serious grounds for concern.

Instead of being used just as a simple palliative, food aid is now widely used as a development resource and a tool for change. This new approach is being put into action, however, without adequate attention to its complex organizational requirements and effects. To be successful, food for development requires trained personnel and a democratic approach—two factors sorely lacking in Central America. In the highly politicized and corrupt context prevailing in the region, these new uses of food aid, instead of promoting development, may actually hold serious dangers for long-term organizational and development efforts.

7

Food for War

*Military efforts [are] not sufficient to win a guer-
rilla war. Such a war is less a fight for territory than
for people.*

AID Mission, San Salvador, 1985

FOOD aid is not politically neutral. Food assistance programs tend to increase
the political power of those who give out the food while modifying the
political responses of those who eat it. And as social situations become more
politically charged, so do food distribution programs.[1]

At the beginning of our investigation we asked, Is U.S. food aid being used
to support U.S.-sponsored military efforts? Through our travels and interviews, we found that the U.S. Food for Peace program is indeed being used to
further war strategies in the region. Three major conflicts dominate Central
America: the Salvadoran civil war, the counterinsurgency offensive in Guatemala, and the contra attacks on Nicaragua. This chapter will look at the uses of
U.S. food aid on all three battle lines, especially that in El Salvador, where
U.S. involvement is particularly extensive.

The use of food aid to pursue war is not new. As discussed in chapter 1, the
South Vietnamese government and military were major beneficiaries of the
Food for Peace program in the 1960s and 1970s. Title I local currencies
helped fund the South Vietnamese military, and distributions of U.S. food
also formed part of the famous hearts-and-minds strategy.[2] Toward the end of
the Vietnam War, however, the U.S. public and Congress became outraged at
the degree to which U.S. food was serving the war effort. Consequently, in the
mid–1970s Congress imposed a number of restrictions and guidelines on the
Food for Peace program intended to limit the military and political applica-

147

tions of food aid and to increase its role in addressing hunger and under-development. Yet in Central America today, both the intent and the letter of that legislation are being violated.

AN LIC WEAPON

Low-intensity conflict (LIC) is a term the Pentagon uses for U.S. military responses that fall below the level of conventional or nuclear war.[3] For the most part, LIC theory is simply an extension of traditional U.S. counterinsurgency and special forces doctrine, which concentrates on isolating insurgents from their base of support in the local population.[4] LIC strategy, however, includes several important new elements and areas of emphasis:
- Heightened caution in involving U.S. troops in Third World conflicts.
- Support for local anticommunist insurgents or "freedom fighters."
- Renewed emphasis on closely linking political and military strategies and coordinating all resources—public and private—to achieve what the U.S. military calls "internal security and development."
- Efforts to control communities in conflictive areas through civic-action programs and psychological operations.
- Constant attention to and shaping of public opinion on the U.S. home front.

Food aid can be used in low-intensity conflicts in a variety of ways. In Central America, U.S. food is used to build up the image of local military, as a form of relief for the intentionally displaced, and as an instrument to control people through food-for-work and resettlement programs. The sale of food aid is also a source of local currency for war-related development or relief projects. Within the United States, this aid also serves a purpose: food aid going to Central America helps to maintain a certain balance, at least on paper, between U.S. military and "humanitarian" aid to this strategic region.

Food aid has two important advantages as a political and military tool. The first is that the U.S. public usually assumes it to be a benign and humanitarian contribution to the well-being of the poor and hungry—an image that AID is quick to promote. "Eliminating world hunger is the central focus of AID," declared the agency's administrator Peter McPherson in 1983. "People who are hungry are fed, regardless of the politics of their country. . . . You cannot blame a child for what his government does. Indeed, a hungry child knows no politics."[5]

Second is the unique role of food as a vital ingredient of human life and as an important leverage factor in human psychology. Hunger can drive people into the arms of their enemies or can get them to work at any task. At the same time, sharing food is an ancient rite of trust and friendship. The provider of food is in some ways taking on the role of a parent or host. Food distribution is thus likely to affect the social attitudes of recipients more than less personally significant forms of aid, such as technical assistance or credit.

Because of its public-relations and psychological impact, food aid constitutes an ideal LIC weapon. We will look first at how this "humanitarian" aid is being used in the civil war in El Salvador, where the United States is deeply involved in backing the Salvadoran government forces. Then we will examine the case of Guatemala, with particular attention of the World Food Programme's role in that country. Finally, we will turn to how the U.S. government has used food aid in supporting the contra campaign waged against Nicaragua from both Costa Rica and Honduras.

EL SALVADOR: THE FISH AND THE SEA

El Salvador, like most of the other Central American countries, has long been characterized by an extremely unequal division of national wealth and power. A ruling class intransigent to reform, which has not hesitated to use repression to defend its interests, has long dominated the country. In the 1970s a variety of factors—including social dislocations provoked by an incipient industrialization process, growing land pressures, and the more active role of the Catholic church—led to the rapid growth of a grass-roots opposition movement intent on demanding long-overdue reforms.

In the face of rising opposition, in the late 1970s a government-sanctioned and government-supported network of terror and assassinations was unleashed upon the Salvadoran population. Until 1983 the Salvadoran armed forces thought they could eliminate the guerrillas by simply relying on their own numerical and financial superiority. Death squads and military massacres did succeed in undercutting the growth and removing the leadership of the unarmed civilian opposition. But the repression also had the boomerang effect of motivating more and more of the population to join the armed resistance or to give moral or material support to the guerrillas.

By 1983 the guerrilla movement had gained considerable strength, and in that year the government responded with a full-scale counterinsurgency campaign. This was to be the "total war"—combining political and military tactics—that LIC strategists had been advocating. On the political side, strong U.S. financial and tactical support was given to the Christian Democratic party and to its base of supporters. Large sums of economic aid flowed into government development and relief programs that were closely associated with the military effort, while military aid itself also escalated.

The military's offensive relied largely on classic counterinsurgency tactics. The main focus was an effort to separate the guerrillas from their civilian supporters. If local communities are the "sea in which the fish swim," as China's Mao Tse-tung put it, then the strategy is obvious: drive the fish out of the sea and/or dry up the water. For the past six years, the Salvadoran army has employed a variety of means to break the link between the guerrillas and their popular base. At the urging of their U.S. advisers, the Salvadoran armed forces have adopted such tactics as aerial bombing and military sweeps of contested and guerrilla-controlled areas. In addition, crops have been burned and supplies to these zones cut off, all in an effort to force the relocation of suspected guerrilla supporters to military-controlled areas. Once displaced, the population is then "aided" by government programs.

Food-aid programs have been an essential element in these counterinsurgency tactics. Donated food has helped sustain and control the deliberately displaced and has been handed out in military/civic-action programs that aim to win rural hearts and minds. Most of the Title I funds going to the Salvadoran government also support the war effort by financing projects better described as holding maneuvers than as development efforts. These include restoring infrastructure destroyed by the guerrillas, funding government "humanitarian assistance" to the displaced, and generating emergency employment.[6] "Despite their innocuous labels," stressed one congressional report, "these [types of] programs are used to prosecute the war and repair its damage, rather than to change the conditions that sparked and continue to fuel the rebellion."[7]

FEEDING THE DISPLACED

Displaced families—the product of rural repression and bombardment— began appearing in the provincial capitals of El Salvador as early as 1979. Since then over half a million Salvadorans, a full tenth of the total population, have been forced to flee their homes for safer areas of the country.[8] These are hungry, malnourished, and dirt-poor people who have been separated from their usual means of subsistence by a civil war now more than a decade old.

Politics and humanitarianism have often come into conflict in programs for the displaced. In recent years, the United States has provided the main material support for both private and government displaced-persons programs. During the very early years of the war, however, AID refused to allow CRS to use PL 480 food to feed the displaced. As a staff member of the Catholic church's Social Secretariat put it, "Back then AID didn't want to recognize the civil war and therefore the displaced population did not exist for them." Apparently AID was concerned about the politics of both CRS and the internal refugees the church was serving. Agency officials demanded to see CRS's beneficiary lists—a request denied by CRS's local Catholic counterpart, which, noting AID's already strong support for the government war effort, feared the lists might be used for intelligence purposes.[9]

By early 1981, however, it became obvious that a full-scale guerrilla insurgency was threatening the United States-backed regime and that the displaced population was going to be a long-term problem. AID funds and food helped set up a government agency called CONADES (National Commission to Aid the Displaced). Its directorate, which includes six representatives of government ministries including Defense, operates under the authority of the Ministry of the Interior.

Given the responsibility of finding coordinated solutions to the swelling problem of the displaced, CONADES's main activity has been simply to give food handouts to any displaced person willing to register with the government—a practice many Salvadorans believe is a method of military intelligence and control.[10] Year after year, with their needs for employment, land, training, and housing largely unmet, El Salvador's displaced lined up for their monthly food handouts. Meanwhile, instances of CONADES corruption and politicization repeatedly surfaced in the press.[11] Nevertheless, as the civil war progressed, CONADES dole registers swelled quickly: from 160,000 in 1982 to a peak of 600,000 in 1986.

Through the years, CONADES's main source of food has been the World Food Programme, which has supplied a continuous chain of six-month emergency allocations. Most of this WFP food, however, was ultimately donated by the U.S. (and of course labeled as such). The commission's budget has been covered largely by Title I local currencies—$10 million worth in 1981–87—as well as by funds generated by the resale of small amounts of food donated by other countries, including the EEC, Italy, and Argentina.[12]

U.S. interest in supporting the displaced did not stop with CONADES, however. Other Salvadoran government programs for the displaced population have received both U.S. funds and direct bilateral food donations. In particular, AID has been supporting several programs of the government's Directorate of Community Development (DIDECO) with both Title I funds and Title II food. (See table 4.) The direct donation of Title II food to a foreign government contrasts with AID's usual practice of channeling this aid through nongovernmental or multilateral agencies, and not surprisingly, these Salvadoran government-run programs have also been highly politicized. DIDECO has channeled the U.S. donations to two government jobs programs as well as to a military/civic-action "psychological operations" program.

The Title II–supplied food-for-work programs, which together have employed tens of thousands of displaced persons at a time, have played an important role in providing food and employment to Salvador's displaced, thus helping to keep these potentially politicized populations under control. As an 1986 AID/State Department evaluation noted: "The U.S. Government-financed employment program for the displaced is the third largest employer in the country after the Government of El Salvador. In a country where internal migration in search of employment is a long-standing custom, where and how these jobs are provided and their eligibility requirements, significantly affect the decisions which the program beneficiaries make about their future."[13]

One of these programs, run by the Christian Democrat–controlled FEDECREDITO office, was set up so that local mayors could hire the displaced to do road work, paying them with a mixture of cash and food. It was discontinued in mid–1987 after damning reports of corruption and party politics surfaced in the U.S. press.[14] The other, run directly by DIDECO, has the displaced building local public works and engaged part time in other local self-help and training activities.

AID has thus given substantial direct support to Salvadoran government programs for the displaced. It has been troubled, however, by the high levels of corruption and mismanagement that characterize the Salvadoran government. In addition, there has also been the problem of the regime's negative image, both at home and abroad. Perhaps these are factors that in the mid–1980s set AID looking for a private partner as well.

An NGO channel would help solve both the image and the management

TABLE 4

U.S. and World Food Programme Distributive Food Aid to El Salvador:
Number of Beneficiaries by Project, 1987 (Thousands of People)

Donor	Agencies	Project Number	Project	Beneficiaries Type	Number
WFP	CONADES	3075 E	FFW-humanitarian relief	Registered displaced	395,000
WFP	CONADES	2806	FFW-integration and resettlement	Registered displaced	60,000
WFP	DIDECO–Ministry of Health	2317 Amp.	Supplementary feeding and nutritional education	Maternal/child	60,000
WFP	DIDECO–Ministry of Education	2690	School feeding	Rural schoolchildren	165,000
WFP	DIDECO-BFA	2146 Amp.	FFW-basic grains	Small farmers	93,000
WFP	DIDECO–Ministry of Public Works	2725	FFW-housing and infrastructure in agrarian reform areas	Rural displaced and AR beneficiaries	330,000
WFP	DIDECO, government	776 Amp. II	Rural and community development	Rural	400,000
				WFP SUBTOTAL:	1,503,000
AID	DIDECO	519-7615 E	FFW-emergency community works	Urban marginal and displaced	85,000
AID	DIDECO-CONARA	5197615 E	Relief	Registered displaced	53,000
AID	DIDECO-FEDECREDITO	519-0281	Community employment	Registered displaced	15,000
AID	CESAD	519-0281	Relief	Unregistered displaced	43,000
AID	CRS-CARITAS	Not available	Supplementary feeding	Maternal/child	130,000
				AID SUBTOTAL:	325,000
				TOTAL:	1,828,000

Sources: USAID and WFP offices, San Salvador.

problems while allowing support for the displaced to continue. The trick, however, was coming up with a reputable private group that would accept working with an AID mission so clearly involved in the war and pacification effort. Ironically, just a few years after criticizing CRS's attention to the displaced, AID switched tactics and began courting CRS to run an AID-sponsored program for this population. But CRS, and a variety of other mainstream NGOs—including the Lutheran church and the Mennonite Central Committee—all reportedly declined the offer on the grounds that AID was not a neutral donor but rather the main support behind one of the parties to the war.[15]

In 1986 AID finally found its channel, the conservative Salvadoran Evangelical Aid and Development Committee (CESAD). Large amounts of Title II food suddenly transformed the obscure CESAD into a significant player on the displaced-persons scene. Ostensibly, the private CESAD was to serve those displaced persons who were afraid to register with the government. CESAD personnel told us, however, that they coordinated all their activities with the other government agencies and the military.[16] With food in hand, CESAD could more easily pump its message of born-again revivalism and anticommunism. In design and administration its projects, often managed at the local level by committees set up by local pastors, left much to be desired. Once again, AID fell short of providing well-managed nonpolitical humanitarian aid to the victims of El Salvador's civil war.

By 1986–87 changing political circumstances forced AID and the Salvadoran government to again adopt new policies in regard to the displaced. Clearly, the existing stopgap programs could not continued indefinitely. Neither the massive CONADES dole program, nor the temporary and part-time jobs programs, nor the scattered CESAD efforts had proved capable of providing adequate alternatives for the displaced. The idea had been simply to keep this population quiet and fed until the war ended—but year after year the conflict dragged on and the costs of these programs continued to mount.

Meanwhile, years on the dole had created a large new subgroup in Salvadoran society completely dependent on outside help and suffering severe social disintegration. The delay in providing a more permanent solution to their problems of subsistence has had an incalculable impact on the economic and psychological well-being of El Salvador's displaced, already suffering from being violently uprooted from their homes and lands. Rural peasants used to farming for a living were reduced to sitting around in urban slums waiting for their next handout. A 1986 WFP evaluation concluded of its CONADES program:

> During the last six years CONADES has supplied humanitarian aid of a welfare nature; by itself, this action has retarded the development of the productive forces of the displaced population, deepening their dependency and thereby strengthening opportunism and conformity. Even when real government and private development programs have been supplied to these population groups, they have been boycotted by an attitude of rejection unlike the usual industriousness of the Salvadoran people. This help has been nothing more than a palliative.[17]

The World Food Programme, seconded by others, pressured the Salvadoran government to cut back food aid, and more importantly, to integrate it into development and resettlement efforts. These efforts bore sudden fruit when another factor came onto the scene: the independent organization of the displaced. Exasperated by years of waiting out the conflict, many of the displaced—especially those who had never registered with the government but had sought help from their families or from private agencies—as well as the Salvadoran refugees who had been living out the war in Honduran refugee camps, refused to continue being passive victims. In 1986 hundreds of Salvadoran refugees and displaced persons began organizing with the support of the Catholic church to return to their homes and lands, whether in contested areas or not.

The Salvadoran government programs were quickly adjusted to meet these new challenges. Straight handout programs were sharply curtailed and replaced with food-for-work projects, under which the beneficiaries were required to undertake community improvements or receive vocational training. Though the developmental impact of these efforts is questionable, given the lack of complementary funds and trained personnel to work in these programs, the switch to food-for-work did bring a sharp falloff in CONADES dole registers. It also provided a vehicle for government organizing efforts, with the leadership of the local CONADES committees paid in food for their participation.

In addition, the government established a resettlement program of its own, which included food aid to tide over the relocated peasants until they could support themselves. In contrast to resettlements supported by the Catholic church and other associated organizations and churches, which aimed to allow people to return to or near their original communities, the government resettlement campaign relocated the displaced in pacification zones selected by the military. The AID-financed resettlement effort, focused on the provincial capital of Suchitoto, emerged in 1986 as the official, tightly controlled alternative to the rise in independent repopulation projects.

For those willing to move to government-sponsored resettlements, WFP provides food while AID supplies building materials and agricultural assistance.[18] Conservative AID-funded NGOs like Project Hope and World Relief provide medical and agricultural assistance. Those who refuse to be included in this new pacification strategy and to move to areas of governmental control, however, are not offered any of CONADES's "humanitarian" assistance.[19] This political litmus test has meant that many hungry Salvadorans have been denied U.S. and WFP aid on basically political grounds.

In sum, while humanitarian concerns have certainly played a role in U.S. support for the Salvadoran displaced, political and military considerations have been tantamount. This should come as no surprise, given that neither the Salvadoran nor the U.S. government is a neutral party to the war. El Salvador's displaced were driven from their homes as part of a deliberate strategy to clear the rural population from areas of guerrilla activity. Even today, displaced people are still viewed as politically suspect. Just as it was the job of U.S. military advisers to direct this counterinsurgency strategy, it fell to AID to help the Salvadoran government care for and manage these internal refugees.

FOOD FOR THOUGHT

Food aid not only is used to pacify, it is also used to sell images. When bags of corn and cans of vegetable oil bearing AID's emblem are proffered to the Salvadoran poor, the food comes with the message that it was donated by the people of the United States. During civic-action programs conducted by the Salvadoran military, the psychological value of food distribution—as a mechanism to create gratitude, trust, and dependency—is exploited to the full.

A typical civic-action program begins early in the morning at the local military base. A caravan of trucks assembles for the drive out to the village selected for that day's civic action. Upon arrival in the town plaza, the battalion's psychological-operations (PSYOPS) team jumps out and hurriedly sets up the microphone and sound system. Soon it begins instructing the gathered crowd about the evils of the subversives and the virtues of the army. A small military band plays the national anthem as well as more popular tunes. But neither the PSYOPS team nor the band is the main attraction. These hungry and malnourished people have mainly come for the free food and medicines being handed out to all who sign up.

AID calls these "combined civic-action programs" because they are sponsored jointly by the military and the National Commission for the Restoration of Areas (CONARA), a pseudocivilian government office set up by AID in 1983. CONARA was originally established to coordinate the National Plan, a pacification plan that focused on the conflictive departments of San Vicente and Usulután. An AID briefing paper described CONARA's origins as follows:

> Early in 1983, military and civilian policymakers saw clearly that military efforts alone were not sufficient to win a guerrilla war. . . . As a result, GOES [Government of El Salvador] policymakers began to map out a strategy for restoring and strengthening the authority of local government over areas that had been subject to guerrilla harassment. That GOES strategy, known as the National Plan, called for an intensive military action to eliminate the guerrillas, followed by a coordinated effort of the central government ministries to strengthen local authority and to assist them in restoring essential public services and promoting development in newly secured areas. CONARA was created to coordinate the civilian ministries and local authorities.[20]

Beginning in 1986, CONARA has coordinated government ministries working under the army's United to Reconstruct (UPR) campaign, a reconstruction and pacification effort focusing on contested and newly secured areas of the country. Where the military situation allows it, CONARA focuses on rebuilding public services and infrastructure. But "in areas with poor security," reads an AID document, "CONARA is limited to coordinating relief activities such as food distribution, medical care, or restoring public services. These activities can be either civic action, using purely military resources, or humanitarian assistance provided by civilian agencies with the support and the assistance of the military."[21] As fits with an LIC approach, CONARA's principal focus is coordinating civilian agencies' resources under military direction. CONARA's municipal-level commissions (known as COMURAS) include military representatives and civic leaders.[22]

In an interview with the civilian head of CONARA, Luis Mejía Miranda, we were told that food-distribution sites were selected by an army officer operating out of the CONARA office, based on requests from local army commanders. Mejía also told us that CONARA's civic-action programs are "basically psychological operations" that "make the people feel that both the government and the armed forces are interested in meeting at least part of their basic needs. Our slogan is, 'People, Government, and Army Together.'"[23] The army is also involved in transporting the food to each distribution site, unloading it from the trucks, and often directly handing it out to recipients.

One U.S. government official portrayed CONARA this way: "The whole program has a political objective, with development objectives being secondary. Projects are chosen by the military using security considerations, and there is an attitude that the military high command knows best."[24] DIDECO itself, the government "community development" office that passes the Title II food on to CONARA, describes this supposedly civilian program as follows: "The Ministry of Defense carries out through CONARA the [project] component of restoring areas destroyed or damaged by the situation of violence in the country, with the support of food rations for the affected families in the conflict areas that participate in the civic actions carried out by CONARA."[25]

Civic-action programs are often part of a larger army campaign to flush guerrillas and guerrilla sympathizers out of an area. People who do not line up for food handouts are suspected of supporting the guerrillas. The same trucks that soldiers use to bring U.S. food into villages have been known to haul away captured suspects after the day's program is over.[26]

One such case was denounced by the Association for the Development of the Communities of Morazán and San Miguel (PADECOMSM) in early 1989. According to a PADECOMSM spokesperson, a detachment from the military base in San Francisco Gotera arrested thirty-one members of the small village of Estancia in the Morazán province shortly after having distributed food aid to the community as part of a civic-action program. "While handing out corn and other cereal, they tried to terrorize the community, telling them that they should quit working with PADECOMSM if they didn't want problems," reported the informant. PADECOMSM, part of a national organization of community organizations, charges that the army's civic-action programs are really "civic-terrorist actions."[27]

In some cases the army camps in a village for a few days during a civic-action program. Such was the case in Guarjila, an independent repopulation site in the department of Chalatenango, where some one hundred soldiers spent three days on a combined intelligence and psychological-operations mission in 1988. The people of Guarjila, however, refused to accept the U.S. food from the soldiers. After threats, a few families finally did line up for the aid, but the rest of the community insisted that the food be placed in a community warehouse where it could be saved for distribution to needy families. One woman said she wasn't about to accept food from soldiers who had killed her son. On hand to witness this U.S.-backed hearts-and-minds action was a U.S. military adviser dressed in combat fatigues.[28]

AID funds and food aid are the backbone of the CONARA program. CONARA is funded by local currency generated by AID's ESF and Title I programs, and it distributes bilateral Title II food.[29] Yet U.S. legislation makes no provision for AID's use of food aid for military purposes.[30] Section 531(e) of the Foreign Assistance Act prohibits Title I local currencies from going to "military or paramilitary purposes." Section 1301 of the U.S. Code also explicitly prohibits the military use of U.S. food aid. Aid can go to military projects only if explicitly intended for that purpose. Since the CONARA "combined civic-action" program is controlled by the military and clearly pursues a military purpose, this use of U.S. food aid is in fact illegal, a point also made by a special congressional mission to El Salvador in 1987.[31]

AID and the Pentagon have tried to evade these prohibitions by claiming that U.S. food and aid-generated funds support only the civilian side of combined military/civic-action programs in El Salvador. AID contends that civic-action activities in El Salvador are controlled by CONARA, that CONARA is a civilian agency operating under the Ministry of Planning, and that the purpose of these operations is only humanitarian relief. In a 1986 policy statement, AID pledged that that it would "not provide financing or supplies for civic-action activities controlled or implemented by the military."[32]

These claims are patently false. The combined civic-action programs we visited in Cuscatlán and Chalatenango, for example, were completely run by the military. Army trucks carried the food to the villages, where soldiers unloaded it. Army PSYOPS teams gathered the people in the town square and spoke to them through loudspeakers throughout the events. Uniformed soldiers handed the food to the beneficiaries. The only civilians involved in the programs we saw were a few CONARA nurses distributing gastrointestinal medicines. One must also doubt the efficacy of any "relief" program that hits each town, according to CONARA, only once or twice a year. Such infrequent incursions might yield psychological results but clearly cannot be expected to have any nutritional or development impact.

According to U.S. statutes, the basic legal test is purpose. Supplies or funds "must be for civilian, not military, purpose." Whatever civilian pretenses CONARA has, its basic objectives are clearly military, not humanitarian.

SELECTIVE ASSISTANCE

Although AID publicly declares that its food-aid program is mainly humanitarian, one gets a different picture at the hundreds of military roadblocks in rural El Salvador. Food aid distributed by AID contractors and government agencies passes easily through the roadblocks, whereas truckloads of food from independent agencies like the Catholic church's Social Secretariat sometimes never reach the intended beneficiaries.

Private organizations and churches that attempt to serve the unregistered displaced and those living in contested areas—-including the International Committee of the Red Cross and the Catholic church's Social Secretariat—are routinely harassed by the Salvadoran army. In some cases the food shipments are confiscated by the military and never recovered.[33] More frequently, though, military commanders just deny the distributing NGOs permission to enter certain areas or delay issuing the necessary "safe conduct" passes. Whereas the church's Social Secretariat complained to us of waiting days for the passes to be issued, the evangelical CESAD reported no delay whatever.

Soldiers often harass independent humanitarian organizations by forcing truckers to repeatedly unload for inspection food shipments destined for communities believed to harbor antimilitary feelings. In at least one instance, a trucker hauling for the Social Secretariat was illegally detained for over a week.[34] Said one CRS official, "There are areas of this country where if you are caught with more than a few pounds of food you are subject to intense military scrutiny."[35] Even the World Food Programme, which maintains good relations with the government, reported trouble in moving supplies for its school-feeding program to all areas of the country.[36]

Reflecting on recent experience in El Salvador, the local CRS director stressed that to be effective, humanitarian aid has to be projected and perceived as being neutral. Instead, he complained, humanitarian aid in El Salvador too often comes in political packages, and as a result, "humanitarian assistance is getting to be seen as a bad word."

GUATEMALA: WAR IN THE HIGHLANDS

During the past three decades, Guatemala has been in an almost permanent state of counterinsurgency. In their unrelenting campaign to stamp out popular rebellion and uphold oligarchic rule, the Guatemalan government and military have been systematically violating human rights since 1954: the year a U.S.-supported coup overthrew a progressive civilian government.

In the mid–1960s, the Guatemalan army with the help of U.S. military advisers wiped out a small band of guerrillas in the eastern part of the country, along with hundreds of local civilians. But resistance to the country's repressive and corrupt government continued and grew over the next decade, in part sparked by the social shake-up caused by a major 1976 earthquake. In the late 1970s the country's impoverished highland Indians began to lend their support to a rapidly growing rural guerrilla movement, rallying behind the banner of agrarian reform and respect for justice and human rights. By the end of the decade, hundreds of thousands of peasants were united in their stand against their repressive government.

Just as in El Salvador, the government response was drastic. Starting in 1981, the Guatemalan army undertook a massive campaign of massacres, scorched-earth tactics, psychological operations, civic-action programs, forced resettlement, and military-directed development projects—concentrated largely on the western highlands. These counterinsurgency tools are much the same the world over. What has distinguished Guatemala has been the utter brutality, the ugly racial dimension, and the relative success of its long-running campaign to maintain a military-controlled society.[37] And once again, food aid has played a role in those efforts.

CRN AND THE DEVELOPMENTALISTS

Since 1954 the armed forces have controlled most aspects of Guatemalan society. Brute force has been the usual response to dissidence. Yet over these past three decades, Guatemalan military officers—trained at counterinsurgency schools in Panama, the United States, Israel, and Taiwan—have gradually come to recognize the value of an integrated response to rural insurgency. Repression has its place, but repression alone, go the new arguments, is insufficient. Effective counterinsurgency needs to integrate military responses with political, social, and economic measures.[38]

The military's integrated approach to social control can be largely traced back to an early morning in 1976 when a severe earthquake shook the western and central highlands. It was the army that took control of subsequent relief and reconstruction efforts. The military high command formed the National Reconstruction Committee (CRN) and installed a general as director. Few objected. After all, the military had controlled the government ever since a 1963 coup, and no other social sector had the organization or resources for such a large undertaking. Foreign volunteers, development experts, the Peace Corps, missionaries, and local churches joined hands with the military and CRN in the food-distribution and reconstruction work that followed the earthquake.

Although the post-earthquake work is long since over, the militarily-linked CRN has endured to this day as a development and relief institution. CRN continues coordinating the different development agencies and responding to "all natural and man-made disasters."[39]

It has been the man-made disasters—especially the havoc wrought by the army's 1981–83 counterinsurgency drives—that have occupied most of CRN's attention during the 1980s. In 1982 CRN was put in charge of the "development" part of the army's 1982 National Security and Development Plan.[40] That same year, a *de facto* military government gave CRN control over all food aid donated to the Guatemalan government, and specifically the food-for-work programs supplied by WFP.[41]

Since 1976 CRN has been a darling of the army's developmentalist faction. The developmentalists are those officers who regard relief and development programs as essential in the fight against subversion. The steady rise of the guerrilla movement in the late 1970s, despite ever greater levels of repression, strengthened the developmentalist arguments. With the coup d'état headed by former Christian Democratic presidential candidate General Efraín Ríos Montt in March 1982, this faction took power and moved into full swing on an ambitious and bloody rural counterinsurgency campaign focused on the western highlands. Development programs, this group argued, were necessary, but first mass repression must be used to force the highlands population under army control.

Under Ríos Montt, widespread massacres and scorched-earth tactics were used throughout the Altiplano. The army's campaign of terror in the highlands—at its height from 1981 to 1984—left over a million Guatemalans displaced and tens of thousands dead. Crops were destroyed, houses burned, and whole communities massacred.[42] The army itself reported over four hundred villages destroyed.[43] To escape this terror, tens of thousands of Indian families fled to Mexico, while those too far to make it to the border tried to hide in the country's isolated mountain forests and lowland jungles.

Army terrorism was designed to wipe out the base of popular support for the leftist guerrillas, breaking the links between the Indians and the armed resistance. But in contrast to their Salvadoran counterparts, the Guatemalan army clearly recognized that terror alone would not succeed in pacifying the highlands. To be truly effective, counterinsurgency violence had to be followed up with programs that addressed the root causes of the rebellion. According to the army, these conditions included endemic hunger, geographical isolation, unemployment, and an inadequate sense of national identity and patriotism. Furthermore, to combat guerrilla infiltration and propaganda, the army had to establish a permanent presence and ongoing mechanisms of intelligence and control.

BEANS AND GUNS

Since 1982 food aid has been an important element of the Guatemalan army's campaign to pacify the Indian highlands, and CRN has been the chosen channel. Food aid has been distributed to paramilitary civil patrols set up by the army, given to displaced persons living under military control, and handed out to Indian workers in food-for-work programs to build "model villages" and roads throughout the highlands. Most of the food distributed in these counterinsurgency-related programs has been U.S. food flowing to CRN through the indirect WFP channel.[44]

Ríos Montt was the first Guatemalan leader to recognize the military value of food aid. Soon after seizing power, he announced his now infamous "Frijoles y Fusiles" (Beans and Guns) pacification campaign, quickly followed by "Techo, Tortillas, and Trabajo" (Shelter, Food, and Work). Central to Ríos Montt's counterinsurgency strategy was the establishment of permanent control over villagers suspected of sympathizing with the guerrilla movement. From this strategy developed the practice of using scorched-earth tactics— including the deliberate destruction of crops and food supplies—to clear the population out of areas of guerrilla activity. Ironically, the massacres and destruction were often followed up by the army's "rescue" of this same population, now left with no means of subsistence and terrorized into compliance. Survivors of army sweeps were often held initially at the local military base and then, when the army deemed it prudent, allowed to return to the ruins of their communities, now to be reconstructed as special "model villages." Designed and supervised by the army, these concentrated and militarized settlements changed living patterns for thousands of displaced Indian families who previously had lived in dispersed communities throughout the mountains and valleys of highland Guatemala.

Army-controlled food aid was used both to feed survivors of the violence and to compensate their forced labor in building the new model villages. Some of this food was simply requisitioned from INDECA (the government's grain-stabilization institute). But most, in a flagrant violation of international standards of neutrality, was World Food Programme food channeled through the CRN.

The World Food Programme has been operating distribution programs in Guatemala since the early 1970s. Up to 1982, these distributions were channeled through the Ministry of Health, but in that year—the same year the Beans and Guns campaign got under way—the military government decreed that all WFP food assistance be controlled by the CRN. Part of that food was handed on to the Ministry of Education, the agricultural extension agency, and other government offices. "Community Development Project" 784, however, CRN decided to administer itself, and it was this food aid that the military-linked CRN used to support the army's counterinsurgency campaign. Food donated by WFP was used by the army to feed those it held in army bases or in the incipient model villages. Through widely heralded CRN-administered "food-for-work" programs, the army justified the forced labor used in constructing the model villages and access roads.[45]

Local WFP officials admit this aid was used to build model villages, but they justify this collaboration with the Guatemalan army's pacification plan by references to the WFP's own "political neutrality."[46] Yet the Guatemalan army, shunned by most other international donors, obviously saw this aid differently. After describing how displaced persons grouped at the Cobán department military base had been fed WFP food, a colonel there told us, "The World Food Programme has been our best friend. Never did it abandon us, even in the toughest years."

Food supplied through WFP's Community Development project was also used in the second element of the military's strategy of control: the improvement in the rural road network. Aside from building model villages, virtually the only development work that the army offered was in labor-intensive road-construction projects. Early each morning, government workers—from either CRN or the roads department—would line up barefoot Indian men in village plazas, pass out picks and shovels, and then cart them off to road-construction sites. For pay, the workers received a weekly WFP food allotment or a small daily wage (less than $1) supplied by AID.[47]

Road building served as the perfect development project for pacification and counterinsurgency in Guatemala. The food and employment supplied by labor-intensive road projects helped maintain Indian communities at a time when the normal social and economic life of the highlands was in chaos. New penetration roads brought an increased government and military presence to conflictive areas. Typically, at the end of each new road the army built a new outpost. Given the high cost of commercial road construction, WFP and AID support allowed the Guatemalan government to extend its road network far beyond what it otherwise would have been able to afford.[48]

WFP officials labeled the road construction "community development," while AID said the new roads would provide employment for the rural poor and promote the marketing of agricultural projects. Yet given CRN's control over all WFP food and the broader interest of Washington in suppressing the Guatemalan insurgency, political and military motives were obviously not far behind any development intent. At the very time that the counterinsurgency campaign was reaching its peak, AID declared that labor-intensive road building was "an ideal type of project to implement with the current Guatemalan highlands environment."[49]

A third element of the Guatemalan army's strategy of permanent control was the establishment of a nationwide civil-patrol system. Starting in 1982, almost all rural males over fifteen years of age, belonging to model villages or not, were forced by the army to organize themselves into local paramilitary patrols. To this day, even under the civilian government that came to power in 1987, the army has continued to maintain the civil-patrol structure in whatever villages it deems fit.

Patrol duty is officially voluntary, but every villager knows that violent reprisals are often taken against individuals and towns that refuse to cooperate. Although this forced service is unpaid, local commanders—especially in the first years of upheaval—have been known to provide a small remuneration in food. In 1987 peasants in the conflictive Ixcán region told us of receiving occasional food donations in exchange for army-imposed tasks such as clearing the roadsides (to prevent ambushes) or repairing roads and bridges. The army has also been known to tell villagers that the delivery of food and other aid to their communities is the direct result of their cooperation in the patrol system.[50]

THE WORLD FOOD PROGRAMME

No discussion of food aid in Central America would be complete without an examination of the United Nations World Food Programme (WFP), which has become so prominent in the region in the 1980s. Food donations from WFP to Central America have increased rapidly over the past decade, jumping from $5.5 million in 1979 to over $60 million today.[51] Currently WFP is the largest food program sponsor in the area.

Multilateral food aid is a normal, fairly predictable response to the serious economic and social crisis affecting Central America. Yet the large degree of integration between WFP and the highly politicized U.S. food-aid program suggests the need for a closer look at the role of WFP in this conflictive region. Distributive food aid from the United States has increased hand in hand with WFP programs in Central America. Indeed, most of the increase in U.S. Title II and Section 416 donations to the area has been channeled through WFP rather than through private agencies or local governments. From 1980 to 1985, the share of total Title II food to Central America distributed through WFP rose from one-fifth to over one-half.[52]

More difficult is calculating what percentage of WFP aid to Central America is U.S. food, since WFP does not normally release country-by-country breakdowns of its assistance flows. Worldwide, the United States contributes approximately a quarter of WFP resources. But in El Salvador, Costa Rica, Guatemala, and Honduras in recent years, the proportion of WFP food supplied by the United States has been at least 70 percent if not 80 percent.[53]

WFP explains this high dependence on U.S. food in Central America on the geographical proximity of the United States to this region, making it logical to call on this donor to supply the region's projects. This argument loses weight, however, when one notes that WFP aid to Nicaragua is supplied entirely by non-U.S. donors. For the other countries, the high dependence of WFP on U.S. donations raises the question of U.S. influence within this multilateral organization. One may also ask why the U.S. government prefers to rely on WFP rather than distributing through its own private and government channels. The answer apparently has to do with WFP's unique role on the food-aid scene.

The World Food Programme is a multilateral food-aid agency set up in 1961–62 under the joint auspices of the United Nations and the Food and Agriculture Organization (FAO). It receives donations of food and cash from over one hundred nations, which it uses in both development and relief efforts around the world. As a UN agency, WFP is careful to maintain official political neutrality. In order not to be seen as passing judgment on the politics of any recipient government, the program allocates its food resources by individual project, not by country. That is, WFP accepts or rejects each project on its own merits, without previously fixing country totals.

WFP projects are initiated, designed, requested, and carried out by government agencies of the host country, in consultation with the local WFP or UN mission. In deciding on project requests, WFP does not consider the political orientation of the host government; it looks only at whether the need for food aid exists and whether the host government has the technical capacity for adequate project management. Hence, in contrast to the political favoritism the characterizes U.S. food-aid allocations, WFP support goes to projects in countries ranging from Cuba to El Salvador. The multilateral WFP thus has a much less politicized image than the bilateral Title II.

This perception of the political neutrality of multilateral WFP is only partially correct, however. It refers only to allocation, not to use. Within each country, bilateral Title II is usually distributed through NGOs such as CARE or CRS and only rarely goes straight to government agencies (usually in emergency projects). In contrast, WFP, following the practice employed by most UN agencies, works directly with local governments. This means that, once within a country, WFP resources lend themselves more easily to government political maneuvering than the aid supplied through AID's partners usually does.

Given its practice of working through local government agencies, WFP should have stronger management and supervision than it currently employs in Central America. WFP-supplied government projects were some of the worst we saw and, on the whole, had weaker management and control than those being administered by AID-supervised NGOs.[54] Corruption and politicization were rife, nutritional education was a joke, and deliveries often were months behind schedule. In Guatemala, for example, the head of the country's

National Reconstruction Committee was forced to resign in February 1987 after the government's General Accounting Office discovered a corruption scandal involving more than two million *quetzales* (roughly $700,000) worth of WFP resources.

Furthermore, evaluations are usually conducted by teams of foreign experts flying in and out in at most three weeks—and almost always giving a favorable review.[55] Emergency projects, such as the six-month displaced-persons projects run by CONADES in El Salvador, are often never evaluated at all, even though in the CONADES case this string of projects went on for a full seven years. One high-level International Labor Office (ILO) employee we interviewed complained that all four WFP-sponsored food-for-work projects he had visited on evaluation missions had lacked proper management, particularly in regard to ILO guidelines on proper worker compensation. He claimed that many in the ILO were unhappy with WFP project management, but that this organization's role as a sister UN agency served to mute open criticism.

More serious still is WFP's demonstrated willingness to collaborate with the highly repressive Central American militaries. Though all UN agencies are careful to maintain good relations with their host governments, other UN agencies in Central America have managed to maintain a much more neutral posture. In El Salvador and Guatemala, WFP sometimes relies on the military for transport.[56]

In Guatemala, a 1982 decree stipulating that all WFP aid must be channeled through the military-affiliated National Reconstruction Committee,[57] and the subsequent assignment of the army model-village program to this agency did nothing to alter subsequent increases in the levels of WFP assistance. Though initially enjoying AID support, the Guatemalan model-village program received such negative international press that the U.S. Congress soon prohibited direct bilateral support for these areas. Today AID in Guatemala reports that it screens all normal PL 480 resources to make sure no food or local currency is going to model-village areas. The World Food Programme, meanwhile, has continued channeling substantial food aid resources—most of them donated by the United States—to those areas.

These special characteristics of WFP projects—their positive apolitical image, their relative lack of administrative controls and requirements, and the direct support they offer to recipient governments—may help explain the increasing share of U.S. food aid to Central America moving through this channel. The use of WFP enables U.S. support to go to projects AID might find it politically inconvenient, or administratively difficult, to support directly. Through WFP, the U.S. government can supply commodities to projects, such as the Guatemalan model-village program, that AID perhaps could not comfortably or even legally support through its regular bilateral program. Furthermore, the involvement of WFP gives any project that extra image boost that AID sponsorship alone just does not have. In El Salvador, for example, AID supplies the government displaced-persons commission CONADES with indirect financial support (Title I and ESF local currencies), but the more visible food supply role, and the headaches of monitoring this notoriously corrupt agency, are left as the responsibility of WFP.

This holds not just for highly politicized resettlement or refugee programs, but even for more benign maternal/child and school-feeding projects. The United States can continue to reap the benefits of donor image (AID requires that "recipients know that U.S. commodities were furnished to WFP by the people of the United States of America") without having to be involved in day-to-day program management or appearing overly interventionist. The projects, meanwhile, continue to have their usual economic and political advantages: building a favorable government image, keeping down social unrest, creating new food habits, and so forth. The United States strongly backed the creation of WFP in the early 1960s precisely because it saw the foreign-policy potential of routing its surplus food through such an apparently apolitical channel.[58]

WFP claims total independence from the United States, but these assertions are contradicted by the evidence. WFP, just like any other multilateral agency, is subject to the political influence of its largest donor, in this case the United States. Local AID mission representatives consult informally with WFP and government officials in designing projects and are instructed to keep Washington informed of any new WFP projects under design, as well as giving their opinion whether the proposed projects coincide with the U.S. objectives for that country. According to the AID handbook on food aid, "WFP has agreed to consult with the [AID] Missions at an early stage in the development of projects." AID, furthermore, notes that "it is in the early stages of project development, preferably before the host country submits a formal request to WFP, that the Mission can have its greatest influence on the project."[59]

Whatever the degree of overall U.S. influence on WFP, there is no doubt that the United States at least maintains substantial control over the uses made of its own donations. Every two years, WFP donors make aid pledges to WFP as a whole, without specifying what countries or projects their resources will be going to. But later, at the moment when WFP actually calls on the United States to release the pledged food for a certain project, the United States can withhold agreement if a project is in conflict with U.S. policy objectives. Usually, however, the situation does not come to that. As explained to us by WFP director James Ingram, "For some countries, such as Nicaragua, we do not even ask the United States to release the food, because we know that the answer would be 'no.' In those cases we must look for food from other sources."

Besides its exercise of veto power, the U.S. government can earmark its donations for specific projects. Every six months, a U.S. representative flies to Rome to review WFP projects awaiting food and to assign U.S. supplies and funds to those it deems acceptable.[60] The procedure for emergency projects allows even more room for Washington to pick and choose. Emergency food does not come out of regular WFP pledges but is sought out case by case. This appears to be true with the controversial WFP emergency program for the displaced in El Salvador, which the AID mission in San Salvador includes in a list of AID's own food programs in the country.[61]

Critics of the politicization of the bilateral U.S. food aid program often suggest that more U.S. food should be directed through WFP, which as a multilateral agency is ostensibly more neutral. That is exactly what is happening in Central America but with less than acceptable results. U.S. food aid going to WFP in Central America has supplied, in numerous cases, highly politicized and often militarized pacification programs.

Although WFP is responsible for the technical success of its projects, U.S. commitments to WFP are made "in accordance with legislative requirements, policies, and procedures applicable to U.S. bilateral donations programs."[62] This means that WFP projects using U.S. food are required to abide by the same guidelines and regulations—such as prohibiting food-aid donations to war-related projects. Yet in Central America these guidelines are simply not being enforced.

AID'S ROLE IN GUATEMALAN COUNTERINSURGENCY

The U.S. role in counterinsurgency efforts is far less in Guatemala than in El Salvador, in both absolute and relative terms. The Guatemalan army prides itself on conceiving and carrying out its counterinsurgency strategies mostly on its own—though it has benefited from counterinsurgency support and training from such countries as Israel, Argentina, and Taiwan. AID mission officers in Guatemala do not express such a clear identification with counterinsurgency as do their counterparts in El Salvador, and U.S. money and food have played a far smaller role in army pacification efforts than they have in neighboring El Salvador.

The reduced intensity and threat of the guerrilla struggle in Guatemala accounts for the more removed attitude of AID. Another factor has been the country's notoriously bad human-rights record. U.S. criticisms of Guatemalan human-rights violations led to a cutoff of direct U.S. military aid from 1977 to 1983. A 1984 congressional prohibition against using AID funds for model villages and development poles has also made the AID mission in Guatemala careful to avoid direct links between its assistance and army programs.

But even though at a relatively low level, U.S. support for Guatemalan counterinsurgency efforts nevertheless does exist, and food aid once again forms part of the picture.[63] First, there is the U.S. practice of allowing its donations to WFP to go to CRN and the model-village program, even after AID withdrew open support from the Guatemalan government's model-village programs. As we traveled throughout the highlands over the past five years, we discovered residents of model villages, displaced persons in army holding camps, and day laborers on road projects all receiving bags and cans of food bearing the familiar red-white-and-blue AID symbol.

Although the AID mission in Guatemala has no official control over what WFP does with its food aid in that country, AID in Washington does exercise decisive influence over the allocation of Title II food to specific WFP programs. AID could, if it wished, refuse to supply PL 480 food to WFP-CRN projects in Guatemala, as it does for political reasons elsewhere. Instead, AID appears to have encouraged these controversial WFP-CRN projects by its continued commitments of U.S. food.

Besides supporting CRN indirectly through WFP, AID has given it direct budgetary support through Economic Support Funds (ESF) and, to a lesser extent, Title I resale funds.[64] In 1985, while the model-village program was still under way, the Guatemalan government assigned nearly three million *quetzales* (about $1.2 million) in Title I local currency to CRN for rural development in the highlands.[65]

The military coordination of civilian ministries—first established under the Interinstitutional Coordination system set up in 1984 and continued today in such plans as the Multisectorial Commission for the Ixil Triangle—also poses problems for bilateral assistance. The military coordination of government efforts means that some of the U.S. aid going to Guatemalan government agencies working in such areas as agricultural development, housing, or road building, as well as CARE food assistance going to the government health and reforestation programs, is probably being used in the counterinsurgency-inspired "development" projects concentrated in conflictive areas.[66]

WINNING HEARTS AND MAYANS

Since 1986, when national elections were held to elect a civilian government, certain changes have been seen in the Guatemalan counterinsurgency model. First there was a deemphasis on the "model villages" per se, and more stress on extending development efforts to villages throughout the conflict areas. Despite initial ambitious army plans, development efforts in these areas have so far not moved beyond providing small-scale social services. There has also been, in some cases, a reduction in army control mechanisms—such as pass systems—in these areas. One reason for these changes is the army's relative success in defeating the guerrillas and reducing their areas of activity. In addition, the ongoing civil-patrol system has proved to be an effective means of control over the population. Indeed, with civil patrols in place throughout the highlands, the distinction between a model village and a regular village has been blurred. Second, the Guatemalan army was not in the end able to capture the quantity of resources it had hoped for, since only a few foreign governments or organizations, such as WFP, Taiwan, and certain U.S. evangelical groups, proved willing to work directly in formal model villages. Finally, a 1986 attempt by the new civilian government to wrest control of the model villages from the army resulted in the army's rather huffily washing its hands of further economic commitments.

Despite these changes, pacification based on food handouts continues to form part of the army's strategy to maintain control over rural Guatemala. In recent years, food aid has been used in two main ways: to help lure in those displaced who continue to hide in the mountains, and to continue local-level community development projects in areas where the army is still trying to consolidate its control.

From 1987 through 1989, the Ixil Triangle army base mounted a major campaign—using both vinegar and honey—to bring in the displaced persons still hiding and living in the mountains to the north. On the one hand, mobile army patrols and civilian patrols, supported by helicopters and bombers, scoured the guerrilla-held area burning crops and capturing any civilians they could find. On the other, army helicopters dropped leaflets and used loud-speakers to offer food, sustenance, and protection to any who turned them-selves in. These efforts bore fruit, and starting in 1987 literally thousands of civilians have been processed through the Nebaj military base. There they are fed, questioned, and given three months of political reeducation. Once re-leased, they can go to any village controlled by the army, where of course they are required to join civil patrols.

Food aid forms a key part of this new strategy. In 1988 the army base used WFP food from CRN (apparently taken from an emergency drought program for eastern Guatemala) and EEC food from the Catholic church's archdiocesan CARITAS program to feed those on the base or in its holding camps. Supplies were tight, however, and sources irregular. In the first months, when condi-tions were at their worst, a group of nuns supplied food to supplement the meager army rations. In early 1989 the government refugee repatriation and displaced-persons program (CEARD), financed and supervised by the United Nations High Commission on Refugees (UNHCR), took charge of caring for the displaced being held under army control. Rations now come largely from CEARD purchases.

The army continues to make use of WFP food aid in food-for-work pro-grams, however. In 1987 CRN's "Community Development" project was renamed "Infrastructure Construction and Productive Activities for Indian Communities." A disproportionate number of these food-for-work projects are directed to the conflict zones. There they support both road building and the provision of basic social infrastructure, such as schools, public clothes-washing sinks, or potable water systems. In the Ixil Triangle, these projects are concentrated in recently secured villages, especially those earmarked by the army for resettlement by the displaced. As for the conflictive Ixcán region, a 1987 CRN promoter's report listed twenty-five FFW projects in the area, several in "model communities." All these activities had been coordinated with the local army base, said the report, because "a full stomach reduces violent activity in this region."[67]

Realizing that hunger fuels rebellion, both the army and the government are strong advocates of food-aid programs. Food aid in areas of army influence helps both to improve the military's image and to draw more people under its control. It is only natural, as a CRN official pointed out to us, that "people look out for where their food is coming from." In the conflictive areas of Guatemala, thanks to international food aid, it is to the army that destitute Indians must often look for food. A report by the U.S. human rights group Americas Watch explained it this way: "International food aid becomes another instrument of military control. That is, hungry peasants must pledge allegiance to the government, work on government projects, and obey military commands in order to obtain food. This situation provides the military with one more form of coercion, with one more weapon in its campaign to consolidate its control and domination of civilian life in the highlands."[68]

HUMANITARIAN AID IN A WAR SETTING

For groups sincerely wishing to aid the victims of Guatemalan army violence, the strict military control of the rural population and the military's attempts to act as relief and development coordinator in those areas pose a serious dilemma. In helping to feed the population living under army control, humanitarian agencies know that to some extent they help perpetuate and reaffirm the military's power. Yet to ignore the needs of that population just because they have come under military control would be to abandon these people to often inadequate care and physical abuse.

Providing aid to this population can give a group access to act as a witness to abuse, thereby serving as a discreet check on human-rights violations. As the International Red Cross told us in El Salvador, "Food assistance permits the IRC to maintain a presence and carry out activities related to protection." To the extent that humanitarian groups make public those abuses or show opposition to army tactics, however, they themselves become suspect—which can pose a danger both to their own workers and to the population they serve. A delicate balancing act is thus required.

In Guatemala the situation has been a special problem because of the very extensiveness and ruthlessness of army control. The International Committee of the Red Cross, traditionally a neutral source of assistance to those caught in the midst of war, was not even allowed into the country until 1988. Really the only important group that has dared to thread its way through these dilemmas has been sectors of the Catholic church. Though itself a victim of army violence and suspicion, the church had the grass-roots network, the national credibility, and the humanitarian tradition to enable it to undertake at least limited relief efforts.

In 1983 CRS arranged for a special U.S. Section 416 powdered-milk donation to aid the victims of the violence. Some of this milk was distributed through questionable government and evangelical organizations selected by AID, but that portion retained by CRS was distributed through the CARITAS church network at a time when the local population found itself truly in crisis. CRS-CARITAS's ongoing "maternal/child" and "other child" programs provided another source of food to destitute widows and orphans, especially in the first years after the violence. Later CRS also distributed EEC food directly to the widowed population. In sum, although extremely limited in comparison to the need, CRS's program did represent a attempt to use food aid for straightforward humanitarian aims.

The context for these programs was, however, particularly difficult. In Guatemala in the early 1980s church and other relief agencies were allowed to remain in operation only if they followed the Guatemalan army game rules: no popular organization, no talk of human rights, and no criticism of the army. In the Quiché department, no church programs operated for almost three years because the entire diocese closed down after a spate of army murders and threats. Many programs were also subject to strict control, such as by posting civil patrolmen right outside the office door to ensure that no beneficiary carried away more food than the army deemed strictly necessary.

Continued distribution in that militarized context obviously required some compromises, especially at the local level. In several cases military personnel made use of church warehouses and the local religious could not prevent it. In other cases local religious decided to take the controversial step of assisting Guatemalans being held directly under army control and supervision. In 1987, for example, one group of nuns helped feed, clothe, and give medical attention to the hundreds of displaced then being brought down from their mountain hideouts and forced to live in army holding camps. The nuns took this action only after considerable internal debate. In the end they decided that the immediate physical needs of the displaced outweighed any political effects their assistance might be viewed as having. They did, however, insist on giving food and clothing to the displaced themselves instead of just handing them over to the army for distribution.

In other cases the national Guatemalan Bishops' Conference managed to draw the line. In 1982 the bishops fought off a military government attempt to place a special administrator in the CARITAS office by threatening to close down the whole program. And in early 1987 the conference withdrew CARITAS from a government plan for the church to handle food distribution for an official refugee repatriation program. The bishops' stated reason, that they did not want CARITAS reduced to a purely logistical role, was taken by most observers as the church's way of indicating its disagreement with the politics of this program, in particular the then active role of the military in receiving and supervising the repatriates.

SURROUNDING NICARAGUA WITH FOOD AID

After the victory of the Sandinista guerrillas over the government of Anastasio Somoza in July 1979, the Carter administration approved a $13 million Title I food-aid package, centered on wheat, to the new left-leaning government. In March 1981 the Reagan administration terminated the agreement, on strictly foreign-policy grounds, before all the food had been delivered. This sudden aid withdrawal was an important blow to the dollar-short Sandinista government, still dealing with the ravages left by the war. Agricultural production was sharply down, just when income redistribution measures and postwar reconstruction were creating a boom in demand. The cutoff in U.S. wheat sales thus contributed to rising shortages and inflation. The suspension of U.S. food aid was, however, only the beginning. Over the next few years the Reagan administration mounted an entire economic, political, and military destabilization campaign designed to undermine the Nicaraguan economy and government. This was to include organizing contra military forces in neighboring Honduras and Costa Rica, mining Nicaragua's harbors, and eventually, mounting a complete trade blockade.

Through the 1980s, Nicaragua has continued to have a strong need for outside food assistance. In 1982 it was hit by drought, and in 1988 a devastating hurricane swept the country's Atlantic coast. The contra war has directly hurt production in conflict areas and, by absorbing enormous amounts of budgetary and dollar resources, has also sharply reduced the funds available for productive imports and agricultural development activities. Food shortages and inflation have continued to plague the population. Yet despite this need, to date Nicaragua receives no U.S.-government food aid of any sort, not

Strategic Private Humanitarianism

The vast majority of the hundreds of private organizations and churches that distribute food aid in Central America are exclusively dedicated to charitable, developmental, or religious concerns. Many, in fact, have made a point of maintaining their political independence and neutrality. Others, however, have consciously integrated their own humanitarian activities into military and political strategies.

In this category are included groups that willingly cooperate in military/civic-action programs and provide services under military auspices in pacification and resettlement zones. Often these groups provide selective assistance only to those sectors of the population cooperating with or controlled by government forces. The evangelical groups in particular engage in ideological or political proselytism. Their efforts, frequently encouraged by the army and AID, fit nicely into the LIC strategy of uniting private and government resources into counterrevolutionary campaigns.

Almost all these groups are involved in some form of food distribution. A few receive Title II food directly or through a cooperating sponsor such as CARE; others receive World Food Programme food from government institutions like the Guatemalan CRN; many rely on their own private sources of supply; and some receive food shipments from the European Economic Community or other foreign donors.

In Guatemala the army has given right-wing and evangelical organizations easy access to the conflictive Ixil Triangle. Indeed, evangelical chief of state General Ríos Montt issued an open invitation to these groups during his 1982–83 reign. Thus, precisely when many mainstream private organizations were forced out of the highlands because of their role in leadership and cooperative formation, conservative groups like the Summer Institute of Linguistics, Air Commando Association, National Defense Council, and Youth with a Mission were given a free rein to expand their activities.[69] Not only did their teaching of obedience to authority, emphasis on individual salvation, and often virulent anticommunism conveniently reinforce the army's own propaganda, but these organizations also frequently provided supplies, technical help, and even translation services for the military.

To a lesser extent, conservative elements of the Catholic church have also cooperated with the army's campaign in the Ixil Triangle and other conflictive zones. The archdiocesan CARITAS program, which operates separately from the more neutral national CARITAS program, has handed over food donations directly to the army for distribution to displaced people being held under military control.[70]

In El Salvador, NGOs and churches that have tried to stay independent of the military and to provide food aid to all needy persons regardless of their suspected political sympathies have been obstructed in their humanitarian work and have themselves been victimized by military repression. Meanwhile, other AID-funded NGOs and churches, especially CESAD, Project Hope, and World Relief, have been playing a key role in the military's United to Reconstruct campaign by providing food or other aid to displaced persons willing to relocate in military-controlled zones. These groups, and right-wing private organizations such as the the Knights of Malta, easily obtain military permission to take their food and other humanitarian supplies into *Continued* areas targeted by the army for pacification.[71] Gerald Coughlin, Salvadoran director of the Knights of Malta, explained targeted food assistance thus: "If you're not eating and a private organization brings you some food, then you're less likely to join the guerrillas."[72]

In Honduras numerous groups, particularly evangelical churches, formed part of a U.S. government-organized effort to back the contras. Organizations like the International Christian Embassy Jerusalem, Gospel Crusade, and Friends of the Americas readily acknowledge providing food and other humanitarian aid to the contras and other Nicaraguans living immediately along the border. Other NGOs like World Opportunities International have supplied civic-action programs sponsored by the U.S. Army.[73]

even humanitarian distributive aid. The CARE Title II program there closed down in 1982. Since 1985 the United States refuses to sell Nicaragua food, or any other item, even on full commercial terms. Clearly, the United States is trying to use withholding food supplies as a weapon against this struggling regime.

The Nicaraguan case shows, however, how the influence of the U.S. "food weapon" has been weakened by the changing structure of international food aid. With the United States no longer the only source of food assistance, Nicaragua has been able to find other donors to help it meet its urgent food needs. WFP runs several large programs in Nicaragua, all supplied with food from non-U.S. donors. Nicaragua also receives substantial food aid from the Soviet Union, the EEC, and other sources. There is even a private U.S. group that helps fund the commercial import of Canadian wheat.

The non-U.S. food-aid programs in Nicaragua are outside the purview of this study. We assume that the same benefits and problems that characterize food-aid programs in the other Central America countries are also seen in Nicaragua. But the management of food aid may be somewhat better in this country than in some of its neighbors. For one thing, the country has several programs, such as the Nicaraguan Food Program (PAN) and the five-year Plan for Food and Nutrition (POAN), that integrate food aid with other multisectorial activities in agriculture, pricing, and nutrition. In addition, the WFP director in Nicaragua commended to us the unusual "honesty and concern" of the Nicaraguan government representatives he works with he works, the innovativeness of some of the WFP-supported programs, and the government's insistence that WFP supply a food basket appropriate to local needs and tastes.[74]

Despite AID claims that the U.S. food-aid program is guided largely by humanitarian and development intent, U.S. food aid to Nicaragua, a country sorely in need of foreign assistance and support, has been blocked by geopolitical considerations. Food for Peace has been used against this country in more indirect ways as well. Increased U.S. aid to Costa Rica and Honduras has helped compensate them for their participation in the anti-Nicaraguan offensive, and some of these supplies have gone to projects that form a direct part of that contra effort.

COSTA RICA: FOCUS ON THE NORTHERN ZONE

Costa Rica, Nicaragua's neighbor to the south, has traditionally not been a major recipient of U.S. food aid. The Costa Rican government distribution network is largely self-supplied, and until the 1980s the country covered its commercial food import needs largely on its own. Starting in 1982, however, Costa Rica began to receive large amounts of both Title I and ESF assistance. These responded to two factors: U.S. concern about the Costa Rican debt crisis and its effect on political stability, and U.S. interest in enlisting Costa Rica's support in the emerging contra war. Starting in this same period, U.S.-financed contras began to set up camp in Costa Rica along the northern border, from which they began to launch attacks and raids against Nicaragua. The extra aid helped secure Costa Rican cooperation in this irregular and illegal endeavor.

ESF and food aid were also used to help directly finance projects relating to the contra war—in particular, the strategic $36 million Northern Zone Infrastructure Development Project begun in 1983.[75] The Northern Zone, a poor and sparsely populated area along Costa Rica's border with Nicaragua, was largely ignored by AID and the Costa Rican government until the contra war started picking up steam. Today this area is the focus of agricultural projects, a colonization program, infrastructure development, and new government services—all paid for by foreign aid, including large sums of Title I local currency.

The security focus of the Northern Zone Project is clear. At the time it was being planned, then-president Luis Monge noted that the zone's "relative isolation from the rest of the country exposes it to foreign influence and infiltration." He proclaimed the proposed development project as part of an effort "to better our system of national security."[76] AID has acknowledged that the project was given priority funding for "geopolitical reasons."[77] A 1984 study by the Inter-American Planning Society (SIAP) concluded that the project's main objective is "the neutralization of the ideological influence of the Sandinista Revolution."[78]

Road construction and maintenance, which observers argue are designed in part to give security forces and contras easy access to the isolated frontier, are the Northern Zone Project's most visible and costly component. The area is also being colonized with landless *campesinos* from elsewhere in the country, with the apparent intention of populating the area with inhabitants who are indebted to the Costa Rican and U.S. governments. AID project evaluations mention "attitude change" as one of the positive results of the program. Agricultural credit and technical assistance are being offered to these new settlers, especially for the production of nontraditional crops, and the U.S.-funded American Institute for Free Labor Development (AIFLD) is forming *campesino* cooperatives in the area. Finally, the project helps finance local potable-water systems and other social services.

Title I has played an important role in funding this strategic project. AID–Costa Rica records of Title I local currency expenditures show at least 39 percent of FY 1984 Title I funds being programmed to Northern Zone activities, with the bulk going to road construction. The Northern Zone Project also figures prominently in the self-help measures stipulated in U.S. food-aid accords with the Costa Rican government. The stated purpose of these measures—"to contribute directly to development progress in poor rural areas"—contrasts sharply with the geopolitical motives for this controversial project.

HONDURAS: ON THE BORDER OF WAR

Wherever you go along the Honduras-Nicaragua border, you are likely to find people eating donated U.S. food. Some rightly goes to civilian Nicaraguan refugees in need of humanitarian assistance. But much of this food has arrived to this area of contra activity to serve not a humanitarian but a political purpose.

The anti-Sandinista contras have long depended on their U.S. backers for both their ammunition and their food. Their rations have come not from the regular PL 480 Title II program, however, but from more obscure private or government sources. Whenever they ventured into Nicaragua, the contras were able to count on supply drops from Central Intelligence Agency planes. In addition, from 1985 onward, the U.S. Congress has approved millions of dollars worth of "humanitarian" assistance (uniforms, foods, and medicines) to be shipped to the contras by a special agency set up within the State Department.

This humanitarian assistance program has one very interesting twist. In 1988 AID, claiming security and logistical problems in getting food to contras within Nicaraguan territory, coined the idea and the practice of "cash-for-food." In practice this program involved direct cash payments to contra leaders claiming to have a certain number of men waiting inside Nicaragua for funds to buy food. Despite the catchy name, of course, there was no way of ensuring that cash-for-food recipients were indeed supporting the number of men they claimed, or that the money would really be spent on troop rations.[79]

Aside from feeding the contra fighters themselves, U.S. food aid has also been used to provide backup insurgency support. In 1982 the United States successfully pressured the UNHCR to set up refugee camps in Honduras for Nicaraguan Miskito Indians, over the objections of many UNHCR workers who felt that food handouts would only encourage the cross-border migration then being encouraged by contra recruiters. The U.S. prevailed, however, and the camps soon filled with the families of contra fighters.[80]

The close links between the Nicaraguan refugee population and the contras, and the fact that both are concentrated in the same areas along the Nicaraguan border, would require Nicaraguan refugee aid programs in Honduras to be extra careful to maintain political neutrality—for example, by moving these camps farther from the border. Unfortunately, the history of these programs is one of flux and manipulation more than of stable and disinterested assistance. CARITAS feeds most of the refugees in Honduras, including Salvadorans, Guatemalans, and non-Miskito Nicaraguans. The strategic Miskito refugees, however, were fed by CARE Title II donations in 1983 and with WFP rations distributed by the conservative World Relief from 1984 onward.[81]

Aside from feeding the contras themselves, U.S. food aid has also been used to provide backup insurgency support, to increase the civic-action capabilities of the Honduran army, and to increase the Honduran government's ability to increase its presence in strategic border areas. One of the first uses of U.S. food aid along the border was when Washington encouraged World Relief in 1982 to set up a refugee camp along the border. Later the United Nations assumed sponsorship of World Relief operations in La Mosquitia, with WFP rations substituting for direct AID donations formerly channeled through NGOs and local government agencies.

Throughout the war, the World Relief camp provided an important organizing and supply point for Miskito contra groups, with U.S. military and CIA advisers frequently holding meetings with contra leaders in the middle of the camp. But U.S. government and private-sector supporters of the contras were not satisfied with the ability of the World Relief camp to meet the infrastructure and supply needs of the Miskito contras.

In 1985 Congress passed an emergency $7.8 million relief program, including community development and road-building projects, for areas immediately along the border where the contras were camped. And even though at least one public health team found no evidence of widespread malnutrition in this border region, AID food aid together with privately supplied food transported by AID and the U.S. military began arriving in the region. CARE food, supposedly destined for government health and education programs, was being distributed by the Friends of the Americas contra-support group in Rus Rus, only a short distance from the Nicaraguan border.[82] One UN official told us: "AID is shipping beans into this area which has always produced enough beans for the Miskitos. Maybe AID thinks transportation [into this isolated and virtually roadless region] increases their flavor." In addition to food donations, Title I local currencies have also been used for projects along the border, whose main purpose, according to some local observers, is to pacify the local Honduran population, which has grown frustrated with the contra presence.

The frontier areas occupied by contra forces have also received frequent food assistance through the Honduran army's civic-action programs and through the army-administered National Emergency Council (COPEN). With assistance from AID and its Office for Foreign Disaster Assistance, COPEN has in the 1980s exhibited a new interest in disaster prevention and relief. The border areas—both in La Mosquitia and farther west near Danlí—have become prime recipients of this disaster aid. Floods in La Mosquitia (where floods are an almost annual event) and "Sandinista invasions" have sparked responses by army civic-action and PSYOPS teams, which are transported to the disaster sites in Huey helicopters often laden with U.S. food aid.[83] COPEN and the closely related military/civic-action program receive their food donations by soliciting U.S. private organizations in Honduras and by dipping into AID food supplies controlled by various government ministries, such as the Ministry of Health.

SUMMARY

The irony of having a program known as Food for Peace used to achieve bellicose objectives has been pointed out before. As the war in Vietnam was winding down, public opposition to the militaristic uses of the PL 480 program forced changes in the Food for Peace authorizing legislation. No longer were U.S. food donations or Title I local currencies to be used for military and paramilitary purposes. Also strengthened were the developmental and humanitarian aims of the program. Yet once again the irony and the tragedy of the Food for Peace program has become evident. In Central America, not only do many food-aid programs fail to achieve the humanitarian intent of the PL 480 legislation, but in some cases they even violate the congressional mandate against the military uses of U.S. food aid.

The main areas of concern that surfaced during our study were the following: the use of Title I local-currency generations to support pacification programs and war-related projects; the use of Title II distributive food in illegal military/civic-action programs; and the degree to which Title II contributions to the World Food Programme are directed to counterinsurgency projects. A related concern is the proliferation of ideologically motivated humanitarian organizations that use private and government food aid in support of their operations.

It is true that one of the stated objectives of the food aid program is to support U.S. foreign policy. But the program also purports to support economic development and assist the poor. In Central America, given the repressive nature of the U.S. government's allies in the region, pursuit of the former largely means neglect of the latter. In a disturbing number of cases, U.S. food aid is being used to help repress and pacify social and revolutionary movements that propose to change the conditions that cause such widespread poverty in the region. In the rush to build strategic roads, pacify restive peasants, and improve the image of local armies, AID has ignored its basic mission to combat world hunger and improve the lot of the poor.

Conclusion

THE ABUSES, weaknesses, and results of the U.S. food-aid program in Central America not only call into question the application of the program in this conflictive region, but also raise serious questions about the merit of entire PL 480 program. Thirty-five years have passed since Congress authorized the first food-aid legislation. Although the program enjoys strong popular support, many observers have decried the self-interested quality of the U.S. food-aid program and detailed its numerous negative consequences. This book, a portrait of what food aid has become in Central America, adds another voice to that growing body of criticism.

Officials from AID, USDA, and other U.S. government offices stress that the U.S. food-aid program benefits donors and beneficiaries alike. It is portrayed as a program where everyone wins. What we saw during our two years of research in Central America, however, did not bear out this comfortable view. In following the food-aid trail from the corridors of Capitol Hill to the impoverished slums and hamlets of Central America, we came to different conclusions.

The harvest of the U.S. heartland is being turned over to politicians, generals, and agroindustries, with only crumbs going to the truly needy. Corruption and inefficiency pervade the program. But most disturbing of all was not the waste or the inevitable siphoning off of food-aid donations, but the overt use of food aid to meet U.S. economic, political, and military ends—even at the expense of local development and regional food security.

BREAKING THE LAW

Food aid is designed to serve a variety of U.S. interests, from surplus disposal to supporting U.S. foreign policy objectives. In the process of responding to the demands of diverse of U.S. sectors and agencies, there have been serious breaches of the PL 480 authorizing legislation.

Human Rights: The legislation prohibits Title I assistance to countries that engage in a consistent pattern of gross violations of human rights. International human-rights organizations like Amnesty International, Americas Watch, and the Inter-American Court on Human Rights have documented that the governments of Guatemala, El Salvador, and Honduras are gross violators of human rights. Any objective interpretation of this human-rights clause would compel a termination of food aid and other forms of U.S. assistance to these countries.

Nonmilitary Purposes: The Foreign Assistance Act of 1973 and the U.S. Code specify that no foreign aid, except for military aid expressly earmarked for that purpose, can be used for military purposes abroad. The U.S. food-aid program in Central America is currently violating that prohibition. In El Salvador, Title II food is being handed out in military/civic-action programs run by army psychological-operations and civil-affairs teams. In both Guatemala and El Salvador, local currency generated by food-aid resales has gone to military-directed pacification campaigns.

Food Security: The legislation regulating U.S. food aid states that these commodities should be used "to enhance food security in developing countries through local food production." Furthermore, AID is obligated to "promote progress toward assurance of an adequate food supply by encouraging countries to give higher emphasis to the production of food crops than to the production of such nonfood crops as are in world surplus." Only rarely in Central America do food-aid programs promote food security and increase local food production. Instead, food aid is fomenting imports and creating disincentive effects for local food production. The funds generated through food-aid resales are being channeled largely to the agroexport production of nonfood commodities and luxury food items like macadamia nuts.

Participation of the Poor: The food-aid legislation and the standard food agreements signed with recipient countries make repeated references to the objective of helping and involving poor farmers. Local-currency agreements are supposed "to increase the access of the poor in the recipient country to an adequate, nutritious, and stable food supply," provide "credit on reasonable terms and conditions for small farmers," and "provide for participation by the poor, insofar as possible, at the regional and local levels."

AID states that the self-help measures it sets forth in food-aid agreements "shall be implemented in poor rural areas and enable the poor to participate actively in increasing agricultural production through small farm agriculture." But while some peasant farmers might benefit from Title I–funded programs, the current stress in AID food-aid agreements is on agribusiness production and trickle-down economics rather than programs that directly meet basic needs. Title I sales agreements, rather than making more credit available to poor farmers, have sought to cut such programs by making credit available only on strictly commercial terms.

Bellmon Amendment: The Bellmon amendment to the PL 480 legislation stipulates that U.S. food aid can be shipped only after USDA has determined that the allocated amounts will not result in substantial disincentives for local production. USDA is complying with this regulation in a highly superficial manner. It approves wheat shipments, for example, without considering how a shift to wheat consumption might affect the demand for other locally produced grains. Yet there is considerable evidence, including that gathered by AID-commissioned studies, that overprogramming and disincentive effects are indeed occurring. The effect of Title II and Section 416 aid on local markets and production has also been given inadequate attention, even though distributive food aid reaches at least a third of the region's population and much of this food could be produced locally.

Usual Marketing Requirement: Long-standing U.S. legislation requires Title I recipients to maintain their normal commercial purchases of the commodities being shipped under each agreement. This is done to protect the usual export levels of both the United States and other food-surplus countries. In Central America, this legal requirement is routinely waived to maximize aid flows to the region. Among those affected are the Central American countries themselves. Easy access to favorable PL 480 credit terms has left their regional agreement, in which they promise to buy from each other before importing from outside the region, in tatters.

Food-aid programs must be held accountable to the laws that govern them. In Central America food-aid programs, in the rush to support the "friendly" governments of the region, are in some cases operating outside the law. Throughout the several decades of PL 480's history, the U.S. Congress has seen fit to add provisions to the legislation to ensure that current food-aid programs do not create the same problems as past ones. These laws should be enforced, or if not appropriate to Central America, amended—but not simply ignored.

GOVERNMENT-TO-GOVERNMENT FOOD AID

Most food aid sent to Central America and other regions supports governments rather than feeding poor people. The goal of both the PL 480 Title I and Section 416 sugar compensation resale programs, which together represent some 80 percent of total U.S. food aid to Central America, is to provide economic support to governments of food-deficit nations. Government-to-government food aid is a rather openhanded form of providing both dollar and local-currency support for Central American governments. This aid has helped local governments maintain import levels, finance their budgets, and hold down food prices.

But such aid does not necessarily go to those nations most in need or to those most concerned about building food security. On the contrary, political considerations are paramount. As a result, large sums of this type of food aid go to governments more interested in managing current crises with food aid than in addressing the long-term food needs of their people. By stepping in to fill the gap, U.S. food-aid programs thereby allow these governments to continue to avoid the reforms needed to ensure national food security and true political stability.

The cheap price of the commodities imported under these aid programs affects food security more directly as well. It does this by promoting the consumption of U.S. commodities at the expense of locally produced goods, thereby lowering the income and eventually the output of local farmers. Meanwhile the aid cultivates a taste and a demand for U.S. agricultural products such as wheat and powdered milk, thus creating pressure for continued imports.

The PL 480 legislation contains some safeguards against food aid's being simply handed over to governments that make no effort to improve their nation's food security. To avoid the "bottomless well" effect, regulations require governments importing under Title I to undertake measures to improve local food production. These conditions often prove ineffective. For one thing, they are difficult to enforce. For another, AID and USDA officials are wont to interpret the regulations according to their own economic and political philosophies. Commonly, they see agricultural development as centered on commercial farmers and agroindustry, not the peasant majority, and on exports, not local grain production. Self-help measures and local-currency projects consequently are used to support such objectives as increased nontraditional agroexport production, privatization of grain-stabilization institutes, and neoliberal structural adjustment.

Recommendations: The Title I program should be suspended. Programs specifically designed for market building and for strategic balance-of-payments support already exist. In duplicating the functions of the CCC and ESF programs, PL 480 Title I only confuses the issue of the type and levels of aid Congress wishes to supply to other countries. Furthermore, Title I has not proved an effective tool for promoting long-term food security in deficit nations. The economic support it provides tempts recipient governments to accept food-aid allocations beyond their countries' true levels of need. The food support it provides enables governments to avoid and delay needed agricultural-sector reforms.

If not repealed, Title I should at least be amended. Several measures could be taken to improve the program and guard against some of its major weaknesses. Before reauthorizing the Title I program, Congress should seek to more closely define its disparate objectives. Currently these include surplus disposal and market development, economic support for U.S. political allies, the encouragement of agribusiness development abroad, the temporary increasing of food supplies in food-deficit countries, and support for rural development efforts that benefit the poor. One or two objectives should be singled out for special emphasis, and the legislation surrounding this program should be rewritten to ensure these are met. As it is, the plethora of aims and interests served by the program results in a lack of accountability. Our specific recommendations for this process are as follows:

– The main objective of the PL 480 Title I program should be to increase food supplies in food-deficit countries, especially those affected by sudden shortfalls. In support of that goal, stricter need criteria should be placed on the allocation of this aid.

– In making Title I aid allocations, current human-rights provisions need to be respected, which means cutting aid to countries that independent international organizations judge to be violators.

– Local-currency and self-help measures need to be rewritten with more specific language to ensure support for local agriculture and food self-sufficiency, in particular small-farmer basic grains production.

- The potential effects of Title I aid on local agriculture should be clearly recognized and regulated. Congress should make explicit that the Bellmon amendment determination should require the study of potential disincentive effects between different commodities—for example, wheat and corn.
- In reconsidering the objectives of Title I, legislation relating to usual marketing requirements should be reviewed and revised in light of the current superficial fulfillment of this obligation. In particular, the effect of Title I imports on regional grain marketing should be considered before making favorable determinations.
- Sufficient reserves and storage space are two associated problems that are affected by Title I aid. The United States should encourage Central American countries to build local and regional reserves and to see that there is adequate storage space for those reserves as well as for seasonal harvests. As it is, year-after-year commitments of Title I assistance discourage governments from adopting strong reserve policies.

DISTRIBUTIVE PROGRAMS

Title II and Section 416 Regular food aid are donations that are distributed directly to poor individuals abroad, either free or through food-for-work programs. U.S. distributive food assistance to Central America has roughly doubled in the past decade. Most of this increase has been channeled through the World Food Programme.

From urban centers to mountain villages, from military bases to churches and clinics, distributive food aid seems omnipresent. More than a third of the Central American population now receives some form of food aid, most from U.S. sources. Yet for all its expansiveness, there is little evidence that distributive food aid is improving the nutritional status of Central Americans. In fact, as land pressures and deforestation increase and economic austerity programs curtail jobs and earning power, malnutrition and hunger are once again on the rise.

Distributive food programs largely throw food at the problems of hunger and poverty. Because they are based more on charitable motives than on any serious reflection about the structural causes of poverty, these programs often end up being both ineffective and wasteful. Distributive food programs also fall short even in the area of improving nutritional status. One reason is that it is nearly impossible to ensure that free rations represent a net addition to the diet instead of simply replacing what probably what would have been eaten anyway. On the whole, these programs are more aptly viewed not as a way to increase overall caloric consumption, but as a form of income transfer.

Nutritional effect is limited by the problem of targeting. In Central America, these programs often do not reach the neediest and most malnourished. They tend to be concentrated in the most geographically accessible areas and in those that already have the social infrastructure needed to administer the program. Beneficiaries are rarely selected by objective criteria of need, such as anthropomorphic measures of malnutrition, but rather are accepted first come, first served or through subjective judgment calls. Much food then, is given to people who do not really need it, while the poorest and most marginal are left out.

AID, recognizing the poor nutritional record of food distribution programs, has in recent years attempted to tie these distributions to nutritional and health education. Following this logic, free food is used as an incentive for attending at health clinics or classes in basic nutrition and sanitation. Most of the nutritional education we saw in Central America, however, was a travesty, consisting of classes on how to prepare the new foreign foods. At other times the educational component described in project proposals simply did not exist.

Food-for-work (FFW) is another strategy for strengthening the development impact of distribution programs. Here the nutritional rationale is replaced by a focus on labor mobilization. But food-for-work can be justified only if the work project truly benefits the individuals involved—a condition frequently not met in Central America. By nature, FFW tends to be imposed from above. Another problem is that some projects ignore workers' rights to a cash income, paying them solely in food even for labor on public works. Finally, though they mobilize labor in the short term, FFW projects in the long term often undermine community organization and participation. These projects are ideal tools for political manipulation. They breed corruption, and they destroy the rationale for voluntary participation in future community development activities.

If the intended nutritional, educational, and developmental benefits of distributive programs are more mythical than real, why do these programs continue to thrive? One reason is that hundreds of government, private, and church agencies in Central America structure their social-service and development activities around food distribution, and their number continues to expand. Both governments and churches sponsor food programs as a way to demonstrate their concern for the poor and to extend their political and ideological influence. Another reason is that food is readily available, whereas money and other resources often are not. As a CARE representative in Honduras quipped, "Why does CARE distribute food? Because the mountain is there!"

Not only are the benefits of these programs unproven, but they also have serious costs and side effects. Food distribution is not free. Program administration requires surprisingly large amounts of both financial and human resources, which are then not available for other tasks. Throughout the region, the time and energy of literally thousands of nuns, nurses, teachers, social workers, and community leaders are taken up in the endless work involved in transporting, repackaging, and distributing food. Beneficiaries, meanwhile, spend endless hours simply standing in food lines.

Outside food aid woos consumer tastes away from traditional diets toward high-cost imported products. Food distributions, even under food-for-work projects, foster a welfare mentality. The population begins to depend on donors rather than on its own initiative and thus people resort to waiting for "help" to arrive rather than seeking their own solutions. The free food can also foster factionalism and corruption as beneficiaries compete among themselves for handouts and "food power."

Year after year, food handouts provide short-term help for long-term and deepening problems. They polish the government's image, enabling it to pretend it is doing something about mass poverty and hunger while glossing over structural class and land-tenure injustices. By acting as a palliative, food aid delays the search for more direct solutions to the problems of poverty and hunger.

Distributive food projects are now being explicitly designed to cushion the social and political impact of structural-adjustment programs. Recognizing that the neoliberal market-economic policies it advocates will weigh most heavily upon the poor, AID is promoting the use of distributive programs to ease this impact and thereby reduce the likelihood of social upheaval. Local armed forces, too, have discovered the palliative and psychological nature of food distribution, and where they are able, they direct these donations preferentially to conflict areas.

AID is well aware of food aid's political role. Food aid is only part of a package that includes both economic and military support for its regional allies. El Salvador, where Washington strongly backs the war effort, is a top recipient of all three types of aid, whereas Nicaragua—despite great need and recurring natural disasters—does not even receive emergency food assistance.

Distributive food assistance deserves congressional and public support. Donating commodities to those in grave need represents an appropriate use of U.S. agricultural wealth and is in keeping with the professed humanitarian ideals of the U.S. government and U.S. citizens. But distributive food aid must be guided by a strict set of conditions and regulations. Otherwise the intended humanitarian benefits of distributive aid may be subverted by destructive political, social, and economic consequences and side effects. Unfortunately, this is too often the case in Central America.

Recommendations

– Food donations should be used preferentially for situations where people are cut off from their normal means of subsistence and must have outside support to survive, especially in short-term emergency situations. Another appropriate use would be the ongoing institutional feeding of the aged, the infirm, and orphans.

– Where food-aid programs are considered necessary, supplies should be purchased, wherever possible, on the local or regional market. This helps ensure that the products are adapted to local needs and tastes, while guarding against creating disincentives for local producers.

– Food aid to achieve "developmental" ends, now so much in fashion, should be reevaluated. Given the importance of grass-roots organization to successful social and economic development, there should be more concern about the possible negative effects of food aid on popular consciousness and organization.

– The benefits of supplementary feeding and food-for-work programs cannot simply be assumed. Their nutritional and income effects should be clearly quantified and weighed against their financial and human costs (including the alternative uses that could be made of these resources) and their possible negative effects on consumption patterns and community organization. Programs that cannot pass muster should be shut down.

– Food distribution programs, to have any chance of being worthwhile, require substantial material, technical, and human resources. No program should be undertaken unless adequate material resources and trained personnel are guaranteed. These resources could come from either the local government, the U.S. government, or its NGO partners.

- Monetization is a problematic solution to the need for complementary resources because of the danger of disincentive effects. If continued, monetization should be closely coordinated and regulated.
- Supplementary food aid should be better targeted to the poorest of the poor. This selection should be made on the basis of some objective criterion such as measurable malnutrition. As Title II guidelines dictate, distributive food aid should be directed only to food-short areas in host countries.
- Supplementary feeding should in every case be accompanied by well-designed nutritional and health education. Sufficient financial resources and trained workers must be earmarked for these tasks.
- Food-for-work should be limited to true self-help projects that directly benefit all of the workers involved. Laborers in public-works programs— including road building—should in no circumstances receive more than half of their pay in food, as stipulated in International Labor Office guidelines.
- The building of places of worship with FFW programs should be stopped. Nor should food aid compensate those who participate in religious activities and instruction.
- In no case should food aid be used for civic-action programs and civil-defense patrols in which the local armed forces play a role, nor should food-aid allocations be made by institutions controlled by the armed forces.
- The food provided by distributive programs should match local diet and spending patterns. In the case of Central America, this would entail eliminating the distribution of cheese and much of the powdered milk, wheat flour, lentils, and other U.S. surplus foods, concentrating instead on providing rice, beans, and white corn.
- Distributive food aid should be allocated by need rather than political standards. Food aid should not be denied needy people living under governments, like that of Nicaragua, regarded as unfriendly by the U.S. government.
- Considering the vast extent of distributive food aid in Central America and the presence of other donors, AID and USDA need to evaluate potential disincentive effects from Title II and Section 416 programs before approving annual allocations.

BETTER OVERSIGHT OF THE WORLD FOOD PROGRAMME

Better oversight is needed over the commitment of distributive food aid to the World Food Programme. Currently there exists little monitoring or serious evaluation of WFP efforts in the region. In Central America, the World Food Programme is using U.S. food donations in ways that would not be permitted under bilateral programs. Indeed, it appears that Washington is sometimes using the World Food Programme to circumvent the restrictions placed on bilateral Title II aid.

The WFP program in Guatemala, largely supplied by U.S. Title II donations, is a case in point. At the same time that the local AID mission was denying any involvement in the military-controlled development poles and model villages, AID at the Washington level was supplying, through WFP, most of the food used by the military and the military-controlled National Reconstruction Committee (CRN) for these pacification activities.

This continuing use of U.S. food-aid resources for military purposes represents a serious lack of compliance by AID with the Food for Peace legislation and the Foreign Assistance Act. Because the U.S. government exercises project-by-project approval over WFP use of its donations, U.S. food aid to military-affiliated projects in Guatemala and elsewhere could easily be stopped.

Since it is the major supplier of WFP worldwide, the U.S. government is also in a position to use its aid as leverage to demand that WFP exercise stricter internal controls to eliminate the military uses of its humanitarian assistance. The project proposals of the World Food Programme often bear little resemblance to the actual use of donated food. For the WFP projects it supports, the U.S. government must insist that project guidelines regarding such areas as nutritional education and community self-government be respected. Washington should also see that international labor regulations are enforced and that WFP takes seriously its stated concern about possible disincentive effects.

FOOD AND FARM POLICY

The agricultural development policy currently promoted by AID through food-aid and development-assistance agreements is not in the best interests of the poor majority of Central America. With its emphasis on agroexports and agribusiness, it represents little more than a refinement of the region's agroexport tradition that for decades has left peasants and local food production out of the development picture. This policy also serves U.S. investors and traders by stressing the primacy of comparative-advantage economics and the elimination of protectionism for local production.

Food aid is increasing the dependence of Central America on food imports from the United States. This is a rich agricultural region that, with a better distribution of land and resources, could easily meet most of its own food needs. Yet to solve their countries' food problems, Central American governments are looking more to food donors than to local food producers. A case in point is the creation by the Guatemalan government of the National Food Council, whose purpose is to "guarantee that consumers will have permanent access to a sufficient quantity of basic foods. . . . There must also be permanent efforts on the part of both governmental and nongovernmental organizations to obtain and optimally utilize the largest quantities of external food aid that countries friendly to us are willing to give until we are able to achieve national food self-sufficiency."[1]

Despite the self-sufficiency rhetoric, Central American governments are not using food aid just as a stopgap measure to tide them over in the case of droughts or other temporary obstacles to increased food production. Instead, food imports are being adopted as a permanent solution to the region's agricultural deficiencies, allowing governments to continue to ignore the serious problems plaguing local food production. By boosting imports beyond what they would have been in the program's absence, food aid is enabling cheap U.S. wheat, as well as other products, to reduce the prices and production of local grains. Food aid, by encouraging new consumption habits that neither family income nor the national treasury can sustain, is undermining not only the region's food production but also its chances for future economic stability.

Recommendations

– U.S. food-aid policy should support local and regional food security goals by promoting local grain production, discouraging food imports that compete directly or indirectly with locally produced food, and backing regional solutions to commodity shortfalls.

– The Central American governments should adopt agricultural development policies that focus on the peasant farmers and the rural landless. This would help alleviate rural poverty, slow rural-urban migration, and boost basic grains production. Such a policy would include land redistribution measures, more rational land use, favorable producer prices, increased credit and technical assistance for small farmers, better local and regional marketing strategies, and the protection of the region's basic grains sector from outside competition. It would also entail more research into basic grains production and efforts to develop processed foods made from locally grown commodities.

– Local governments might wish to place tariffs or stronger direct controls on the foods, such as wheat, that will continue to be imported because they cannot be produced locally. Low-priced imported foods accelerate changes in consumption patterns and foment long-term import dependency. Protective tariff measures not only would help hold down imports, by making imported foods that much more expensive, but could also generate increased tax revenue. While such measures would not be in the best interests of U.S. exporters, the U.S. government should not, as it now does, block such attempts to maintain traditional consumption patterns and protect domestic agriculture.

– The U.S. government should encourage Central American countries to adopt agricultural development policies that seek a balance between local and export-oriented production. Aid resources should be directed to both ends.

– Rather than seeking to reduce the role of the grain-stabilization institutes and other programs for basic grains growers, AID should help strengthen and reform Central American agricultural agencies to enable them to accomplish their objectives of supporting rural income and basic grains production, while guaranteeing stable supplies for consumers. Support for national grain-stabilization institutes would be an appropriate use of local currency generated from food-aid resales.

– The United States should base its food-aid program not on availability (surplus) in the U.S. domestic market, nor on a desire to conquer new markets, but rather on the real and expressed needs of recipient countries.

The tremendous flow of food aid into Central America during the 1980s has contributed to the U.S. economic bailout of the region, as part of its strategy of containment of revolution. There is no doubt that this injection of food aid has benefited the governments of Central America. Their balance-of-payments crises were somewhat alleviated, budget deficits were made less extreme, and the handouts helped them claim a commitment to social welfare. Food prices were held down, and millions of poor families received a little help in stretching their budgets to meet their monthly needs.

As a temporary measure, food assistance can be an appropriate response to shortfalls and disaster. But as a major, long-term response to profound economic, military, and political crisis, food aid is inappropriate. Concessionary sales and donations are currently being used as part of the U.S. government's three-pronged economic-aid strategy for Central America—stabilization, pacification, and private-sector support. As such, it is allowing Central American governments to postpone sorely needed reforms in the region's agricultural structure, its food distribution system, and its political and economic structures.

As now administered, U.S. food aid is actually, in many cases, blocking prospects for long-term peace and development in Central America. The program as a whole is indifferent to the needs and wishes of the poor, with most food entering commercial markets, where it is largely out of the reach of the hungry and malnourished. The little that is distributed to the poor often goes to those considered of the most political importance, as a means of quelling political unrest. By bolstering the strength of unpopular governments and their armed forces, food aid is undermining the Central American poor's prospects for a better life, and in the process it is feeding the region's deepening crisis.

Appendix

TABLE 5

U.S. Food Aid[a] to Costa Rica, by Program, Compared with Total
Agricultural Imports from the United States, 1954–88
(Millions of Dollars)

| | PL 480 Title I | PL 480 Title II | Section 416[b] Regular | Section 416[b] Sugar Quota | Mutual Security Aid | Total Food Aid | Export Promotion GSM-102 | Total Agricultural Imports from U.S. | Percentage of Total U.S. Agricultural Imports Food Aid | Percentage of Total U.S. Agricultural Imports GSM-102 |
Fiscal Year										
1954–79	—	15.8	—	—	0.4	17.2[c]	0.2[d]	321.0	5	0[c]
1980	—	0.3	—	—	—	0.3	—	64.2	0	—
1981	0.0	0.8	—	—	—	0.8	4.1	48.1	2	9
1982	17.2	1.5	—	—	—	18.7	15.7	53.9	35	29
1983	25.1	0.3	—	—	—	25.2	—	40.6	62	—
1984	23.0	—	—	—	0.3	23.3	2.8	51.8	45	6
1985	19.6	0.2	—	—	1.5	21.3	—	43.1	49	—
1986	11.9	0.3	1.4	—	0.7	13.1	—	35.8	37	—
1987	10.5	0.0	—	1.2	0.1	11.9	—	49.7	24	—
1988	0.0[e]	n.a.	—	4.4	n.a.	n.a.	—	78.0	n.a.	n.a.

Source: USDA. *Food for Peace Annual Report on Public Law 480*, 1980–86, for all Section 416 regular figures and 1987 Title II and total U.S. agricultural import figures, USDA; for remaining 1987 and 1988 (and all Section 416 SQ figures), U.S. Agricultural Attaché.
[a]Figures represent export value of commodities shipped, not amounts approved. [b]CCC cost. Includes transportation. [c]Includes $1.0 million in barter. [d]Twelve-month GSM-5 financing. [e]Congress approved $15.0 million in Title I for FY 1988, but none was shipped because of delays in approval by the Costa Rican Legislative Assembly.

TABLE 6

U.S. Food Aid[a] to El Salvador, by Program, Compared with Total Agricultural Imports from the United States, 1954–88
(Millions of Dollars)

Fiscal Year	PL 480 Title I	PL 480 Title II	Section 416[b] Regular	Section 416[b] Sugar Quota	Mutual Security Aid	Total Food Aid	Export Promotion GSM-102	Total Agricultural Imports from U.S.	Percentage of Total U.S. Agricultural Imports Food Aid	Percentage of Total U.S. Agricultural Imports GSM-102
1954–79	0.6	29.6	—	—	0.7	31.7[c]	0.9[d]	389.8	8	0
1980	2.9	2.4	—	—	—	5.3	3.9[d]	50.2	11	8
1981	11.9	6.9	—	—	—	18.8	14.3	62.2	30	23
1982	22.9	4.6	—	—	—	27.5	26.6	65.4	42	41
1983	42.7	8.1	—	—	—	50.9	19.3	84.9	60	23
1984	48.8	3.4	—	—	—	52.2	30.5	98.3	53	31
1985	33.4	8.7	—	—	—	43.9	23.0	85.1	52	27
1986	32.6	7.8	0.3	—	—	40.7	12.1	88.3	46	14
1987	25.9	6.1	1.1	2.5	0.1	35.6	17.4[c]	84.8	42	21
1988	35.5	n.a.	3.2	6.0	—	n.a.	17.0	n.a.	n.a.	n.a.

Source: USDA. *Food for Peace Annual Report on Public Law 480,* 1980–86, for 1988 (and GSM and Section 416 figures), USDA (preliminary).
[a]Figures represent export value of commodities shipped, not amounts approved.   [b]CCC cost. Includes transport costs.   [c]Includes $0.8 million in barter.   [d]Twelve-month GSM-5 financing.   [e]This year El Salvador also received $0.1 million in GSM-103 financing.

TABLE 7

U.S. Food Aid[a] to Guatemala, by Program, Compared with Total
Agricultural Imports from the United States, 1954–88
(Millions of Dollars)

Fiscal Year	PL 480 Title I	PL 480 Title II	Section 416[b] Regular	Section 416[b] Sugar Quota	Mutual Security Aid	Total Food Aid	Export Promotion GSM-102	Total Agricultural Imports from U.S.	Percentage of Total U.S. Agricultural Imports Food Aid	GSM-102
1954–79	1.0	52.4	—	—	8.8	66.6[c]	10.8[d]	485.3	14	2[c]
1980	—	3.2	—	—	—	3.2	—	71.2	4	—
1981	—	7.3	—	—	—	7.3	—	85.1	9	—
1982	—	5.5	—	—	—	3.7	0.5	65.0	6	1
1983	—	5.2	—[e]	—	—	5.5	32.1	67.1	8	48
1984	1.2	7.8	—	—	—	6.4	51.9	81.9	8	63
1985	11.7	4.6	0.3	—	—	20.5	39.4	86.6	24	45
1986	4.9	7.8	1.7	3.8[f]	—	11.4	20.5	73.7	15	28
1987	18.7	8.1	3.8	6.0	—	36.6	11.9	98.2	37	12
1988	13.9	n.a.	0.7	3.8	—	n.a.	8.0	n.a.	n.a.	n.a.

Source: USDA. *Food for Peace Annual Report on Public Law 480*, 1980–87, for 1988 (and GSM and Section 416 figures), USDA (preliminary).
[a]Figures represent export value of commodities shipped, not amounts approved.   [b]CCC cost. Includes transportation.   [c]Includes $4.4 million in barter.   [d]Twelve-month GSM-5 financing.   [e]Powdered milk of unknown value brought in this year and distributed to victims of the violence.   [f]Contrary to usual practice, $2.4 million of this sugar quota shipment was distributed to NGOs.

TABLE 8

U.S. Food Aid to Honduras,[a] by Program, Compared with Total Agricultural Imports from the United States, 1954–88

Fiscal Year	PL 480 Title I/III	PL 480 Title II	Section 416[b] Regular	Section 416[b] Sugar Quota	Mutual Security Aid	Total Food Aid	Export Promotion GSM-102	Total Agricultural Imports from U.S.	Percentage of Total U.S. Agricultural Imports Food Aid	Percentage of Total U.S. Agricultural Imports GSM-102
1954–79	9.0	24.7	—	—	0.4	34.4[c]	1.4[d]	263.4	13	0[c]
1980	0.6	2.8	—	—	—	3.4	—	50.2	7	—
1981	5.1	4.3	—	—	—	9.4	1.0	44.7	21	2
1982	5.0	2.4	—	—	—	7.4	—	37.1	20	—
1983	11.1	4.9	—	—	—	16.1	4.1	37.5	43	11
1984	14.4	4.4	—	—	—	18.9	—	44.7	42	—
1985	10.0	3.8	—	—	—	13.8	5.7	45.6	30	13
1986	8.5	3.2	0.2	—	—	12.1	5.0	45.2	27	11
1987	10.9	3.0	0.9	n.a.[e]	—	14.8	5.3	56.0	26	9
1988	12.0	n.a.	0.9	n.a.	—	n.a.	17.3	n.a.	n.a.	n.a.

Source: USDA. *Food for Peace Annual Report on Public Law 480*, 1980–87, for 1988 (and GSM and Section 416 figures), USDA (preliminary).
[a]Figures represent export value of commodities shipped, not amounts approved.   [b]CCC cost. Includes transport costs.   [c]Includes $0.3 million in barter.   [d]Twelve-month GSM-5 financing.   [e]Agricultural Attaché reports Section 416 SQ donations approved at $2.7 million in FY1986 and $5.6 million in 1987, though actual shipments lag considerably.

Notes

CHAPTER ONE

1 *Report of the National Bipartisan Commission on Central America* (1984). Also see U.S. Department of State, AID/OMB (1987), "A Plan for Fully Funding the Recommendations of the National Bipartisan Commission on Central America."

2 See tables 5–8 for yearly calculations for each country under study. The 30 percent figure is calculated on data from USDA, FAS (1980–86), *Food for Peace: 1986 Annual Report on Public Law 480*.

3 USAID, ROCAP (1985), *Technical Support for Food Assistance Programs*, 10, 13. This document calculates that in 1983 more than 200,000 tons of food were distributed to 5.2 million Central Americans, not including refugees, representing 24 percent of the region's population. The United States is far and away the largest supplier of food aid to Central America. In government-to-government resale aid it stands nearly alone, and in distributive aid it dominates the field. For 1985, AID estimated bilateral U.S. assistance to represent 27 percent of total distributive food assistance to the four countries under study, with the World Food Programme (WFP) (supplied largely by the United States), making up another 55 percent. Other donors, including European Economic Community (EEC) and the Federal Republic of Germany, represented only 17 percent of distributive food donations for that year. Ibid., 15. International food-aid figures for 1985, not by program but by ultimate country donors, show the U.S. tonnage share to be 78 percent. Authors' calculations based on FAO (n.d.), *Food Aid in Figures, 1987*, no.5.

4 See table 4 on Salvadoran distribution programs in chapter 7.

5 Although most Title II and Section 416 regular food is donated directly to needy individuals, certain sections of the law do provide for limited resale. Section 206 of Title II mentioned above allows for resale by recipient governments. In addition, nongovernmental organizations (NGOs) are currently allowed to sell portions of

their Title 11 and Section 416 shipments to generate local currency for use in their food distribution and development programs. This practice is known as monetization.

6 USAID, *Front Lines*, August 1984.

7 McPherson (1983), "Stalking Hunger," 16.

8 Cathie (1982), *The Political Economy of Food Aid*, 6–24; International Trade and Development Education Foundation (1985), *The United States Food for Peace Program: 1954–1984*, 5–9; Wallerstein (1980), *Food for Peace: Food for War*, 3–20.

9 For the legislative history of PL 480, see International Trade and Development Education Foundation (1985). For general discussions of program evolution, see Cathie (1982), Wallerstein (1980), and Gilmore (1982), *A Poor Harvest: The Clash of Policies and Interests in the Grain Trade*.

10 For more on the creation of the World Food Programme, see Cathie (1982) and Wallerstein (1980, 90–118).

11 Morrell (1977), "The Big Stick," 9; Wallerstein (1980, 130–32).

12 Burbach and Flynn (1980), *Agribusiness in the Americas*, 72; Cathie (1982, 22); Wallerstein (1980, 134–35).

13 Wallerstein (1980, 15).

14 This restriction still guides Title 1 food aid. USDA defines it this way: "A minimum of 75 percent of the commodities allocated under Title 1 in any fiscal year must go to countries that meet the minimum per capita GNP level for lending established by the International Development Association of the IBRD [World Bank], and which are also unable to secure sufficient food through their own production or commercial imports. The requirement may be waived if it is determined that 75 percent of the food aid cannot be used to effectively carry out the purposes of Title 1." USDA, FAS (1984b), *PL 480 Concessional Sales*, 33.

15 Other political restrictions on Title 1 recipients are that aid must go to a "friendly country" that is not "dominated or controlled by a foreign government or organization controlling a World Communist movement." Nor can food aid go to a country regarded as "an aggressor, in a military sense, against any country having diplomatic relations with the United States." These restrictions apply only to Title 1 and not Title 11, so that donations can still go to individuals living under communist regimes such as that ruling Poland.

16 USDA, FAS (1984b, 21–30).

17 Wennergren et al (1986), *Solving World Hunger*, 26.

18 The human-rights clause was added to the 1954 Agricultural Trade Development

and Assistance Act in 1977 and updated to include the reference to disappearances in 1980.

19 USDA, FAS (1984b, 4–7); Wing (1987), *U.S. Food Aid Programs and the Guatemalan Experience,* 7–8, 16.

20 National Security Decision Document (NSDD) 167, "Food for Progress Program Implementation," 29 April 1985, and NSDD 156, "U.S. Third World Food Aid: A Food for Progress Program," 3 January 1985. (These two NSDDs were released to the Center for Investigative Reporting in San Francisco.) Food for Progress was included in the Food Security Act of 1985. More discussion of this measure follows in chapter 2.

21 For a discussion of the links between U.S. economic aid and security interests in Central America, see Danaher, Berryman, and Benjamin (1987), *Help or Hindrance? United States Economic Aid in Central America.*

22 USDA, FAS (1980–86), *Food for Peace: 1986 Annual Report,* 7–8. In fiscal year 1985, $44 million in Title I aid was shipped to El Salvador, followed in Latin America by $35 million to Jamaica, $30 million to the Dominican Republic, and $20 million apiece for Peru, Costa Rica, and Bolivia. Of the Latin American total of $226 million, El Salvador received 19.5 percent.

23 Title II assistance allocated in 1985 for El Salvador was 17.6 pounds per capita, compared with just 0.4 in Ecuador, 2.7 in the Dominican Republic, and 5.4 in Peru, all countries with higher infant mortality and comparable levels of calorie availability per capita. Authors' calculations based on data from World Bank (1987), *World Development Report, 1987,* and USAID (1983–88), *Congressional Presentation, 1987.*

24 In Guatemala, for example, more than 38,000 people have disappeared in the past fifty years, and at least another 50,000 were murdered. For documentation on the violation of human rights in Central America, see the numerous publications by Amnesty International, Americas Watch, and the Interamerican Commission for Human Rights of the Organization of American States.

25 Brown (1985), *With Friends Like These,* 12–23; Americas Watch (1982), *U.S. Reporting on Human Rights at Odds with Knowledge;* and Americas Watch (1985), *Guatemala Revised: How the Reagan Administration Finds "Improvements" in Human Rights in Guatemala.* For the administration's version of the human-rights situation in these countries, see the State Department's annual *Country Reports on Human Rights Practices.*

26 Amnesty International (1989), *Human Rights Violations under the Civilian Government.*

27 Sanford (1989), *Central America: Major Trends in U.S. Foreign Assistance,* 30–31. Note that these figures refer to aid allocations, whereas the figures used in this book refer to actual aid shipped.

28 USDA, Economic Research Service (1986–89), *World Food Needs and Availabilities,* for 1984, 1986–87, and 1987–88.

29 Authors' calculations based on USDA, FAS (1980–86), *Food for Peace: 1986 Annual Report,* 7–8, and IDB (1987), *Economic and Social Progress in Latin America,* 421.

CHAPTER TWO

1 From 1979 to 1987, approximately one-fifth of the total volume of Title I and Section 416 Sugar Quota food aid to Central America was yellow corn, tallow, and soybean products, used mostly for animal feed. (Tallow is also used in making soap and margarine.) Authors' calculations based on Title I sales agreements and USDA Agricultural Attaché reports.

2 Danaher, Berryman, and Benjamin (1987, 60–64), citing USAID, *Congressional Presentations,* various years. This calculation varies depending on the time frame and whether one uses AID *Congressional Presentation* figures (aid allocated) or USDA *Food for Peace Annual Report* figures (aid actually sent). Throughout this book, unless otherwise noted we will be using USDA figures on commodities shipped.

3 See Garcia et al. (1987), *Agricultural Development Policies in Honduras,* and Norton and Benito (1987), *An Evaluation of the PL 480 Title I Program in Honduras* chap.2, pp.14–15.

4 Interestingly, though Title I's role as a form of balance-of-payments and budgetary support is widely recognized in the literature and is obvious from the design of the program itself, this function is referred to only obliquely in the official statement of program objectives in the preface to PL 480, with the phrase "to encourage economic development in the developing countries, with particular emphasis on assistance to those countries that are determined to improve their own agricultural production."

5 The commodities exported under Title I are not, as many assume, government-held surpluses, but are regular market items. The function of bringing down government-held stocks is carried out by the Title II and Section 416 donation programs, both supplied from Commodity Credit Corporation (CCC) stockpiles.

6 Title III of PL 480, "Food for Development," was set up in 1978 and was oriented specifically toward the poorer countries. Title III forgives Title I dollar repayments for low-income countries (currently those with a per capita GNP of U.S. $790 or

less) that agree to undertake development projects and policy reforms specified in a special multiyear Title III agreement. In general, however, the increased administration and monitoring required for Title III (straining the resources of both the low-income recipient government and the local USAID mission) have limited the use of this program. In Central America, so far only Honduras has received Title III, probably because it is practically the only one with a low enough per capita income. In the late 1970s and early 1980s, the Honduran government was forgiven $12 million in Title I repayments under this program.

7 For an explanation of AID economic-stabilization strategy, see USAID, Latin America Bureau (1983), *Regional Strategic Plan for Latin America and the Caribbean*.

8 USAID, Office of Planning and Budgeting (1989), *U.S. Overseas Loans and Grants, Obligations and Loan Authorizations, July 1, 1945–September 30, 1987*.

9 Cathie (1982, 6–24); International Trade and Development Education Foundation (1985, 5–9); Wallerstein (1980, 3–20).

10 Data on the economic crisis in Central America can be found in Inforpress, *Centroamérica 198–* (various years); CEPAL, *Notas para el estudio económico de América Latina y el Caribe* (annual country overviews); the annual country reports of the Economist Intelligence Unit; and Gallardo and López (1986), *Centroamérica: La crisis en cifras*.

11 These savings assume that in the absence of food aid the Central American countries would still have imported, on commercial terms, the same large quantities of food. There is no doubt that the Central American governments have in recent years wanted high levels of food imports to help keep food prices down; however, stiffer commercial sales terms would undoubtedly have reduced this quantity by some unknown degree. See Clay and Singer (1982), *Food Aid and Development: The Impact and Effectiveness of Bilateral PL 480 Title I–Type Assistance*, 21, for a further discussion of import additionality.

12 Calculating the grant element of concessional sales programs involves comparing the value of concessional and commercial sales when each has been discounted at the appropriate interest rate. Grant elements for various Central American countries were reported to us by the Commerce Department at 68 percent. For further discussion of the grant element concept, see Huddleston (1984), *Closing the Cereals Gap with Trade and Food Aid*, 70–72.

13 Hatfield, Leach, and Miller (1987), *Bankrolling Failure: United States Policy in El Salvador*, 30, citing U.S. embassy figures.

14 Norton and Benito (1987), chap.3, pp.1–2).

15 Public Law 480, Sections 106(b) and 109. A good concise review of the entire Title I program is USDA, FAS (1984b).

16 Norton and Benito (1987, chap.3, pp.2–6). Title I funding not only failed to increase the net revenues of this low-priority ministry, it was also unable to prevent a decline in its overall effectiveness. Among other problems was the lack of programmatic focus in the diverse agricultural projects Title I was used to support.

17 U.S., GAO (1984d), *U.S. Economic Assistance to Central America*, 5. Also see U.S., GAO (1984a), *AID Needs to Strengthen Management of Commodity Import Programs*.

18 U.S., GAO (1985b), *USAID/Costa Rica's Monitoring of and Controls over Dollar and Local Currency Resources*; U.S., GAO (1984c), *Monitoring Dollar and Local Currency Resources . . . in Honduras*; and U.S., GAO (1985a), *Providing Effective Economic Assistance to El Salvador and Honduras: A Formidable Task*. Also see USAID, Regional Inspector General for Audit (1985a), *Audit of Private Sector Support Program and PL 480 Local Currency Generations USAID–El Salvador*.

19 Source wishes to remain anonymous, but this person's observations were later confirmed by U.S. press reports, including James LeMoyne, "Salvador Candidate Is Suspected in Misuse of $2 Million in U.S. Aid," *New York Times*, 6 March 1988.

20 Author interview with Javier Vargas, 2 February 1988.

21 Leach, Miller, and Hatfield (1985), *U.S. Aid to El Salvador: An Evaluation of the Past, a Proposal for the Future;* and Hatfield, Leach, and Miller (1987).

22 Hatfield, Leach, and Miller (1987, 17–18).

23 Central government current revenues as a percentage of gross domestic product in 1985 were 16.6 percent for Costa Rica, 15.6 percent for Honduras, 13.4 percent for El Salvador, and 7.8 percent for Guatemala. Over two-thirds of the Latin American countries, in contrast, had rates of over 15 percent, and many had rates of 20–30 percent. Only Bolivia had a lower rate than Guatemala. IDB (n.d.), *Economic and Social Progress in Latin America, 1987*, 437.

24 Hanrahan (1988a), *The Effectiveness of Food Aid*, 80.

25 This figure corresponds to CCC-reported exports, not to Section 416 aid allocated, and thus may be less than figures reported elsewhere. CCC export figures tend to lag behind amounts allocated.

26 Title I sales agreements for Guatemala, Honduras, Costa Rica, and El Salvador, 1985–87.

27 USAID (1983f), "Regional Strategic Plan," 25.

28 Dell (1980), *The Balance of Payments Adjustment Process in Developing Countries*, 135–36.

29 U.S. GAO (1986), *Foreign Assistance: U.S. Use of Conditions to Achieve Economic Reforms,* 36.

30 Newfarmer (1986), "The Economics of Strife," 222.

31 Ibid.

32 Oxfam America (1986), "Third World Debt: Payable in Hunger"; Helleiner (1985), *Stabilization Policies and the Poor;* Hanrahan and Epstein (1987), *Foreign Food Aid: Current Policy Issues,* 20.

33 The burgeoning literature on food aid in economic adjustment includes Franco, Sukin, Shaw, and Singer, and Mellor, all in a special February 1988 issue of *Food Policy;* Gilmore and Bremer-Fox, in Hanrahan (1988a); and Hanrahan and Epstein (1987). Not just AID, but also the World Food Programme and the World Bank are exploring the use of food aid in structural and sectoral adjustment. See WFP (n.d.), *1986 in Review,* 13.

34 USAID-Guatemala (1986c), *FY 1987/88 Action Plan,* 30.

35 Title 1 sales agreements, and USAID–Costa Rica (1986), *Action Plan/Annual Budget Submission,* 60.

36 A 1978–79 study from Honduras found that Hondurans living in the principal cities (whose average incomes are several times those of the rural population) consume nearly five times the quantity of wheat and fourteen times the quantity of poultry and eggs, on a per capita caloric basis, than those eaten by rural consumers. Garcia et al. (1987), chap.4, pp.9–11, table 4.19).

37 Sukin (1988), "U.S. Food Aid for Countries Implementing Structural Adjustment," 102.

38 Pines, King, and Lowenthal (1988), *Evaluation of Guatemalan PL 480 Programs,* i.

39 Author interview, March 1989.

40 Norton and Benito (1987, chap.2, pp.17–21).

41 Public Law 480, Sections 2 and 109.

42 Agricultural marketing institutes, also known as grain-stabilization institutes, are semiautonomous government agencies established since the 1950s to regulate the basic grains market in each Central American country. Their role is to guarantee small farmers a fair price for their grain and to ensure that consumers have year-round access to affordable basic grains.

43 See Title 1 sales agreements for Guatemala, El Salvador, Costa Rica, and Honduras, 1985–87.

44 The Food Security Act of 1985 added to PL 480 two special sections designed to increase the lending of Title 1 local currencies to the private sector. Section 108, the

one now being used in Central America, requires a minimum set aside of 10 percent of the aggregate value of worldwide Title I sales contracts for immediate repayment in local currency to the U.S. government. The U.S. government then directs the currency to intermediate financial institutions that lend to the country's private sector. Section 106, suggested at 10–15 percent of the Title I program (and not yet being implemented in Central America) specifies that the local government set aside a certain portion of its own local-currency generations for private-sector use. For further information, see USAID, Bureau for Private Enterprise, Office of Food for Peace, "PL 480, Title I, Section 108 Workshop."

45 Under Section 108(f), a specified percentage (usually 5 percent) of Section 108 local currencies goes to technical assistance, including agricultural market development.

46 Another U.S. export subsidy program is the 1985 Export Enhancement Program, which was designed to counter what the United States considers unfair competition from subsidized European sales by matching the European price. In Central America, however, thus far only the region's brewers, who import barley malt, are participating in this subsidy program.

47 *Report of the National Bipartisan Commission on Central America* (1984), 70.

48 The GSM-102 program started in early 1981 and expanded rapidly to help counteract the world slump in U.S. agricultural exports registered in the late 1970s. By 1987 program size had reached $2.6 billion. GSM-102 sales to Cental America—concentrated mostly in Guatemala and El Salvador—expanded from $19.4 million in 1981, the first year of the program, to a high of $88.5 million in 1984, declining to $29.3 million by 1987. (Authors' calculations based on CCC export trade reports.) This decline was due in part to the countries' falling behind on repayments, causing temporary suspensions in the program (this is especially a problem with Honduras). Another reason for the reduction in GSM-102–supported sales to Central America was that many of these commercial exports were replaced by sales made under the more concessional PL 480 aid program.

49 Author interview with USDA representative in Guatemala, April 1988.

50 Another new PL 480 program called Food for Progress, was included in the Food Security Act of 1985 as a mechanism to use existing food-aid resources (from either Title I or Section 416) in support of governments that agree to undertake structural adjustment measures in their agricultural sector. The program awards additional food assistance, in the form of either grants or loans, to countries "that have made commitments to agricultural policy reform during a period of economic hardship.

Food for Progress is designed to expand free enterprise elements of the economies of developing countries through changes in commodity pricing, marketing, import availability, and increased private-sector involvement." No Central American country has yet applied for Food for Progress assistance, although Guatemala and El Salvador have been approached by AID.

CHAPTER THREE

1 According to FAO calculations, each of the Central American countries, except densely populated El Salvador (which is borderline), could now grow more than enough food for its population using intermediate technology and inputs if sufficient land were dedicated to that purpose. If current population and production trends continue, however, by the year 2000 El Salvador will be able to support its population only with a high level of inputs, and Guatemala will have lost its margin of safety. Accelerated land degradation in Guatemala and El Salvador, caused in great part by inequalities in landholdings that force peasants to farm marginal areas, introduces an addtional factor of risk. FAO (1984b), *Land, Food, and People.*

2 Imports of cereals into Central America (here defined to include Mexico and the Caribbean) swelled from 2 million metric tons in 1961–63 to 5.8 million MT in 1976–78, to 11.2 million MT in 1981. Huddleston (1984, 20), citing FAO Year-books.

3 USDA, Economic Research Service (1986–89), *World Food Needs and Availabilities, 1987/88,* 152.

4 USAID, ROCAP (1985, 7–8), estimates that 60 percent of children under five in Central America and Panama suffer from some degree of malnutrition and that moderate to severe malnutrition ranges from a low of 7 percent in Costa Rica to a high of 29.5 percent in Guatemala and Honduras.

5 The unweighted average of per capita availability (production plus net trade) of basic grains in the four countries under study fell sharply in the period 1980–85: corn availability declined from 428.7 to 325.1 kg/year, rice from 80.5 to 67.7, beans from 41.0 to 40.5, and wheat from 111.9 to 110.7. INCAP, PROPAG (1986, 39), citing national food balance sheets.

6 There is a vast and growing literature on agricultural systems and inequities in Central America, including Williams (1986), *Export Agriculture and the Crisis in Central America;* Barry (1987), *Roots of Rebellion;* and Weeks (1985), *The Economies of Central America;* USAID (1983c), *Land and Labor in Guatemala.*

7 On the relation between agroexport production and poverty, see Hintermeister

(1984), *Rural Poverty and Export Farming in Guatemala;* Barry (1987); Browning (1971), *El Salvador: Landscape and Society;* Brockett (1984), "Malnutrition, Public Policy, and Agrarian Change in Guatemala."

8 Some 40 percent of all the region's agricultural exports are shipped to the United States, and about 50 percent of the region's agricultural imports come from the United States. USDA (1982), *Farmline,* 7.

9 Many of the problems of U.S. agriculture have to do with its unique economic structure compared with other industries. With long production lead times, few alternative uses for productive assets, and an atomized market where individual farmers cannot exert any influence on price, farmers often respond to falling prices not by producing less or shifting to other industries, but rather by producing more, so as to compensate for low unit profits with high volume of sales. Thus increased production has been the farmer's reaction in times of both boom and bust. Furthermore, owing to the influence of weather agricultural supplies are variable, but demand for food is quite constant, causing wide price swings from year to year. The lack of information and uncertainty that characterize commodity markets only add to the farm industry's problems. Ray and Plaxico (1988), *The Economic Structure of Agriculture.*

10 Much of this discussion of U.S. farm policy is based on "Straight Talk on Agriculture: A Conversation with Mike Ritchie," *Multinational Monitor,* July–August 1988.

11 Henningson (1981), "Agricultural Exports and the Farm Economy: A Full Accounting Needed," citing USDA figures.

12 See Working Group on Farm and Food Policy (1984), *Beyond Crisis,* and "Family Farm Act of 1987," S.658 H.R. 11425 (also known as the Harkin-Gephardt bill).

13 The world cereal market, for example, was 176 million metric tons in 1986, of which developing countries absorbed almost 100 million—10 percent of this in food aid. Arias (1989, 2), citing WFP figures. In the industrial world, slow population growth and the peaking of per capita food consumption, as well as the increasing use of synthetic food products, have slowed the demand for food.

14 Paarlberg (1988), "U.S. Agriculture and the Developing World: Opportunities for Joint Gains."

15 League of Rural Voters (1985), "U.S. Farm Policy and World Hunger: The Deadly Connection," 7.

16 For an overview of the use of food aid in market development, see Gulick (1987), *How U.S. Food Aid Programs Help American Agricultural Exports.*

17 Since Title I purchases are concentrated in April through September, U.S. exporters might even realize some extra benefit by having captive buyers during a period when grain prices are normally a little higher.

18 USDA dedicates a large section of its *1984 Food for Peace Annual Report* to this process of "building commercial expertise."

19 Over 8.2 million people in El Salvador, Guatemala, Costa Rica, Honduras, and Nicaragua receive distributive food aid. Arias (1989, 53), citing INCAP, PROPAG (1986);

20 In Guatemala, for example, school-lunch enrollment is up to nearly a million (about one-eighth of the total population).

21 U.S. Congress, House, Select Committee on Hunger (1987), *Enhancing the Developmental Impact of Food Aid*, 46.

22 The Bellmon amendment reads: "No agricultural commodity may be financed or otherwise made available under the authority of this Act except upon a determination by the Secretary of Agriculture that: (1) adequate storage facilities are available in the recipient country at the time of exportation of the commodity to prevent the spoilage or waste of the commodity, and (2) the distribution of the commodity in the recipient country will not result in a substantial disincentive to or interference with domestic production or marketing" (7 USC 1731).

23 Minutes no. 36 of the Twenty-ninth Ordinary Meeting of the Central American Marketing and Price Stabilization Commission (CCMEP), Tegucigalpa, Honduras, 27–29 November 1985 (certified version). Translation by authors.

24 Minutes no. 37 of the Thirtieth Ordinary Meeting of the Central American Marketing and Price Stabilization Commission (CCMEP), San José, Costa Rica, 9–10 April 1987 (preliminary version). Translation by authors.

25 Resolution VIII-08. Seventh Ordinary Meeting of the Regional Council for Agricultural Cooperation (CORECA). Members are Guatemala, El Salvador, Honduras, Nicaragua, Costa Rica, Panama, Mexico, and the Dominican Republic.

26 USAID (1983a), *AID Handbook 9*, 4–7.

27 In Guatemala, average annual consumption of wheat varies from 66 to 132 pounds per person in urban areas, while the consumption of wheat by rural residents averages about 18 pounds a year. In contrast, the average annual consumption of corn is 132 pounds in the city and 414 in rural areas. ("Callejon sin salida," *Crónica*, 26 November 1987, 29). In Costa Rica in 1982, wheat products represented 10.7 percent of caloric intake for urban families and 7.6 percent for rural families (Costa Rica, OCAF, SIN [1985], *Estudio de caso sobre la situacion alimentaria y nutricional de Costa Rica*).

28 Garcia et al. (1987, 21).

29 Guatemala, SEGELPLAN Departamento de Sectores Productivos (1983), *Análisis del subsector alimentario con respeto al trigo . . .*, 40; Garcia et al. (1987), table 4.13.

30 USDA, Economic Research Service (1986–89), *World Food Needs and Availabilities, 1987/88.*

31 Authors' calculation based on 1982–85 wheat import data of the Secretaría Permanente del Tratado General de Integración Económica Centroamericana (SIECA); and from 1986 and 1987, U.S. Agricultural Attaché Reports.

32 The price of a metric ton (f.o.b. Gulf Port) dropped from $161/MT in 1982 to $105/MT in April 1987.

33 Garcia et al. (1987, chap.8, p.12).

34 Norton and Benito (1987, 6–9).

35 Consumption studies for Honduras for 1970–84 show apparent per capita consumption of corn, beans, bananas, cassava, and potatoes falling, whereas that of wheat, rice, sugar, plantains, vegetable oils, and poultry is on the rise. These changes are attributed to "the availability of PL 480 imports, the effects of opportunities to increase exports of some items [i.e., bananas], lack of yield increases in others (beans, for example), urbanization, and relative price shifts" (Garcia et al. 1987, chap.4, pp.1–2).

36 USDA, FAS, Agricultural Attaché–Costa Rica (1987), "Costa Rica Grain and Feed Annual," 7.

37 INCAP, PROPAG (1986, 39), citing food balance sheets, shows per capita wheat availability holding steady from 1980 to 1985 (see n.6). Other sources, however, have detected an increase. Guy Christophe, head of commercialization studies for the CADESCA-CEE food security program, has carried out preliminary calculations showing per capita availability of wheat rising 2.1 percent per year for Honduras (1979–86), 7.7 percent a year for El Salvador (1975–85), 1.1 percent a year for Guatemala (1982–87), and 4.4 percent a year for Costa Rica (1981–87).

38 Norton and Benito (1987, 2–6).

39 Between 1950 and 1985, according to CEPAL, the urban population increased 8.5 times while the total regional population increased 2.97 times.

40 Ahern et al. (1987), *Assessment of the CRS/CARITAS PL 480 Title II Program in Honduras,* 21.

41 Robert R. Nathan Associates, Inc. (1984), *An Inventory of Policies Affecting Agriculture in El Salvador,* 43.

42 USDA, FAS (1989), "Costa Rica Agricultural Situation Annual, 1988," 21–22, 27.

43 USDA, FAS (1987).

44 USAID–Honduras (1984), *Project Evaluation Summary: PL 480 Title II*, annex I, citing audit report prepared in May 1984 by Morales, Palao, Williams, and Associates at the request of AID–Honduras.

45 FAO (1987b), *Informe técnico.*

46 El Salvador, Ministerio de Agricultura, DEA (1986a), "Diagnóstico de la leche en El Salvador."

47 "La industria lechera en periodo de vacas flacas," *Crónica,* 2 June 1988, 30.

48 Inforpress Centroamericana (1987a), *Centroamérica 1987,* CR:20–21.

CHAPTER FOUR

1 USAID (1978), *Agricultural Development Policy Paper.*

2 Gilmore (1988), "Food Aid in Latin America," 83.

3 These policies can be found, for example, in USAID (1983–88), *Congressional Presentations;* USAID, Latin American Bureau (1983).

4 For an overview of peasant opposition to food aid and associated agricultural policy, see CENAP et al. (1988), *No hay paz sin alimentos.*

5 USDA, FAS (1980–86), *Food for Peace: 1986 Annual Report,* 9–10.

6 For information on food distribution programs in Costa Rica, most of which are supplied locally through the CNP, see INCAP, PROPAG (1986, 49–88).

7 See discussion in CENAP et al. (1988, 32), based on CNP purchase and sales figures.

8 For details of AID's offensive against the CNP, see Title I sales agreements, 1984–88, and USAID (1986, 22–24, 58–63); CADESCA-CEE, Programa de Seguridad Alimentario del Istmo Centroamericano, Eje III: Comercialización de Granos Básicos (1987), *Propuesta de síntesis de la primera fase.*

9 USAID (1987), "Program Strategy Summary," 1.

10 AID has specifically targeted government-sponsored credit programs for structural adjustment in the agricultural sector. "AID, together with other financial organizations, has supported important macroeconomic changes . . . among which can be mentioned: large reductions in the number of institutions and programs that receive subsidized credit." USAID (1985), "La cooperación internacional de AID." Statistics from the Central Bank of Costa Rica show that between 1985 and 1987, government credit to the farm sector fell from 19.8 percent to 13.5 percent of total credit authorized. Small farmers received a diminishing part of this lower amount of government agricultural credit, their percentage dropping from 14.2 percent in

1985 to 13.0 percent in 1987. CENAP et al. (1988, 19–24). Although the credit available to small farmers from the government is decreasing rapidly, there is an abundance of credit being authorized for personal consumption and commercial activity.

11 USDA, FAS, Agricultural Attaché–Costa Rica (1987). "Not official USDA data."

12 USDA, FAS, Agricultural Attaché–Costa Rica (1989, 35). "Not official USDA data."

13 For a critique of government agricultural policies, see CENAP et al. (1988).

14 For a valuable discussion of these different political tendencies, see CENAP et al. (1988, 50–51).

15 Letter from a coalition of *campesino* organizations to Costa Rican president Oscar Arias Sánchez, 3 September 1987.

16 UCADEGUA/UPAGRA/FEDAGRO (n.d.), *El plan del maiz.*

17 CENAP et al. (1988, 30).

18 USAID–Honduras (1987), "PL 480 Title I and I/III Local Currency Generations, as of May 31, 1987" (table).

19 Economic Perspectives, Inc. (1986a), *Honduras: Basic Grains Policy Options;* and Hanrahan (1983), *Some Impacts Associated with Selected Honduran Basic Grain Policies.* For more discussion of Honduran agricultural pricing policies, see Garcia et al. (1987) and Honduras, IHMA, DIAMER/CADESCA-CEE (1987), *Funcionamiento del sistema de comercialización pública y privada de granos básicos.*

20 Bustamante (1988), *Análisis de la politica de precios.* Also see Garst (1986a), *Background Information for Basic Grain Imports.*

21 Arias (1988), *La ayuda alimentaria y el desarrollo agrícola de granos básicos en Guatemala,* 111–12.

22 Another possibility is that INDECA's stabilization role would be assumed by the National Supply and Price Institute, a branch of the Ministry of the Economy, which would mean an increased orientation toward consumer as opposed to producer interests.

23 INDECA documents show more than eight million *quetzales* worth of grain channeled to the army in the period 1982–86. The value of this grain in dollars is difficult to calculate, since the *quetzal* was devalued, with fluctuations, from Q1:$1 to about Q3:$1 during that period. Guatemala, INDECA: *Organo informativo de la institución* 1:5, (15 September 1986), and Guatemala, INDECA (n.d.), *Memoria de labores,* 1983–86.

24 Author interviews of SIECA's agricultural department, the Guatemalan Ministry of

Agriculture's Sectorial Unit for Agricultural Policy (USPADA), and INDECA. Also see National Poultry Producers Association's (ANAVI) paid advertisements dated 3, 13, and 24 March 1987, and paid advertisement by the Organized Producers of Basic Grains, dated 28 March 1987, in *Prensa Libre;* and "Hay o no hay maiz en Guatemala?" *El Gráfico,* 8 February 1987.

25 Guatemalan wheat production and prices are regulated not by INDECA, but rather through a mixed governmental–private-sector board. Local production is protected from competition by imports by tying the right to import to the purchase of a certain amount of Guatemalan wheat.

26 Gilmore (1982, 20).

27 For an analysis of the interrelation between agorexport production and underdevelopment, see De Janvry (1981), *The Agrarian Question and Reformism in Latin America;* Browning (1971); Weeks (1985). Brockett (1984, 490), for example, concluded in a recent study of Guatemala: "Land concentration is directly related to export cropping, food supply deficiencies, and, therefore, malnutrition."

28 *Frontline* (AID), August 1984. Cauterucci subsequently became AID director in Guatemala.

29 Norton and Benito (1987, chap.4, p.1).

30 Pines, King, and Lowenthal (1988, 6).

31 Arias (1989, 76, 116).

32 OIT, PREALC (1983), *Producción de alimentos básicos y empleo en el istmo centroamericano,* 38–39.

33 In 1980, 46 percent of the total rural population of Central America and Panama did not have an income sufficient to cover even their basic food needs, much less funds to invest in capital-intensive nontraditional production. CEPAL (1983b), *Satisfacción de las necesidades básicas de la población del istmo centroamericano,* 9.

34 Braun, Hotchkiss, and Immink (1989), *Nontraditional Export Crops in Guatemala,* 14.

35 USDA, FAS, Agricultural Attaché–Costa Rica (1989, 17). "Not official USDA data."

36 In February 1989, peasant cardamom producers in the Ixcán, Playa Grande Region of Guatemala reported to us that the price of cardamon had fallen by half over the past few years, leaving them with serious losses and no alternative means of cash income. Author interviews.

CHAPTER FIVE

1 Agricultural Trade Development and Assistance Act of 1954 (PL 480), Title II, Section 201.

2 USAID, ROCAP (1985, 10, 13). ROCAP's 5.2 million beneficiary figure does not include refugees.

3 Arias (1989, 53), citing INCAP, and PROPAG (1986).

4 Inforpress Centroamericana (1987b), "La ayuda alimentaria a Guatemala." For El Salvador calculation, see table 4 in chapter 7.

5 These figures refer only to the countries of the region under study: Guatemala, El Salvador, Honduras, and Costa Rica.

6 In 1985 the main donors, in order, to the four countries under study were the United States, EEC, Canada, the Netherlands, Norway, and Switzerland. West Germany also has food-aid programs in Guatemala and Honduras, but this food is purchased locally. FAO (n.d.), *Food Aid in Figures* (1985).

7 WFP projects in Central American are directed to agricultural development and settlement, community development (especially small-scale infrastructure and road building), emergency aid to refugees and the displaced, maternal/child health, and school feeding.

8 USAID, Bureau for Food for Peace and Private Voluntary Assistance (1988b), *Voluntary Foreign Aid Programs, 1985–1987.*

9 A small CRS Panamanian program was terminated in the mid-1980s.

10 Ahern et al. (1987).

11 Ahern et al. (1987).

12 CARE (1983), "CARE International," 2.

13 USAID, Bureau for Food for Peace and Private Voluntary Assistance (1988b). The U.S. care *Annual Report 1988* shows that "agricultural commodities, including ocean freight, donated by the U.S. Government and others" increased from 58 percent of its budget in 1987 to 64 percent in 1988, showing a continuing and even increasing reliance on food distribution programs.

14 Authors' calculations based on PL 480 *Annual Reports*. In Honduras, CARE's program rose from 5,422 MT in 1982 to 10,658 MT in 1987. Ahern et al. (1987, table 3).

15 Winrock International (1987), *Implementation and Impact Evaluation of PL 480 Title II Program*, 1–2, also reported CARE–Honduras having 10,000 beneficiaries in food-for-work and refugee feeding programs.

16 CARE–Honduras reported CARE maternal/child donations as going to forty private feeding centers through the "Programa de Alimentación Materno Infantil JNBS/CARE." These included programs supported by World Vision, Assemblies of God, World Gospel Mission, and the Santidad church. Other private groups that

receive AID/CARE food include Iglesia de Dios, Avance Misionero en Honduras, and Iglesia Elim Pentocostal. Most of these private day-care and feeding centers acquire the CARE food from the First Lady's Government Social Welfare Board (JNBS). In addition, it appears that CARE itself also passes some food directly on to private local groups through its "Community Program." Interview with Bruce Lustman, director of CARE's Feeding Programs in Honduras, 9 March 1988. Interview with Marty Schwartz, CARE mission official in Honduras, 23 July 1987. Also see INCAP (1986), *Programas de alimentación a grupos,* 165; Ahern et al. (1987, 10); and Winrock International (1987, 3). In Guatemala, local CARE officials report that CARE food is distributed to some ninety private agencies, including church groups, through their "other child" feeding program. These groups include World Vision, Christian Children's Fund, El Verbo church, Shaddai Church, New Dawn Center, Latin America Evangelical Institute, and the New Jerusalem church. Interview with Carlos Garcia, CARE's administrative assistant, 13 May 1987. Interview with Heather Nesbitt, Maternal Child Program director, 3 June 1987. Interview with Christian Nill, CARE's assistant director in Guatemala, 15 January 1987. The AID 1988 evaluation of food aid in Guatemala reported that CARE's Other Child Feeding Program provides Title 11 food for beneficiaries in 123 institutions, noting that most of these institutions are church and community groups, including evangelical churches. Pines, King, and Lowenthal (1988, 13).

17 According to AID's *Voluntary Foreign Aid Programs* report (1980 and 1986–87— last available year), U.S. government contributions to CARE increased from $40.2 million to $62.3 million in freight, from $91.8 million to $121.8 million in PL 480 food, and from $4.8 million to $32.7 million in grants—for a total increase of $78 million. During the same period, private contributions increased only $5.8 million, from $26.9 million to $33.7 million. A *Fortune* overview of U.S. philanthrophy reported that of $397 million in total revenues in 1986, $340 million came from "government payments," most of which were contributions of surplus food. Gwen Kinkead, "America's Best-Run Charities," *Fortune,* 9 November 1987. In response to assertions that CARE is heavily dependent on AID, CARE states that it has been diversifying its funding base since the early 1980s and that it is now demonstrating a greater degree of political neutrality in its Central American operations. Letter from CARE to the University of Nebraska's General Counsel, 22 November 1989.

18 CARE reports that a "strategic objective for the 1990–1995 period" is to develop "increased levels of cooperation with indigenous nongovernmental organizations."

Letter from CARE to the University of Nebraska's General Counsel, 22 November 1989.

19 USAID–Honduras (1984), *Project Evaluation Summary: PL 480 Title 11*, 9–10, reports 12,000 Miskito refugee beneficiaries in this program in FY 1983. According to CARE, CARE responded to a request by World Relief, the U.S. evangelical relief organization, to provide PL 480 food to some 7,000 beneficiaries in La Mosquitia. CARE says it "interpreted its assistance to World Relief as being purely humanitarian in nature." CARE reports that in the mid-1980s it turned down AID requests for undertaking another project in the region. Letter from CARE to the University of Nebraska's General Counsel, 22 November 1989.

20 CARE disputes descriptions of its projects in Playa Grande as being "controversial," describing the colonization project initiated under the military regime of General Romeo Lucás Garcia as a "humanitarian effort" and saying that its subsequent agricultural projects in the development pole of Playa Grande represented a shift "towards more development-oriented activities in Playa Grande." Letter from CARE to the University of Nebraska's General Counsel, 22 November 1989. The role of food aid in counterinsurgency and pacification in Guatemala is covered in chapter 7. For information on the function of development poles like Playa Grande in the counterinsurgency war see the following: Carmack (1988); Black (1984); Simon (1988), Guatemala, Junta Militar (1982); Guatemala, Estado Mayor (1982); Americas Watch (1984, 1986); Guatemala, Ministerio de Defensa (1985); Guatemala, Ministerio de Defensa (1984); Krueger and Enge (1985); Krueger (1987); Manz (1986, 1988).

21 CARE–Guatemala (1986), "Urban FFW Project Proposal for July 1986–January 1988." The proposal states: "The Guatemalan government has expressed concern that the successful implementation of the reforms might be jeopardized if the austerity measures provoke a violent response, particularly from the urban poor. The Guatemalan government is seeking ways to alleviate some of the negative effects that the reforms are likely to have temporarily on this segment of the population. An urban FFW program is one of the means proposed." An AID-contracted evaluation of PL 480 Title 11 programs in Guatemala describes the political context of the new urban food programs: "The political context, in which a new, more democratic government must increase taxes and reduce spending to restore economic growth and financial stability, justifies the use of Title 11 to alleviate consequences of structural adjustment for the poor." Pines, King, and Lowenthal (1988, i). According to AID official Harry E. Wing, "Under the direc-

tion of CARE, the USAID Mission undertook an emergency Food-for-Work program in 1986 [the year Cerezo took office] which contributed to the economic stabilization of Guatemala." Wing (1987, 37). In a 15 January 1987 interview, Christian Nill, CARE's assistant director in Guatemala, acknowledged that the urban FFW program had a "pacification" component related to the new government's economic package.

22 From 1980 to 1986, the CCC value of Title II donations plus ocean transport costs averaged $700 million a year. USDA, FAS (1980–86), *Food for Peace: 1986 Annual Report,* 57.

23 USAID, ROCAP (1985, annex 9, p.21).

24 Epstein (1985), *U.S. Bilateral and Multilateral Food Assistance Programs,* 22–23.

25 The funds CCC uses to finance Section 416 are earned in other programs. One should also note that Section 416 donations, though these involve some CCC outlay, also save it long-term storage costs.

26 Descriptions of the working of the Section 416 regular program include Epstein (1987), *Food for Peace, 1954–1986;* USDA, FAS, (1987), "Section 416 of the Agricultural Act of 1949, as Amended" (fact sheet); and *Federal Register* 53, no. 243 (19 December 1988): 51032–41. Also see Remy Jurenas, "Section 416 Foreign Donations Program Activity in Central America," 30 June 1988 memo to Senator Tom Harkin, Washington, D.C., Congressional Research Service, Environmental and Natural Resources Division.

27 USDA, FAS, "CCC Reports of Section 416 Export Donations Program," for FY 1983–88 (table).

28 USAID, Regional Inspector General for Audit (1986a), *Audit of Idle United States Donated Dairy Commodities Observed in Panama.*

29 Strangely enough, these Guatemalan powdered-milk shipments, worth over $10 million, do not appear on CCC export records, although Harry Wing of AID–Guatemala and other sources confirmed that they did occur. USDA's table "Section 416 Dairy Donation Exports Action Summary . . . for FY 1983" shows that in FY 1983 agreements 3019 and 4019 were signed with CRS for such a quantity. Also see Epstein (1987), citing USDA, Foreign Agricultural Circular, February 1985, 13.

30 AID reports that it is further exploring the possibility of channeling Title I local currencies to these programs. USAID (1983–88), *Congressional Presentation, Fiscal Year 1988,* 179.

31 In 1982 the WFP monetized wheat in Honduras to generate funds for women's participation in an agrarian reform basic grains project.

32 U.S. Congress, House, Select Committee on Hunger (1987); USAID, Bureau for Food for Peace and Private Voluntary Assistance (1988a), *Monetization Field Manual.*

33 For more information on CARE monetization see Garst (1986a, 28, 48–49); and Pines, King, and Lowenthal (1988, 21–25, 48–49).

34 Martin (1986), "Some Thoughts on Monetization," 6.

35 Price, Ledogar and Townsend (1984), "Supplementary Feeding Programs for School Age Children."

36 Winrock International (1987, 18).

37 USAID, PVA/PPE (1985), *PL 480 Title II Evaluations, 1980–1985.* Also see USAID, ROCAP (1985, 9–10). Jackson (1982), *Against the Grain,* 41–72, pulls together much of the more negative evidence. Also see Clay and Singer (1985), *Food Aid and Development,* 89–104; and Beaton and Ghassemi (1987), "Supplementary Feeding Programs for Young Children in Developing Countries," 413–28.

38 See AID, ROCAP, (1985, annex 9, pp. 32–35), for a case study of misdirected food resources in a Panamanian school-feeding program, showing that more than half the children being served were not malnourished.

39 AID, ROCAP (1985, 8), reports, "For children under the age of five in [Central America and Panama], recent studies on growth retardation (an accepted indicator of nutritional status) have estimated that approximately 60 percent suffer from mild, moderate or severe malnutrition. The incidence of moderate and severe malnutrition—defined as weight for age below 75 percent of the standard median weight for the respective age and sex—ranges from a low of 7 percent in Costa Rica to a high of 29.5 percent in Guatemala and Honduras."

40 AID, ROCAP, (1985, 13).

41 Programa Mundial de Alimentos–El Salvador (1986), *Análisis de la problemática y costos actuales del sistema logístico,* 52–55, reports a disproportionate concentration of food resources in the better-off and more accessible regions. Poor geographical and individual targeting was also reported by Ahern et al. (1987, 31–43).

42 Food line at the offices of the Sisters of Charity, Colonia Betania, Zona 12, Guatemala City, 22 August 1987.

43 By law, processed commodities currently must constitute at least 75 percent of world Title II nonemergency tonnage.

44 U.S. Congress, House, Select Committee on Hunger (1985c), *Special Report on Applying United States Food Surpluses to the Problems of Hunger,* 67.

45 USAID (1983a, chap. 10, p. 3).

46 Author interview with World Share–Guatemala staffer Luz Mercedes Arce, 1988. Recipes taken from World Share handout.

47 National Reconstruction Committee (CRN) training class for departmental-level CRN promoters. Author visit 5 June 1987.

48 Latham (1984), "Strategies for the Control of Malnutrition and the Influence of the Nutritional Sciences," cites several influential studies that emphasize the shortage of energy rather than protein deficiencies in causing protein-energy malnutrition (PEM).

49 Milk causes diarrhea and flatulence in many Central American children and adults because their digestive systems produce too little of an enzyme (lactase) needed to digest lactose (milk sugar). Approximately three-quarters of the world's population—with the exception of northern European Caucasians and certain African tribes that have historically consumed a diet rich in milk—lose the capacity to produce significant quantities of this enzyme once they are out of infancy. Spiro (1977), *Clinical Gastroenterology,* 495–503; and Woodruff (1978), "Intolerancia a la Leche." Given the large Native American and black population in Central America, lactose intolerance should certainly be a concern for food-program planners, especially since diarrhea is a major factor undermining nutritional well-being. Spiro (1977, 499) reports, for example, "In children, sugar intolerance is usually manifested as a failure to thrive. The infant has diarrhea and remains thin and malnourished, improving only after the elimination of the specific sugar from the diet." Nevertheless, AID was able to offer us no data on lactose intolerance in Central America, nor does it adequately discuss the problem in its Food for Peace Office's *Commodities Reference Guide* (1988). The only recommendations (sect.1, p.5) are that "milk or milk products . . . are best used in combination with local foods such as porridges or bread," and that "NFDM [nonfat dry milk] should be used with caution in age groups or areas not accustomed to drinking milk."

50 There are actually two issues at stake in the discussion of bottle feeding. One, described above, is the danger of bottle feeding itself, independent of whether this replaces breast-feeding. The second danger is that the easy availability of powdered milk (or the assumption that powdered milk is nutritionally superior to breast milk) will encourage mothers to give up breast-feeding altogether, with even more serious effects. The child is deprived of the antibodies contained in human milk and is forced to rely totally on an artificial ration, often too watered down to meet nutritional needs. The danger of insufficient intake is especially great if the donated milk rations are frequently delayed or cut off. It is important to note that most

Central American families could not afford to purchase enough powdered milk on commercial terms.

51 In Honduras, we encountered several U.S. private organizations, including Friends of the Americas and the Knights of Malta, distributing Slim Fast.

52 Visit to Hermanas de la Caridad (Sisters of Charity) program, Colonia Betania, Zone 12, Guatemala City, 22 August 1987. The formula was apparently donated by CARITAS–Belgium.

53 Norton and Benito (1987, chap.2, p.6).

54 Author interview with a supervisor of the CONADES social promotion department, San Salvador, 18 October 1987.

55 Bunch, McKay, and McKay (n.d.), *Problems with Food Distribution Programs: A Case in Point.*

56 Cuny (1983), *Disasters and Development;* Oxfam (1985), *The Field Directors' handbook.*

57 Jackson (1982, 7–22).

58 Bunch, McKay, and McKay (n.d.).

59 USAID (1983a, chap.7, pp.10–11). See USAID–Honduras (1984).

60 Author interview with CESAD officials Rosa Emilia de Seballos and Blanca Betida de Menjivar, 13 November 1987. Various other informants in El Salvador complained to us that CESAD engages in proselytism and distributes rations preferentially to protestants, but CESAD personnel denied these allegations.

61 Untitled typewritten pages listing NGO powdered-milk recipients, the first from a FY 1983 donation, the second from FY 1987. The FY 1983 donation agreement, according to USDA Section 416 agreement records, was signed with CRS. The CRS office in Guatemala, however, told us it was AID that wrote up the list of agencies the food would go to. The 1987 donation formed part of a Section 416 Sugar Quota Set Aside program that, contrary to the usual practice of putting these commodities on the market, was used in distribution programs. Wing (1987, 41).

62 See food-aid country overviews collected in INCAP, PROPAG (1986). Also see USAID, ROCAP (1985).

63 Guatemala, Presidencia (1987), *Plan de reorganización nacional,* 45.

64 Food-aid policy proposals include El Salvador, MIPLAN, Asesoria Técnica (1987), "Lineamientos para una política de ayuda alimentaria"; Guatemala, MDUR (1987), *Bases de una política nacional para el uso de la ayuda alimentaria";* and Honduras, CONSUPLANE (1987), "Taller: Enfoque de la alimentación a grupos en el plan nacional de desarrollo."

65 Author interview with Patrick Ahern, CRS director in Honduras, 7 July 1987.

66 An all-day December 1988 evaluation conducted by the local social pastoral committee listed first among project drawbacks the extraordinary amount of time needed for program management. In addition, the team judged that the program did not reach the poorest members of the community; that it fomented corruption and divisions; and that, because of substitution effects and the use of foreign foods, it did not significantly improve beneficiaries' nutrition. Furthermore, the main work being done under the project—sweeping the streets—had not been chosen by the beneficiaries themselves and was considered low priority. The project's main benefit was the small level of material support it provided to one thousand of this poor neighborhood's families. (Information based on author's attendance at the evaluation.)

CHAPTER SIX

1 For discussions of the emerging role of distributional food aid in development, see Schneider (1978), *Food Aid for Development;* Clay and Singer (1985); Singer, Wood, and Jennings (1987), *Food Aid: the Challenge and the Opportunity;* Hopkins (1984), "The Evolution of Food Aid"; and Hopkins (1987), "Aid for Development."

2 "AID policy emphasizes the need to concentrate U.S. resources, including PL 480 programs, in an integrated approach to solving priority development problems. . . . AID views Title II resources as interim assistance to reach specific objectives to combat hunger, alleviate malnutrition, improve economic and social development, and/or increase food production and improve its distribution." USAID (1983a, chap.3, pp.3–4). Current pressures for reorientation of food-aid programs in Central America are clearly seen in Pines, King, and Lowenthal (1988) and Ahern et al. (1987).

3 For discussions of the WFP's promotion of food-for-work, see Cathie (1982, 65–95); and WFP (1983), *Food Works: Twenty Years.* As described by the *AID Handbook 9,* "The WFP seeks to use food aid as a capital input which, added to other forms of capital and local labor, will yield a lasting gain in the economic and/or social betterment of the recipients." USAID (1983a, chap.12, p.1).

4 Hopkins (1987, 153–60).

5 "A major emphasis of AID policy dealing with Title II is the need for close and continuing attention to program management and control. Since Title II deals with the utilization of expensive and perishable resources, effective program management and control is essential." USAID (1983a, chap.3, p.4).

6 Pines, King, and Lowenthal (1988, 53–54).

7 Ahern et al. (1987).

8 USAID, ROCAP (1985, 12).

9 USAID (1983a, chap.10, p.3).

10 Honduras, CONSUPLANE/PMA (1985), *Análisis de los programs de ayuda alimentaria,* table 7; Winrock International (1987, 30); and Ahern et al. (1987, 35–37). For El Salvador, see El Salvador, MIPLAN, SECONAN (1984b), *Estudio sobre el funcionamiento,* 45–47.

11 Author interview with consultant for Title 11 Enhancement Program for CARE–Latin America, Honduras, 15 March 1988.

12 Interview with a local development worker who had participated in a WFP evaluation tour for projects 2705 and 784, Guatemala, 1 June 1987.

13 Jackson (1982, 57–64).

14 Interestingly, one recent overview of school-feeding studies from around the world found that the more rigorously designed the study, the less conclusive the evidence. The poorly designed, impressionistic studies, on the other hand, gave favorable reports almost across the board. Levinger (1986), *School Feeding Programs in Developing Countries.*

15 Ibid.

16 USAID (1983a, chap.10, p.4).

17 USDA, FAS (1980–86), *Food for Peace, 1984 Annual Report,* 2.

18 Such was the case of WFP project 2806 in El Salvador, a resettlement program for the displaced, with a six-month food-aid time frame. Employees we interviewed at CONADES, the government commission in charge of the program, were pessimistic about the chances that the displaced could achieve self-sufficiency within those six months, especially since they are given productive inputs only for one *manzana* of land (0.69 hectare) and because many are being relocated in agrarian reform cooperatives where those who arrived first are known not to welcome newcomers.

19 ILO (1949), *Protection of Wages Convention, no. 95.*

20 OIT, Programa Mundial de Empleo (1981), *Pautas para la organización de programas especiales de obras públicas*"; and ILO (1975), "International Labour Standards and WFP Projects: The Distinction between Wage-Labour Schemes and Self-Help Projects." AID's guidelines vary from those of the OIT, however, in that the payment mixture depends not on who benefits from the project but on whether the "workers are employed for full-time over an extended period of time." USAID (1983a, chap.10, pp.5–6).

21 World Share Guatemala (1988), "Municipality of Guatemala-Clinic Plan: Food for Work Projects" (computer printout).

22 World Share, a Catholic humanitarian organization with offices in San Diego, was contracted by AID in 1987 to supply this Guatemala City government food-for-work project with Section 416 food, even though the mayor's office already had a food-for-work project with CARE. A recent evaluation, noting this duplication of programs, has proposed putting World Share in charge of coordinating AID "other child" donations to the smaller distribution agencies and church groups. Pines, King, and Lowenthal (1988, 54).

23 The food for the Salvadoran program comes through WFP project 718, "Rural Development and Rehabilitation through Self-Help." For Honduras, see INCAP, PROPAG (1986, 154).

24 Jackson (1982, 23–40).

25 In El Salvador, personnel at the displaced-persons programs CONADES and CESAD told us that they are now transferring all their programs, including CESAD's program for nutritionally vulnerable groups, to food-for-work. In Guatemala, an EEC-supplied relief program for the displaced is also food-for-work. Ahern et al. (1987, 27–28) also reported various Honduran diocesan maternal/child health programs now using food-for-work.

26 Pines, King, and Lowenthal (1988, 21, 26).

27 Stevens (1979), *Food Aid and the Developing World,* 117.

28 Shantytown visits and interviews with directors of two urban community development groups, October and November 1987.

29 CARE–Guatemala (1986, 3–4).

30 U.S. GAO (1985b), *USAID/Costa Rica's Monitoring of and Controls over Dollar and Local Currency Resources,* 7.

31 Interview with peasant from Playa Grande, 26 March 1988.

CHAPTER SEVEN

1 Various studies have discussed the use of food aid as an instrument of international foreign policy. Probably the best of these is Wallerstein (1980), *Food for Peace: Food for War.* Literature relating to the political uses of food *within* nations is, however, much scarcer. Gayle Smith (1987), "Ethiopia and the Politics of Famine," and (1988), "Rethinking Humanitarian Aid," is one of the few researchers who has focused on this issue.

2 Wallerstein (1980, 134–35, 193–97).

3 U.S. Army (1985), "U.S. Army Operational Concept for Low-Intensity Conflict." For further discussion of LIC, see Bermúdez (1987), *Guerra de baja intensidad,* and Barry (1986b), *Low Intensity Conflict: The New Battlefield in Central America.*

4 Waghelstein (1985), "Post-Vietnam Counterinsurgency Doctrine."

5 McPherson (1983, 19).

6 AID–El Salvador directed 56 percent of Title I funds for FY 1985 to public-service restoration, employment generation (basically working on those same restoration programs), and assistance to the displaced. Only 12 percent of Title I funds for that same year went to agricultural development projects. See U.S. AID–El Salvador (1986c), "Report to the Congress"; and USAID–El Salvador (1986a), *Amendment No. 1 to the Memorandum of Understanding,* 11–13. For an even more detailed breakdown, see El Salvador, MIPLAN, SETEFE (1987), "Situación financiera del presupuesto extraordinario."

7 Hatfield, Leach, and Miller (1987, 4).

8 For information on the number and situation of El Salvador's displaced, see Montes (1984), "La situación de los salvadoreños desplazados y refugiados"; "Inforpress Centroamericana (1986), "Informe especial: Los desplazados salvadoreños"; Contracting Corporation of America (1985), *Encuesta de base de la población desplazada.*

9 Interviews with CRS and archdiocese Social Secretariat officials, September and November 1987.

10 Though its own programs cover only registered displaced persons living in areas of government control, one should note that CONADES has also channeled small amounts of food to the politically neutral International Committee of the Red Cross for distribution to nonregistered displaced persons living in conflict areas.

11 See, for example, Chris Hedges, "U.S. Food for Displaced Salvadoreans [*sic*] Diverted by Corruption and Bad Management," *Christian Science Monitor,* 6 March 1984; Sam Dillon, "In Salvador, 'Loving Hand' has Political Strings Attached," *Miami Herald,* 17 December 1984.

12 El Salvador, MIPLAN/CONADES (1987), *La población desplazada: Acción gubernamental, 1980–1987.*

13 Gersony, Lynch, and Garvelink (1986), *The Journey Home: Durable Solutions for Displaced Families,* 35. The heavy political overtones of programs for the displaced in El Salvador are also suggested by the classification as "privileged material," and deletion from the public version, of more than two-thirds of this entire report.

14 U.S. Congressional Research Service, Foreign Affairs and National Defense Division (1989), *El Salvador, 1979–1989: A Briefing Book,* 71; Hatfield, Leach, and Miller (1987, 6–7), citing the *Wall Street Journal* and the Gersony Report; USAID–El Salvador (1986, 1987), "El Salvador Title I and Title II PL-480 Food Programs" (press handouts).

15 CRS-CARITAS of El Salvador has for many years run a maternal/child food program with AID-supplied Title II food. This program, relatively apolitical, currently continues at the traditional level. CRS also continues to aid the displaced, but with EEC rather than U.S. food. This assistance is channeled through the archdiocese Social Secretariat office, which has made clear its resistance to working with AID in feeding displaced persons.

16 Author interview with CESAD, 11 November 1987.

17 Programa Mundial de Alimentos–El Salvador (1986, 95), authors' translation. Also see Montes (1984, 9–12). Severe social disintegration was also reported to us by a supervisor in CONADES's social promotion office interviewed in October 1987.

18 See El Salvador, Ministerio del Interior, CONADES (1987e), "Lista de proyectos del 2806, por comunidad," and the project 2806 proposal: El Salvador, Ministerio del Interior, CONADES (1987a), "Asistencia de rehabilitación a la población desplazada."

19 CONADES argues that it cannot aid communities in contested areas because the guerrillas would attack its trucks. Given that CONADES is a politicized government agency, this is probably true. But neither have WFP and AID found less political channels for their donations. Except for a small amount of WFP aid channeled by CONADES through the politically neutral International Committee of the Red Cross, and the aborted AID-CRS program back in 1981, no U.S. aid has gone to truly humanitarian organizations that might be able to serve all the displaced impartially.

20 Shepard (1986), United States Government Memorandum, USAID 10 39/86 "El Salvador: The National Plan."

21 Ibid. For more information on CONARA, see El Salvador, Ministerio del Interior, CONADES (1987b), *Directorio de las instituciones;* and U.S. Congressional Research Service, Office of Research Coordination (1989), "Background Information on CONARA and U.S. Food Assistance in El Salvador."

22 USAID–El Salvador (1986), "The National Plan: Questions and Answers." In this press handout, AID goes on to downplay the military's role in combined civic action: "Often civic action and humanitarian relief through civil agencies and supported logistically by the military are undertaken. . . . AID is not directly involved with civic action. However, AID-supported humanitarian activities might be undertaken in conjunction with military civic action in conflicted zones in which the military provides security and logistics support."

23 Author interview with CONARA general coordinator Luis Mejía Miranda, San Salvador, 11 November 1987.

24 Interview with U.S. government official working in San Salvador, 17 September 1987.

25 El Salvador, Ministerio del Interior, DIDECO (1987), "Plan de acción para el proyecto GOES/AID," 2, authors' translation. (Spanish says: El Ministerio de Defensa a través de CONARA ejecuta el componente dirigido a la restauración de areas destruidas o deterioradas por la situación de violencia en el pais, con el apoyo de raciones alimentarias para las familias afectadas en las areas conflictivas y que participan en las acciones civicas que realiza CONARA.)

26 See, for example: "Marjorie Miller, "Test for Salvador Civilians: Survival in Guerrilla Area," *Los Angeles Times,* 18 January 1988.

27 Author interview with PADECOMSM spokesperson, 30 January 1989 and PADECOMSM press release (21 January 1989).

28 Author interviews in March 1988 with social-service workers associated with Social Secretariat. For an excellent report on the repopulation movement in El Salvador, see CARECEN (1988), "The Journey Home."

29 U.S. Congressional Research Service, Office of Research Coordination (1989), reports that ESF and Title I funding to CONARA was approximately $16.4 million in calendar year 1986.

30 PL 480 Section 106(b) (1) states that "proceeds from the sale of the commodities in the recipient country are used for such economic development purposes as are agreed upon in the sales agreement or any amendment thereto. In negotiating such agreements with recipient countries, the United States shall emphasize the use of such proceeds for purposes which directly improve the lives of the poorest of their people and their capacity to participate in the development of their countries.

31 Hatfield, Leach, and Miller (1987, 9–10). AID may also have been misrepresenting the true size and nature of this civic-action program. The AID mission in El Salvador reported this "humanitarian relief" program as serving 20,000 persons in 1986 and 52,500 in 1987, whereas CONARA reported to us well over ten times that number of beneficiaries. For U.S. figures, see USAID–El Salvador (1986), "El Salvador PL 480 Programs," 2, and USAID–El Salvador (1986, 1987, 4, 5). As for CONARA, interview figures supplied by Mejia Miranda worked out to a high 144,000 families a year, whereas a CONARA paid advertisement (*El Diario de Hoy,* 10 May 1987) reported an even higher 118,460 beneficiary families in January, February, and March 1987. The discrepancy may also be explained by CONARA's

distribution of non–U.S. food. Informants from both the U.S. government and DIDECO told us that CONARA also distributed WFP food, even though no such WFP project exists.

32 USAID–Washington (1986), "LAC [Latin America and Caribbean] Policy in Support of Military Civic Action in El Salvador."

33 CARECEN (1988). Archdiocese Social Secretariat press release, February 1989.

34 Author interview with Laura Guzmán of the Archdiocese Social Secretariat, San Salvador, 11 November 1987.

35 Author interview with CRS official, San Salvador, 1 November 1987.

36 Author interview with WFP country mission head Francisco Roque Castro, San Salvador, 17 September 1987.

37 See Carmack (1988), *Harvest of Violence;* Black (1984), *Garrison Guatemala;* Simon (1988), *Eternal Spring, Eternal Tyranny.*

38 See, for example, Guatemala, Junta Militar de Gobierno (1982), "Objectivos Nacionales Actuales."

39 Interview with director of CRN cited in Barry (1986a), *Guatemala: Politics of Counterinsurgency.*

40 Guatemala, Estado Mayor General del Ejército (1982), "Plan Nacional de Seguridad y Desarrollo."

41 Government Accord 44-82, published in the official government newspaper 18 June 1982, reads: "The National Reconstruction Committee is charged with the coordination of all the food distribution projects carried out in the Republic of Guatemala by the government, including food-for-work projects" (authors' translation).

42 Americas Watch (1984), *Guatemala: A Nation of Prisoners.* Also see Garst (1986b), *Análisis de la situación económico y social de Guatemala,* 256–60, for a summary of government figures on the number of orphans (150,000 to 200,000) and the number of assassinations recorded in Ministry of Health files (20,980 in 1980–83).

43 Guatemala, Ministerio de Defensa Nacional (1985a), *Revista cultural del ejército: Edición especial dedicado a los polos de desarrollo,* 21.

44 Infopress Centroamericana (1987b) reports $36.4 million in WFP donations for 1981–87. Though exact figures are not available, interview data and comparisons of U.S. aid to WFP in Guatemala with the total size of the WFP program in the country make it clear that since 1981 the great majority of WFP aid to Guatemala has actually been from the United States.

45 Guatemala, Ministerio de Defensa Nacional (1984), *Polos de desarrollo,* lists nu-

merous model villages built with food-for-work programs between October 1983 and September 1984. The army's 1985 *Revista cultural del ejército: Edición especial dedicado al labor del* CRN not only shows the army's close ties with CRN and CRN's work in building the model villages, but lists WFP as the only source of CRN food (p.13). For indications of WFP assistance to the model village of Acul, see Krueger and Enge (1985), *Security and Development Conditions in the Guatemalan Highlands,* 44; and "Polos de desarrollo" (1986, 2, 7).

46 Author interview with WFP–Guatemala interim director Claudia Von Rohl, 4 June 1987.

47 Barry and Preusch (1988), *The Soft War,* 129–33. A 1984 AID–Guatemalan government agreement stipulated that Title 1 local currency be used to pay for 20,000 person-months of labor on highland roads.

48 For a review of AID-financed road building, largely concentrated in conflict areas, see USAID (1983b), *Guatemala Project Paper: Small Farmer Development.* As to WFP support, information supplied to us by WFP–Guatemala shows that during the first two and a half years of the WFP-CRN food-for-work "Community Development" project (GUA-784), participants constructed 3,725 kilometers of rural roads—three and a half times the stated goal.

49 USAID (1983b, 11).

50 Interviews with two *campesinos* from the Playa Grande, Ixcán region, 26 March 1988, and with a community development worker, Chichicastenango region, June 1988.

51 Tables supplied by WFP, "WFP Shipments by Recipients for Development Projects and Emergency Operations," 1978–87. Also see FAO (n.d.), *Food Aid in Figures,* 1987, no.5.

52 USDA, *Food for Peace Annual Reports,* various years.

53 Calculations based on USDA, *Food for Peace Annual Reports,* various years; tables supplied by WFP–Rome: "WFP Shipments by Recipients for Development Projects and Emergency Operations," 1978–87; FAO (n.d.), *Food Aid in Figures,* 1987. no.5; and summary tables published by each WFP country mission.

54 Wallerstein (1980, 106–9) and Cathie (1982, 97–120) discuss some of the reasons behind WFP's "management mediocrity."

55 A notable exception would be the quite thorough, and critical, PMA–El Salvador 1986 evaluation.

56 Author interview with Rosa Inés de Antolin, WFP–El Salvador, 10 November 1987; newspaper report appearing in *La Prensa Gráfica* (San Salvador), 11 November 1987, 3; author interviews with rural development workers in Guatemala.

57 Acuerdo Gubernativo 44–82, 29 June 1982.

58 Wallerstein (1980, 167–71) and Cathie (1982, 36). Other reasons behind the U.S. World Food Programme proposal were growing U.S. surpluses and the desire to promote more burden sharing.

59 USAID (1983a, chap. 12, pp. 1–9). In the course of this investigation, several WFP officials did admit to us that the U.S. embassy may in the past have played a dominant role in WFP projects in Honduras, El Salvador, and Guatemala, but they claimed that such bilateral control is no longer being exercised.

60 Wallerstein (1980, 107) writes: "The United States, alone among all other donors, continues to insist on the right of prior scrutiny for each individual WFP project; this is the case despite the fact that U.S. contributions now represent only 25 percent of WFP's total resources." This practice was confirmed by USDA and AID officials we interviewed.

61 USAID–El Salvador (1986, 1987), "El Salvador Title I and Title II PL 480 Food Programs." In its 1987 description of food-aid programs in El Salvador, AID stated that Title II food commodities are distributed to 670,000 Salvadorans, with 51.4 percent being channeled through WFP and the balance through AID's bilateral programs. In 1986 AID had reported 64 percent of its Title II aid to El Salvador flowing through WFP.

62 USAID (1983a, chap. 12, p. 2).

63 Since 1982 AID has focused over 90 percent of its development assistance to Guatemala on the highlands. Admittedly this is the most impoverished region, but AID'd interest in the highlands is political as well as developmental in nature (Barry and Preusch [1988, 119–24]) In its 1984 *Congressional Presentation,* AID noted that its development priorities coincided with those of the military government in power. It told Congress economic assistance was urgently needed to "improve the current economic situation and to address the political unrest in the Altiplano" (USAID 1983–88).

64 For more information on ESF assistance to the Guatemalan government, see Barry (1986a, 41–46). Also see various local currency agreements between AID and the Guatemalan government, 1984–88.

65 Wing (1987, 13–15).

66 A November 1984 decree by the military government of Mejía Victores, "The Organic Law of the National System of Inter-institutional Coordination for Reconstruction and Development," established the Inter-Institutional Coordinating Committees, which were to supervise all development efforts in the country as part

of the army's pacification plan. With the coming to power of the civilian government in 1986, the IICCs were officially put under civilian control. Nevertheless, military coordination mechanisms still continue. The pseudo-civilian Multisectorial Commission for the Ixil Triangle (officially headed by the Ministry of Public Works) is currently channeling and coordinating government and international resources (including EEC and WFP food aid) in the still-conflictive Ixil area. See AVANCSO (1988), *La politica de desarrollo del estado guatemalteco, 1986–1987.*

67 Untitled report of CRN activities in the municipality of Ixcán, Playa Grande, signed by CRN promoter Edgar Francisco Girón Méndez and dated November 1987.

68 Americas Watch (1984).

69 Davis and Hodson (1982), *Witness to Political Violence in Guatemala: The Suppression of a Rural Development Movement;* Inter-Hemispheric Education Resource Center (1988b), *Directory and Analysis: Private Organizations with U.S. Connections—Guatemala,* 7–13; Stoll (1990), *Is Latin America Turning Protestant?*

70 CARITAS Arquidiocesana (1988), *Informe Anual de Labores, 1987,* 47.

71 Inter-Hemispheric Education Resource Center (1988a), *Directory and Analysis: Private Organizations with U.S. Connections—El Salvador,* 7–17.

72 Interview with Gerald Coughlin of the Knights of Malta, 4 September 1987.

73 Inter-Hemispheric Education Resource Center (1988c), *Directory and Analysis: Private Organizations with U.S. Connections—Honduras,* 8–15.

74 Under the Assistance to Hospitals project, WFP food donated to Nicaraguan hospitals and health centers frees budgeted funds then used to improve hospital infrastructure and administration. Another WFP food-for-work project is designed to boost the local production of milk. Author interview with Raul González Vigil, director of WFP program in Nicaragua, 19 March 1988. Also see Programa Mundial de Alimentos (1986), *Conclusiones y recomendaciones de la misión de evaluación . . . del proyecto Nicaragua 2536.*

75 An initial $15 million Northern Zone Infrastructure Development Project was followed by a $21 million consolidation project.

76 Granados and Quezada (1984), "Los intereses geopolíticos y el desarrollo de la zona norte, 22.

77 USAID (1983d), *Northern Zone Infrastructure Development Project Paper.*

78 Granados and Quezada (1984, 14).

79 U.S. Congress, House, Committee on Foreign Affairs, Subcommittee on Western Hemisphere Affairs (1988), *The Implementation of the Humanitarian Assistance Package for Central America,* 30, 34, 42, 43.

80 Barry and Preusch (1986a), *The Central America Fact Book,* 43.

81 Programa Mundial de Alimentos, CFA, (1985), *Examen de algunas experiencias nacionales,* 9–10, reports World Relief as assisting 9,000 to 15,000 Miskito refugees in 1984.

82 Atlanta Center for Disease Control (1984), "International Trip Report: Nicaragua Indian Refugees in Honduras." The two U.S. lawmakers responsible for getting additional AID funds into the La Mosquitia region, former senator Jeremiah Denton (R–Ala.) and state representative Robert Livingston (R–La.), were both cohorts of the directors of Friends of the Americas (FOA), which has operations in the very area targeted by the emergency AID program, a location FOA has called "the most strategic place in the world" (FOA fund-raising letter of 27 October 1986).

83 Author interview with COPEN's General Oswaldo López Arrellano, August 1987. Honduras, Fuerzas Armadas de Honduras/COPEN (1989), "Informe Final de Actividades de COPEN: 1986."

CONCLUSION

1 Guatemala, Presidencia de la República (1987), *Programa de reorganización nacional,* 45.

Glossary

Appropriated funds: Funds to cover the cost of U.S. government programs, approved each year by Congress.

Bellmon amendment: The requirement that the U.S. Secretary of Agriculture certify that adequate storage facilities are available to handle proposed amounts of PL 480 or Section 416 food aid, and that these commodities will not create disincentives for local agricultural production, before they can be shipped.

Cargo Preference Act: Legislation requiring that a certain percentage of U.S. exports (including those financed under PL 480 Title I) be shipped on U.S.-flagged vessels. Because freight rates on U.S.-flagged vessels exceed those of foreign-flagged vessels, the CCC reimburses importers for the additional costs (known as the Ocean Transportation Differential) created by this requirement.

Commodity Credit Corporation (CCC): A corporate body and a U.S. government agency within the U.S. Department of Agriculture, charged with helping to maintain adequate internal market supplies; stabilizing, supporting, and protecting U.S. farm income and prices; and aiding in the export of U.S. agricultural commodities. The CCC is charged with financing the sale and export of commodities under PL 480, and it also runs the Section 416 donation program.

Concessional sale: A sale in which the buyer is allowed payment terms that are more favorable than those obtainable on the open market.

CCC cost: The gross cost to the CCC of financing the sales and export of U.S. agricultural commodities under PL 480 Title I. This includes that portion of the cost of the commodities financed by the CCC plus the ocean transport differential.

Cooperating sponsor: A U.S. private voluntary organization or an intergovernmental agency that acts as a channel for Title II or Section 416 food. Cooperating sponsors may distribute food themselves or pass it on to be distributed by other private and government agencies.

Disincentive effects: The depressive effect of food-aid imports on local agricultural prices and production, created by its addition to supply.

Dumping: The sale of products below their cost of production, or donations made into market channels. Prohibited under international trade law as unfair competition.

Export market value: The market value of a commodity based on world prices.

Food for Progress: A legislative mechanism to channel additional Title I or Section 416 food to countries undertaking structural adjustment measures related to their agricultural sector.

Local currency: The funds generated by the sale of food aid on the internal market of the recipient country. Usually refers to the government-held local currencies generated under Title I or Section 416 Sugar Quota Set Aside sales, which may be used only for purposes stipulated in advance under special bilateral agreements.

Monetization: The sale of food aid on the internal markets of recipient countries in order to generate funds for running food programs or for other development uses. Usually refers to sales of Title II or Section 416 commodities by private or intergovernmental agencies.

Ocean transport differential: See Cargo Preference Act.

Per capita income requirement: A minimum of 75 percent of the commodities allocated under Title I in any fiscal year must go to countries with a per capita GNP level low enough for them to be eligible for the concessional loan programs of the International Development Association of the World Bank. In FY 1988 this level was $790.

Public Law 480 (PL 480): Also known as Food for Peace. The legislative authority for the official U.S. government food aid program. Established in 1954 and periodically amended.

Section 106: A private-sector support program under PL 480 Title I, funded by Title I local currencies belonging to recipient governments.

Section 108: A private sector support program under PL 480 Title I, funded by Title I local currencies recipient governments have paid back to the United States.

Section 206: A government-to-government monetization program under PL 480 Title II.

Section 416: A program to donate surplus CCC-held commodities. Authorized under the Agricultural Act of 1949 and extended under the 1985 farm bill.

Section 416 Sugar Quota Set Aside: A program under Section 416 to donate surplus CCC-held commodities to governments of countries affected by recent cuts in their U.S. sugar sales quota. Similar to Title I.

Self-help measures: A series of measures that a recipient government must agree to undertake in order to be eligible for Title I assistance. These measures vary case by case, but generally revolve around improving the production, storage, and distribution of its agricultural commodities.

Structural adjustment programs: A series of measures designed to improve the short-term balance-of-payments position of countries with serious debt problems. These measures usually include currency devaluation, reductions in public-sector spending, and price liberalization. Food aid programs are frequently used to support these programs.

Title I: The PL 480 concessional sale program. This provides foreign governments with credit to finance purchases of selected U.S. commodities. Recipient governments resell those commodities on domestic markets to obtain local currency.

Title II: The PL 480 food donation program. Donates both food and the costs of its transport to the foreign point of entry, where it is picked up by cooperating sponsors. A small part of this food is monetized, but most is distributed directly to the local population through private or government agencies.

Title III: A program that converts PL 480 Title I sales to grants for low-income countries that meet a certain set of conditions. Also known as Food for Development.

Usual marketing requirement (UMR): The requirement that countries importing under Title I continue their normal commercial imports, from any source, of those same agricultural commodities. Basically an antidumping measure.

References

Ahern, Patrick, et al. 1987. *Assessment of the* CRS/CARITAS PL 480 *Title II program in Honduras*.

Americas Watch. 1982. *U.S. reporting on human rights at odds with knowledge*. New York.

———. 1984. *Guatemala: A nation of prisoners*. Washington, D.C.

———. 1985a. *Little hope: Human rights in Guatemala, January 1984–January 1985*. Washington, D.C.

———. 1985b. *Guatemala revised: How the Reagan administration finds "improvements" in human rights in Guatemala*. New York.

Amnesty International. 1989. *Human rights violations under the civilian government*. New York.

Archdiocese Social Secretariat. February 1989. Press Release. San Salvador.

Arias, Salvador. 1987. La perspectiva de la biotecnología en la agricultura y la producción de alimentos en América Central. Doctoral thesis, University of Paris VIII at Saint Denis.

———. 1988. *La ayuda alimentaria y el desarrollo agrícola de granos básicos en Guatemala: Perspectivas al año 2000*. Guatemala City: CADESCA-CEE, Programa de Seguridad Alimentaria del Istmo Centroamericano.

———. 1989. *Seguridad o inseguridad alimentaria: Un reto para la region centroamericana: Perspectivas al año 2000*. Guatemala City: CADESCA-CEE, Programa de Seguridad Alimentaria del Istmo Centroamericano.

Arriaga, Udoboro. 1986. Evolución reciente de la política agraria en Honduras. In *Honduras: Realidad nacional y crisis regional*, 279–87. Tegucigalpa: Centro de Documentación de Honduras/Universidad Internacional de la Florida.

Asociación para el Avance de las Ciencias Sociales en Guatemala (AVANSCO). 1988. La política de desarrollo de estado guatemalteco, 1986–87. Guatemala City.

Atlanta Center for Disease Control. 1984. International trip report: Nicaragua Indian refugees in Honduras. Atlanta.

Austin, James E. 1981. *Nutrition programs in the Third World: Cases and readings.* Cambridge, Mass.: Oelgeschlager, Gunn and Hain.

Ayuda Memoria: Reunión de coordinación de donantes de ayuda alimentaria a Honduras. 1988. 29 January. Typescript.

Banco Mundial. 1988. Reporte y recomendación del presidente del Banco Internacional de Reconstrucción y Fomento . . . Costa Rica.

Barraclough, Solon, and Peter Marchetti. 1985. Agrarian transformation and food security in the Caribbean basin. In *Towards an alternative for Central America and the Caribbean,* ed. George Irvin and Javier Gorostiaga, 154–93. Boston: Allen and Unwin.

Barraclough, Solon, and Michael F. Scott. 1987. *The rich have already eaten.* Transnational Issues 3. Amsterdam: Transnational Institute.

Barry, Tom. 1986a. *Guatemala: The politics of counterinsurgency.* Albuquerque: Inter-Hemispheric Education Resource Center.

———. 1986b. *Low intensity conflict: The new battlefield in Central America.* Albuquerque: Inter-Hemispheric Education Resource Center.

———. 1987. *Roots of rebellion: Land and hunger in Central America.* Boston: South End Press.

Barry, Tom, and Debra Preusch. 1986a. *The Central America fact book.* New York: Grove Press.

———. 1986b. *El Salvador: The other war.* Albuquerque: Inter-Hemispheric Education Resource Center.

———. 1988. *The soft war: Uses and abuses of U.S. economic aid in Central America.* New York: Grove Press.

Beaton, George H., and Hossein Ghassemi. 1987. Supplementary feeding programs for young children in developing countries. In *Food policy: Integrating supply, distribution, and consumption,* ed. J. Price Gittinger, Joanne Leslie, and Caroline Hoisington, 413–28. Baltimore: Johns Hopkins University Press for the World Bank.

Becker, Geoffrey. 1984. *The 1985 farm bill: A summary.* Issues Brief no. 86013. Washington, D.C.: Library of Congress, Congressional Research Service, Environment and Natural Resources Policy Division.

Bermúdez, Lilia. 1987. *Guerra de baja intensidad: Reagan contra Centroamérica.* Mexico City: Siglo XXI.

Black, George. 1984. *Garrison Guatemala*. New York: Monthly Review Press.

Bloomfield, Iririangi C. 1983. National food strategies and food policy reform. *Food Policy*, November, 287–96.

Braun, Joachim von, David Hotchkiss, and Maarten Immink. 1989. *Nontraditional export crops in Guatemala: Effects on production, income and nutrition*. Research Report 73. Washington, D.C.: International Food Policy Research Institute.

Bremer-Fox, Jennifer. 1988. Food aid and structural adjustment. In *The effectiveness of food aid: Implications of changes in farm, food aid and trade legislation: Proceedings of a CRS workshop held on April 25, 1988*, ed. Charles Hanrahan. Report for Congress (88–493 ENR). Washington, D.C.: CRS.

Brockett, Charles D. 1984. Malnutrition, public policy and agrarian change in Guatemala. *Journal of Interamerican Studies and World Affairs* 26, 4(November): 477–97.

Brown, Cynthia. 1985. *With friends like these: The Americas Watch report on human rights and U.S. policy in Latin America*. New York: Pantheon Books.

Browning, David. 1971. *El Salvador: Landscape and society*. London: Oxford University Press.

Bunch, Roland, M. McKay, and P. McKay. n.d. *Problems with food distribution programs: A case in point*. Fact sheet. Oklahoma City: World Neighbors.

Burbach, Roger, and Patricia Flynn. 1980. *Agribusiness in the Americas*. New York: Monthly Review Press.

Bustamante, Antonio. 1988. *Análisis de la política de precios: Granos básicos*. Documento de trabajo para discusión sectorial interna. Guatemala: FAO/USPADA, Unidad de Estudios Básicos.

Cáceres, Miguel. 1986. Tecnología y crisis alimentaria. Paper presented at VII Congreso Centroamericano de Sociología, 2–7 November. Tegucigalpa, Universidad Nacional de Honduras.

CADESCA-CEE. Programa de Seguridad Alimentaria del Istmo Centroamericano, Eje III: Comercialización de Granos Básicos. 1987. *Propuesta de síntesis de la primera fase (Recopilación de información)*. Guatemala City.

Cameron, Bruce P., and Christopher D. Ringwald. 1983. Aid to Guatemala: Violating human rights. In *International policy report*. Washington, D.C.: Center for International Policy.

Cardoza de Márquez, A. D. 1982. *Análisis de convenios de los programas de ayuda alimentaria en El Salvador*. San Salvador: SECONAN.

CARE. 1983. CARE International. Typescript.

————. 1985a. *CARE's use of food aid: Policy and guidelines*. Abridged February 1985 edition. New York.

————. 1985b. *CARE and the Food for Peace program: Thirty years of achievement*. New York.

CARE–Costa Rica. n.d. a. Costa Rica: Overview country strategy fact sheet. Typescript.

————. n.d. b. CARE managed low energy extrusion cooking (LEC) food processing plant. Typescript.

————. n.d. c. CARE International in Costa Rica. Typescript.

CARE–Guatemala. 1986. Urban FFW program: Project proposal for July 1986–January 1988. Guatemala City.

CARECEN. 1988. *The journey home*. Washington, D.C.

CARITAS Arquidiocesana. 1988. *Informe anual de labores 1987*. Guatemala City: Arzobispado de Guatemala.

Carmack, Robert, ed. 1988. *Harvest of violence*. Norman: University of Oklahoma Press.

Carrancho, Felix. 1987. Manual operacional para la elaboración de hojas de balance de alimentos. Paper presented at CADESCA-CEE Seminario Taller sobre Hojas de Balance de Alimentos, 27–31 July, Guatemala City.

Carrasco de Bermúdez, Odilia. 1986. Programa de seguridad alimentaria para Panamá. Bogotá: FAO/Colombia, Ministerio de Salud, ICBF. Paper presented at Segunda Mesa Redonda Internacional sobre SISVAN de América Latina y el Caribe, 1–5 December 1986, Bogotá.

Castillo de Arevalo, Yolanda C. 1987. Comportamiento de la producción de Centroamérica de los principales alimentos que componen la canasta básica. Paper presented at CADESCA-CEE Seminario Taller sobre Hojas de Balance de Alimentos, 27–31 July, Guatemala City.

Cathie, John. 1982. *The political economy of food aid*. Aldershot, Hampshire: Gower.

Catholic Relief Services. 1984. *CRS 1983 Annual Report*. New York: CRS.

CEDECO. 1986. La agricultura y la crisis en los ochenta. Documento interno de trabajo. San José, Costa Rica. Typescript.

CEDOH (Centro de Documentación para Honduras). n.d. *Los refugiados salvadoreños en Honduras*. Tegucigalpa.

CEIG (Centro de Estudios e Investigaciones para Guatemala). 1986. *Contrainsurgencia y desarrollo rural en Guatemala, 1965–1985*. Mexico City: CEIG.

CENAP/CEPAS/Justicia y Paz/Extension ESEUNA. 1988. *No hay paz sin alimentos: Los pequeños productores por el derecho de producir*. San José, Costa Rica.

Central America provisions in the FY 86–87 foreign aid authorizations bill in the mark-up of the House Subcommittee on Western Hemisphere Affairs. N.p. 19 March 1985. Typescript.

CEPAL (Comisión Económica para América Latina). 1981. *Naturaleza y alcance de la pobreza en Guatemala*. Mexico City: CEPAL.

———. 1983a. *La agroindustria y el sistema alimentario centroamericano*. L.24. Mexico City: CEPAL.

———. 1983b. *Satisfacción de las necesidades básicas de la población del istmo centroamericano*. L.32. Mexico City: CEPAL.

———. 1986. *Centroamérica: Crisis agrícola y perspectivas de un nuevo dinamismo*. L.27 Mexico City: CEPAL.

———. n.d. *Notas para el estudio económico de América Latina y el Caribe: 198–* Mexico City: CEPAL. Country overviews, various years.

CEPAL/FAO. División Agrícola Conjunta. 1986. Los sistemas alimentarios como contexto general para la vigilancia alimentaria y nutricional. FAO/ICBF. Presented at Segunda Mesa Redonda Internacional sobre SISVAN de América Latina y el Caribe, 1–5 December 1986, Bogota.

CEPAL/FAO/OIT/IICA/SIECA/OEA. 1973. *Tenencia de la tierra y desarrollo rural en Centroamérica*. San José, Costa Rica: Editorial Universitaria Centroamericana.

CEPAS (Centro de Estudios para la Acción Social). 1988a. La crisis agraria y la protesta campesina. *Costa Rica: Avance-Balance de la Situaciún*, July, 2–5.

———. 1988b. El carácter nacional de la lucha campesina. *Costa Rica: Balance de la Situación* 26(June–July): 12–16.

———. 1988c. Protesta campesina en la Costa Rica de los ochenta: Características, significado social y perspectivas futuras. By Rolando Rivera y Isabel Roman. Ponencia al VII Congreso Centroamericano de Sociología. Guatemala, 10–15 October.

———. 1988d. *UNSA: Por el derecho a producir*. Cuaderno de Estudio no.8 San José, Costa Rica.

———. 1989. El costo social de la agricultura de cambio. *Costa Rica: Balance de la Situación*, April–May, 6–11.

Chávez Avila, Henri Ernesto. 1986. Diagnóstico del polo de desarrollo Pueblo Nuevo Chacaj, Municipio de Nenton, Departamento de Huehuetenango. Huehuetenango, Guatemala: Instituto Nacional de Cooperativas, 1a Subregión. Typescript.

Christophe, Guy. 1987. La substituabilidad de cereales en la alimentación en el istmo

centroamericano (preliminar). Guatemala: CADESCA-CEE, Programa de Seguridad Alimentaria. Typescript.

———. 1988. Consideraciones sobre la demanda de granos básicos del istmo centroamericano. Guatemala: CADESCA-CEE, Programa de Seguridad Alimentaria.
Typescript.

Clark, John. 1986. *For richer, for poorer: An Oxfam report on Western connections with
world hunger*. Oxford: Oxfam.

Clay, E. J. 1986. Rural public works and food-for-work: A survey. *World Development*
14, 10–11(October–November): 1237–52.

Clay, E. J., and Hans Singer. 1982. *Food aid and development: The impact and effectiveness
of bilateral PL 480 Title I–type assistance*. AID Program Evaluation Discussion Paper
15. Washington, D.C.: USAID.

———. 1983. Food as aid: Food for thought. *IDS Bulletin* 14, 2(April) (special issue
devoted to food aid).

———. 1985. *Food aid and development: Issues and evidence (a survey of the literature since
1977 on the role and impact of food aid in developing countries)*. Occasional Papers 3.
Rome: World Food Programme.

Colom de Morán, Elisa. 1987. *Ordenamiento y análisis de la legislación en materia de
seguridad alimentaria-nutricional y previsión de cosechas: Informe final*. Guatemala:
CADESCA-CEE, Eje VI-Legislación, Programa Especial de Seguridad Alimentaria
para el Istmo Centroamericano, Comité Especial de la Seguridad Alimentaria-
Guatemala.

Committee on Government Operations. 1988. *Poor management is impeding the Food
for Peace program*. Washington, D.C.: 100th Congress, 2d session, House Report
100–537. (Fortieth Report, 29 March 1988, Union Calendar 334.)

Contracting Corporation of America. 1985. *Encuesta de base de la población desplazada*.
San Salvador: USAID.

Contrainsurgencia y régimen constitucional. 1985. *Temas de la Realidad Guatemalteca*
1, 1(October–December).

CORECA (Consejo Regional de Cooperación Agrícola de Centroamérica, México,
Panamá y la República Dominicana). 1987. *Resolución VII–08: Sobre los efectos de la
ayuda alimentaria*. VII Reunión Ordinaria. Guatemala: CORECA.

Corrales, Jorge. 1985. *Políticas de precios y de subsidios en Costa Rica*. Estudios 3. San
José, Costa Rica: Academia de Centroamérica.

Costa Rica. 1988. *Convenio entre el Gobierno de los Estados Unidos de América y el
Gobierno de Costa Rica para la venta de productos agrícolas*. San José, Costa Rica.
Typescript signed 3 March by the relevant officials of each government.

Costa Rica. Asamblea Legislativa. 1985. Ley no.7019 ... Convenio entre el Gobierno de los Estados Unidos de América y el Gobierno de Costa Rica para la venta de productos agrícolas. *La Gaceta: Diario Oficial* 57, 247(26 December).

———. 1987. Ley no. 7059 ... Convenio entre el Gobierno de los Estados Unidos de América y el Gobierno de Costa Rica para la venta de productos agrícolas. *La Gaceta: Diario Oficial* 59, 63(1 April).

Costa Rica. OCAF (Oficina de Control de Asignaciones Familiares). SIN (División Sistema de Información en Nutrición). 1985. *Estudio de caso sobre situación alimentaria y nutricional de Costa Rica, 1982: Informe final.* San José, Costa Rica: Ministerio de Salud.

Costa Rica. SEPAN/MIDEPLAN. 1986. Taller: Definición y establecimiento de estrategias nacionales para la integración de los PAG en el plan nacional de desarrollo, 23–24 October.

Cuny, Frederick C. 1983. *Disasters and development.* New York: Oxford University Press.

Curry Foundation. 1986. *United States agricultural exports and Third World development: The critical linkage.* Washington, D.C.

Danaher, Kevin, Phillip Berryman, and Medea Benjamin. 1987. *Help or hindrance? United States economic aid in Central America.* San Francisco: Institute for Food and Development Policy.

Danby, Colin. 1989. Aiding Central America: An alternative for equitable and sustainable development. Washington, D.C.: PACCA (Policy Alternatives for the Caribbean and Central America).

Davis, Bob, et al. 1986. *An analysis of the Guatemalan wheat and bread industry.* Report prepared for AID Guatemala under the Technical Support Mission Work Order 12 with Texas Tech. University.

Davis, Shelton, and J. Hodson. 1982. *Witness to political violence in Gutemala: The suppression of a rural development movement.* Boston: Oxfam America Impact Audit.

Deaton, B. J. 1980. Public Law 480: The critical choice. *American Journal of Agricultural Economics* 62.

De Janvry, Alain. 1981. *The agrarian question and reformism in Latin America.* Baltimore: Johns Hopkins University Press.

Dell, Sidney Lawrence. 1980. *The balance of payments adjustment process in developing countries.* Oxford: Pergamon Press.

Della Torre, Mirna Lievano, and Roger D. Norton. 1988. *Food imports, agricultural policies and agricultural development in El Salvador, 1960–1987.* Work performed under contract with AID. Washington, D.C.: Robert R. Nathan Associates.

Democratic Policy Committee. 1987. *Foreign aid to Central America,* FY 1981–1987. Special Report.

El desarrollo de los programas de alimentación a grupos y la ayuda alimentaria extranjera: Documento país-Nicaragua. n.d. Paper presented to the Seminario Subregional sobre Programas de Alimentación a Grupos en Centroamérica y Panamá.

Dethier, J., and K. Funk. 1987. The language of food: PL 480 in Egypt. *Middle East Report,* March–April.

De Walt, Billie R. 1985. The agrarian bases of conflict in Central America. In *The Central American crisis: Sources of conflict and the failure of U.S. policy,* ed. K. Coleman and G. Herring. Wilmington, Del.: Scholarly Resources.

Durham, William. 1979. *Scarcity and survival: Ecological origins of the Soccer War.* Stanford: Stanford University Press.

Economics Perspectives, Inc. 1986a. *Honduras: Basic grains policy options.* Report prepared on contract for USAID-Honduras.

———. 1986b. *Una evaluación del Instituto Hondureño de Mercadeo Agrícola (IHMA).* Report for USAID-Honduras.

Ek, Carl. 1987. *Cargo preference and agriculture: Background and current issues.* CRS Report for Congress 87–134 ENR. Washington, D.C.: Congressional Research Service.

El Salvador. Ministerio de Agricultura. DEA (Dirección General de Economía Agropecuaria). 1986a. Diagnóstico de la leche en El Salvador. San Salvador. Unpublished typescript.

———. 1986b. *Economía Agropecuaria* 6(July–December).

———. 1986c. *El cultivo del arroz en El Salvador,* by Margarita Grande Zuniga. San Salvador.

———. 1986d. *El cultivo del frijol en El Salvador.* San Salvador.

———. 1986e. *El cultivo del maíz en El Salvador,* by Margarita Grande Zuniga. San Salvador.

———. 1987. *Economía Agropecuaria* 7(January–June).

El Salvador. Ministerio del Interior. CONADES (Comisión Nacional de Asistencia a la Población Desplazada). 1982. ¿Qué es CONADES? Hoja Divulgativa 1. San Salvador.

———. 1987a. Proyecto 2806: Asistencia de rehabilitación a la población desplazada. San Salvador. Typescript.

———. 1987b. *Directorio de las instituciones internacionales, privadas y gubernamentales que prestan servicios a la población desplazada de El Salvador.* San Salvador.

―――. 1987c. Comunidades participando en el Proyecto 3075, por región. San Salvador. Typescript.

―――. 1987d. Informe sobre el desarrollo de las actividades de ejecución del proyecto PMA/ELS/3075E. San Salvador. Typescript.

―――. 1987e. Lista de proyectos del 2806, por comunidad. San Salvador. Typescript.

―――. 1987f. Solicitud de segunda expansión del proyecto PMA/ELS/3075E-Asistencia alimentaria a la población desplazada en El Salvador. San Salvador. Typescript dated September.

El Salvador. Ministerio del Interior. DIDECO (Dirección de Desarrollo de la Comunidad). 1987. Plan de acción para el proyecto GOES/AID 519 7615: "Ayuda alimentaria comunal de emergencia para comunidades marginales urbanas y rurales" April 1987–March 1988. San Salvador.

El Salvador. MIPLAN (Ministerio de Planificación), Asesoría Técnica. 1987. Lineamientos para una política de ayuda alimentaria. Documento de uso restringido.

El Salvador. MIPLAN/CONADES (Comité Nacional de Ayuda para Desplazados de El Salvador). 1987. *La población desplazada: Acción gubernamental, 1980–1987.* San Salvador.

El Salvador. MIPLAN. CONARA (Comisión Nacional de Restauración de Areas). 1987. Paid advertisements on its program achievements in *El Diario de Hoy*, 10 May, and *La Prensa Gráfica*, 13 July.

El Salvador. MIPLAN/Ministerio de Salud. 1987. *Política de ayuda alimentaria: Propuesta.* San Salvador.

El Salvador. MIPLAN. SECONAN (Secretaria Ejecutiva de la Comisión Nacional de Alimentaciún Nutrición). 1984a. *Diagnóstico alimentario nutricional de El Salvador: Resumen.* San Salvador.

―――. 1984b. *Estudio sobre el funcionamiento de los programas de ayuda alimentaria ejecutados por el gobierno de El Salvador.* Documento no. 6. 1984. San Salvador.

―――. 1985. *Plan de alimentación y nutrición, 1985–89, y estrategias a largo plazo.* Documento de trabajo no. 4, preliminar. San Salvador.

El Salvador. MIPLAN. SETEFE (Secretaria Técnica del Financiamiento Externo). 1987. Situación financiera del presupuesto extraordinario para reactivación económica al 30 de junio de 1987. San Salvador.

Epstein, Susan. 1984. *Primer on P.L. 480 program history, description and operations: A brief compilation of explanatory documents.* Report 84–803 ENR. Washington, D.C.: Congressional Research Service.

―――. 1985. *U.S. bilateral and multilateral food assistance programs.* Report 85–114 ENR. Washington, D.C.: Congressional Research Service.

————. 1987. *Food for Peace, 1954–1986: Major changes in legislation*, revised. CRS Report for Congress 87–409 ENR. Washington, D.C.: Congressional Research Service.

Falcon, Walter P. 1987. Aid, food policy reform, and U.S. agricultural interests in the Third World. *American Journal of Agricultural Economics* 69, 5(December): 929–35.

FAO. 1984a. *Agricultural price policies in Latin America and the Caribbean*. LARC/84/5. Paper presented at Eighteenth FAO Regional Conference for Latin America and the Caribbean, 6–15 August, Buenos Aires.

————. 1984b. *Land, food and people*. Based on the FAO/UNFPA/IIASA report: Potential population supporting capacities of lands in the developing world. Rome.

————. 1985. *World Food Report, 1985*. Rome.

————. 1987a. *1986 Production Yearbook*. Vol. 40. Rome.

————. 1987b. *Informe técnico: Capacitación rural en derivados lacteos*. Informe preparado por el consultor del FAO Enrique Canut, del Programa de Cooperación Técnica: Capacitación y asistencia técnica para el fortalecimiento de las empresas rurales en el sector reformado. TCP/ELS/6651: Informe Técnico. San Salvador.

————. n.d. *Food aid in figures/La ayuda alimentaria en cifras*. Rome. Various years.

FAO. CFS. 1982. *Informe del director general sobre la seguridad alimentaria mundial: Reconsideración de los conceptos y métodos*. CFS 83/4.

FAO. Commodities and Trade Division. 1983. *Assessing food aid requirements: A revised approach*. Economic and Social Development Paper 39. Rome: FAO.

FAO. Misiún de Alto Nivel. 1983. *Examen de las políticas y estrategias de desarrollo rural en Guatemala*. Borrador preliminar. Guatemala City.

FAO. Oficina Regional para América Latina y el Caribe. n.d. *Papel de la vigilancia alimentaria nutricional en la seguridad alimentaria*.

————. 1986. *Antecedentes sobre la situación alimentaria y agrícola en America Latina y el Caribe*. LARC 86/INF/4.

Feinberg, Richard E. 1982. The International Monetary Fund and basic needs: The impact of stand-by arrangements. In *Human rights and basic needs in the Americas*, Margaret E. Crahon. Washington, D.C.: Georgetown University Press.

Ferguson, Donald. 1988. Food security and private sector lending under sections 106 and 108 of PL 480. N.p.: USDA Office of International Cooperation and Development, Technical Assistance Division.

Fledderjohn, David C., and David C. Thompson. n.d. *Final report: Northern Transversal Strip land resettlement project (AID project no. 520–0233 Small Farmer Development)*.

Work performed under contract with AIDS. N.P.: ACDI (Agricultural Cooperative Development International).

Flores, Marina. 1986. Consideraciones generales sobre las hojas de balance de alimentos. Paper presented at CADESCA-CEE Seminario Taller sobre Hojas de Balance de Alimentos, 27–31 July 1987, Guatemala City.

FMLN/FDR (Farabundo Martí National Liberation Front/Democratic Revolutionary Front). 1985. *La situación de los derechos humanos en el conflicto armado salvadoreño (January–September 1985)*.

Franco, Marc. 1988. Food security and adjustment: The EC contribution. *Food Policy*, February, 90–97.

Gallardo, María Eugenia, and José Roberto Lúpez. 1986. *Centroamérica: La crisis en cifras*. San José, Costa Rica: Instituto Americano de Cooperación para la Agricultura/Facultad Latinoamericana de Ciencias Sociales.

García U., Magadalena, et al. 1987. *Agricultural development policies in Honduras: A consumptionist perspective*. Report prepared on contract for USDA/USAID.

Garst, Rachel. 1986a. *Background information for basic grain imports*. Report prepared on contract for Catholic Relief Services. Guatemala City.

———. 1986b. *Análisis de la situación económico y social de Guatemala*. Guatemala City: UNICEF.

Garzón, José M. 1984. Food aid as a tool of development: The experience of PL 480 Title III. *Food Policy*, August, 232–44.

George, Susan. 1977. *How the other half dies*. Montclair, N.J. Allenheld, Osmun.

———. 1979. *Feeding the few: Corporate control of food*. Washington, D.C.: Institute for Policy Studies.

———. 1984. *Ill fares the land: Essays on food, hunger, and power*. London: Writers and Readers Publishing Cooperative.

George, Susan, and Nigel Paige. 1982. *Food for beginners*. London: Writers and Readers Publishing Cooperative.

Gersony, Robert, Raymond Lynch, and William Garvelink. 1986. *The journey home: Durable solutions for displaced families*. El Salvador: U.S. AID and U.S. Department of State.

Gilmore, Judith W. 1988. Food aid in Latin America. In *The effectiveness of food aid . . . proceedings of a CRS workshop held on April 25, 1988*, ed. Charles E. Hanrahan. CRS Report for Congress 88–493 ENR. Washington, D.C.: Congressional Research Service.

Gilmore, Richard. 1982. *A poor harvest: The clash of policies and interests in the grain trade*. New York: Longman.

Gittinger, J. Price, Joanne Leslie, and Caroline Hoisington, eds. 1987. *Food policy: Integrating supply, distribution, and consumption*. Baltimore: Johns Hopkins University Press for the World Bank.

Glazer, Lawrence K. 1986. Provisions of the Food Security Act of 1985. Agriculture Information Bulletin 498. Washington, D.C.: USDA, Economic Research Service.

González Suárez, Enrique González Guevara, and Fabio González Guevara. n.d. Crisis alimentaria y participación popular en Nicaragua, 1979–1985. *Cuadernos de Investigación* (Managua, INIES), 1:13–21.

Granados, Carlos, and Liliana Quezada. 1984. Los intereses geopolíticos y el desarrollo de la zona norte nor-atlántica costarricense. Paper presented at SIAP, Primer Encuentro Centroamericano-Mexicano sobre Problemas, Perspectivas, y Planificación para el Desarrollo de las Regiones Fronterizas, November.

Guardia, Jorge. 1988. El mito de la autosuficiencia alimentaria. *La Nación*, 5 April.

Guatemala. Banco de Guatemala. 1983. Algunas tendencias de la producción de los alimentos básicos en Guatemala. *Informe Económico* 30(January–March): 43–81.

Guatemala. Congreso de la República. 1974. Decreto 40–74: Ley obligatoria y de fomento para el cultivo de granos básicos. *Diario Oficial*, May.

Guatemala. DGE (Dirección General de Estadística). 1977–81. *Hojas de balance de alimentos, serie 1976–80*. Guatemala City.

Guatemala. Estado Mayor General del Ejército. 1982. *Plan nacional de seguridad y desarrollo*. Guatemala City.

Guatemala. INDECA. n.d. *INDECA: Organo informativo de la institución*. Guatemala City: INDECA.

———. n.d. *Memoria de labores*. Guatemala City: INDECA. Various years, 1980, 1983–86.

———. 1985. *¿Qué es INDECA: Objetivos, organización y funcionamiento*. Guatemala City: Ministerio de Agricultura, Ganadería y Alimentación. INDECA.

Guatemala. INDECA. Dirección de Operaciones. 1988. *Informe de realizaciones institucionales año 1987*. Guatemala City.

Guatemala. INE (Instituto Nacional de Estadística). 1981–86. *Hojas de balance de alimentos, serie 1980–83, 1985*. Guatemala City.

Guatemala. Junta Militar de Gobierno. 1982. Objetivos nacionales actuales. Guatemala City.

Guatemala. Ministerio de Agricultura, Ganadería y Alimentación. Programa de Seguridad Alimentaria. 1988. *Análisis de perspectivas y discusión de alternativas de política encaminadas al desarrollo del sistema subsectorial maíz en Guatemala*. Guatemala City.

Guatemala. Ministerio de Defensa Nacional. 1984. *Polos de desarrollo*. Guatemala City: Editorial del Ejército.

———. 1985a. *Revista cultural del ejército: Edición especial dedicada a los polos de desarrollo*, January/February. Guatemala City: Ejército de Guatemala, Relaciones Públicas.

———. 1985b. *Revista cultural del ejército: Edición especial dedicada a la labor institucional del Comité de Reconstrucción Nacional*. Guatemala City: Ejército de Guatemala, Relaciones Públicas.

Guatemala. MDUR (Ministerio de Desarrollo Urbano y Rural). 1987. *Bases de una política nacional para el uso de la ayuda alimentaria*. Informe general y anexos del Seminario Nacional, 22–24 September 1987, Antigua and Guatemala City.

Guatemala. Ministerio de Educación. USIPE/INCAP. 1986. *Primer censo nacional de talla de escolares de primer grado de primaria de la República de Guatemala, 1986*. Guatemala City.

Guatemala. Ministerio de Salud Pública y Asistencia Social/INCAP. 1986. *Encuesta nacional simplificada de salud y nutrición materno-infantil*. Guatemala City: INCAP.

Guatemala. Presidencia de la República. 1987. *Programa de reorganización nacional*. Guatemala City.

Guatemala. SEGEPLAN (Secretaria General del Consejo Nacional de Planificación Económica). 1984. *Agricultura, población y empleo en Guatemala*. Proyecto GUA/79/PO3-OIT/FNUAP. Serie resultados no.5 Guatemala City.

Guatemala. SEGEPLAN. Departamento de Sectores Productivos. 1983. *Análisis del subsector alimentario con respeto al trigo y productos derivados de consumo final: Informe preliminar, 1a version*, by J. A. Carrera. Proyecto SEGEPLAN/USPADA-PNUD/FAO-GUA/81/001). Guatemala City: SEGEPLAN.

Guatemala. SEGEPLAN. Departamento de Sectores Productivos/MAG. Unidad Sectorial de Planificación Agrícola. 1985. *Antecedentes cuantitativos y análisis del subsector maíz-sorgo*. Proyecto de Fortalecimiento del Sistema de Planificación Agrícola y Formulación de Proyectos, GUA/81/001. Guatemala City.

Gulick, Lewis. 1987. *How U.S. food aid programs help American agricultural exports*. Study commissioned by AID. N.p.: Bureau for Food for Peace and Voluntary Assistance.

Hanrahan, Charles. 1988a. *The effectiveness of food aid: Implications of changes in farm, food aid and trade legislation*. Proceedings of a CRS workshop held on 25 April 1988. CRS Report for Congress 88–493 ENR. Washington, D.C.: Congressional Research Service.

———. 1988b. *Foreign food aid programs: Effectiveness issues.* Issue Brief IB88057. Washington, D.C.: Congressional Research Service.

———. 1989a. *Foreign food aid: Reauthorization issues.* CRS Issue Brief (updated 23 May, 1989; order code IB89097). Washington, D.C.: Congressional Research Service.

———. 1989b. Agriculture and food aid in Central America. CRS Memo, 3 February. Washington, D.C.: Congressional Research Service.

Hanrahan, Charles E., and Susan B. Epstein. 1987. *Foreign food aid: Current policy issues.* CRS Report for Congress 87–923 ENR. Washington, D.C.: Congressional Research Service.

Hanrahan, Michael S. 1983. *Some impacts associated with selected Honduran basic grains policies.* Prepared for the Food and Agricultural Development Office, USAID-Honduras.

Hatfield, Mark O., Jim Leach, and George Miller. 1987. *Bankrolling failure: United States policy in El Salvador and the urgent need for reform.* Report to the Arms Control and Foreign Policy Caucus. Washington, D.C.: U.S. Congress, Arms Control and Foreign Policy Caucus.

Helleiner, Gerald K. 1985. *Stabilization policies and the poor.* Toronto: University of Toronto, Department of Economics.

Henningson, Berton E., Jr. 1981. Agricultural exports and the farm economy: A full accounting needed. Statement before the U.S. House of Representatives, Committee on Agriculture, Subcommittee on Department Operations, Research and Foreign Agriculture, 8 July, 1981, Washington, D.C. (Reproduced in *News from National Farmers Organization.*)

Hernández E., Gonzalo Adolfo. 1987. Estadísticas básicas para la elaboración de hojas de balance de alimentos. Paper presented to CADESCA-CEE. Seminario Taller sobre Hojas de Balance de Alimentos, 27–31 July 1987, Guatemala City.

Hintermeister, Alberto. 1984. *Rural poverty and export farming in Guatemala.* World Employment Programme Research Working Paper, no.71. N.p.: International Labor Office.

———. 1985. Modernización agrícola y pobreza rural en Guatemala. *Polémica* 17–18:25–45.

Holt, J. F. J. 1983. Ethiopia: Food for Work or Food for Relief. *Food Policy,* August, 187–201.

Honduras. Congreso Nacional. 1987. Decreto no.68–87: Ley de la Dirección de Alimentación y Nutrición de la Secretaria de Estado en el Despacho de Salud Pública. *La Gaceta: Diario Oficial de Honduras* 61, 2(3 July 1987).

Honduras. CONSUPLANE (Secretaria Técnica del Consejo Superior de Planificación Económica)/PMA. 1985. *Análisis de los programas de ayuda alimentaria que funcionan en Honduras*. Tegucigalpa. (Reproduced in INCAP, PROPAG, *Programas de ayuda alimentarias: Experiencias en país*, Documentos Técnicos 2, Reproducciones.)

———. 1987. *Taller: Enfoque de la alimentación a grupos en el plan nacional de desarrollo*. Tegucigalpa, Honduras (workshop).

Honduras. Fuerzas Armadas de Honduras/COPEN. 1987. Informe final de actividades de COPEN: 1986. Tegucigalpa, Honduras.

Honduras. IHMA (Instituto Hondureño de Mercadeo Agrícola), DIAMER/Programa de Seguridad Alimentaria CADESCA-CEE. 1987. *Funcionamiento del sistema de comercialización pública y privada de granos básicos: Primera Fase: Eje III: Comercialización*. Tegucigalpa: IMHA.

Honduras. Ministerio de Agricultura. 1985. *Encuesta agrícola nacional, 1984*. Tegucigalpa.

Honduras. SAPLAN (Sistema de Análisis y Planificación de Alimentación y Nutrición). 1982. Proyecto de desarrollo de una estrategia alimentaria-nutricional para Honduras: Diagnóstico multisectorial. Tegucigalpa.

Honduras. Secretaria de Recursos Naturales/PMA. 1982. Proyecto de producción de alimentos básicos por grupos organizados de agricultores. SRN Hoja Divulgativa no.84. Tegucigalpa.

Hopkins, Raymond. 1984. The evolution of food aid: Towards a development first regime. *Food Monitor*, November, 345–62.

———. 1987. Aid for development: What motivates the donors? In *Poverty, development and food*, ed. Edward Clay and John Shaw, chap. 8. London: Macmillan.

Huddleston, Barbara. 1984. *Closing the cereals gap with trade and food aid*. Research Report 43. Washington, D.C.: International Food Policy Research Institute.

———. n.d. Confronting world hunger. *CARE Briefs on Development Issues* 3.

IDB (Interamerican Development Bank). N.d. *Economic and social progress in Latin America, 198–* . Yearly. Washington, D.C.

ILO (International Labour Office). 1949. *Protection of Wages Convention, No.95*. Geneva.

———. 1975. International labour standards and WFP projects: The distinction between wage-labour schemes and self-help projects. Item 1c; note by the ILO presented by K. T. Samson. Third ILO/WFP Intersecretariat Meeting, 7–8 May 1975, Geneva.

INCAP (Instituto de Nutrición de Centroamérica y Panamá)/ALAN. 1978. *Conocimientos actuales en nutrición*. Guatemala City.

INCAP/Guatemala. SEGEPLAN. 1980. Regionalización de problemas nutricionales en Guatemala. Guatemala City.

INCAP. PROPAG (Proyecto de Apoyo Técnico a Programas de Alimentación de Grupos). 1985. Análisis de los programas de alimentación a grupos (PAG) para personas desplazadas, refugiadas y en situaciones de emergencia: Informe final.

———. 1986. *Programas de alimentación a grupos: Su integración a programas y estrategias de desarrollo en Centroamérica y Panamá.* Memorias del Seminario Subregional, 21–25 June, Antigua, Guatemala. Guatemala City: INCAP.

———. n.d. *Boletín del INCAP para la Difusión de Información y Temas del Proyecto de Apoyo Técnico a Programas de Alimentación a Grupos.* Guatemala City: INCAP. (Quarterly, since January–April 1987.)

Inforpress Centroamericana. 1986. Informe especial: Los desplazados salvadoreños. *Inforpress* 692 (5 June).

———. 1987a. *Centroamérica 1987.* Guatemala City.

———. 1987b. La ayuda alimentaria a Guatemala. *Informe Especial* 744 (25 June).

Inter-Hemispheric Education Resource Center. 1988a. *Directory and analysis: Private organizations with U.S. connections—El Salvador.* Albuquerque.

———. 1988b. *Directory and analysis: Private organizations with U.S. connections—Guatemala.* Albuquerque.

———. 1988c. *Directory and analysis: Private organizations with U.S. connections—Honduras.* Albuquerque.

International Trade and Development Education Foundation. 1985. *The United States Food for Peace program, 1954–1984: A compilation of informational materials on United States Public Law 480.* Arlington, Va.: International Trade and Development Foundation.

Isralow, Sharon. 1983. Beyond better nutrition: A closeup of potential multiplier effects of food aid in Costa Rica. *Horizons*, October, 22–27.

Jackson, Tony (with Deborah Eade). 1982. *Against the grain.* Oxford: Oxfam.

Klare, Michael T. 1986. Low Intensity Conflict: The new U.S. strategic doctrine. *Nation*, 28 December 1985–4 January 1986.

———. n.d. Doctrina de la contrainsurgencia. Proyecto Lázaro Cardenas sobre la Condición Estratégica del Petroleo en el Hemisferio Occidental. Mexico City: CONACYT/UNAM/PEMEX.

Knowles, L. L. 1984. *A guide to world hunger organizations.* Georgia: Seeds/ Alternatives.

Krueger, Chris. 1987. The Guatemalan highlands: Democratic transition or the continuation of war? Washington, D.C.: Washington Office on Latin America.

Krueger, Chris, and Kjell Enge. 1985. *Security and development conditions in the Guatemalan highlands.* Washington, D.C.: Washington Office on Latin America.

Lardizabal Guilbert, Fernando. 1986. Política agrícola o política agraria: Mitos y realidades de la política agropecuaria hondureña. In *Honduras: Realidad nacional y crisis regional,* 289–303. Tegucigalpa: CEDOH.

Larson, Donald W. *Feasibility of handling larger size shipments of Public Law 480 bulk wheat in Honduras.* Prepared under contract no. PDC-1406-1-26-1142-00 for USAID Honduras. Minneapolis: Experience Incorporated.

Latham, Michael C. 1984. Strategies for the control of malnutrition and the influence of the nutritional sciences. In *Food policy: Integrating supply, distribution, and consumption,* ed. J. Price Gittinger, Joanne Leslie, and Caroline Hoisington, 332–33. Baltimore: Johns Hopkins University Press for the World Bank.

Leach, Jim, G. Miller, and M. Hatfield. 1985. *U.S. aid to El Salvador: An evaluation of the past, a proposal for the future.* Report to the Arms Control and Foreign Policy Caucus. Washington, D.C.

League of Rural Voters. 1985. U.S. farm policy and world hunger: The deadly connection. Minneapolis.

Leogrande, William M. 1987. Central America: Counterinsurgency revisited. NACLA *Report on the Americas* 20, 3 (January–February): 3–5.

Leonard, Jeffrey. 1987. *Natural resources and economic development in Central America.* Washington, D.C.: Conservation Fund.

Levinger, Beryl. 1986. *School feeding programs in developing countries: An analysis of actual and potential impact.* AID Evaluation Special Study 30. Washington, D.C.: USAID. (Views are author's, not agency's.)

López Grande, Carlos Mauricio, and Ana Daysi Cardoza de Márquez. 1984. *Estudio sobre el funcionamiento de los programas de ayuda alimentaria ejecutados por el gobierno de El Salvador.* San Salvador: SECONAN/MIPLAN.

McPherson, M. Peter. 1983. Stalking hunger. *Horizons* 2, 9:16–19.

Manarolla, Jerre. 1988. Preliminary estimates of the costs associated with food aid. AID/PPM/PAD Memorandum, 11 October.

Manz, Beatriz. 1986. *Guatemala: Community change, displacement and repatriation.* Cambridge: Center for International Affairs.

———. 1988. *Refugees of a hidden war: The aftermath of counterinsurgency in Guatemala.* New York: State University of New York Press.

Martin, Terence M. 1986. Some thoughts on monetization. Draft. New York: Catholic Relief Services.

Martínez Echeverría, Alberto. 1987. *Costa Rica: Política y regulación de los precios de los granos básicos*. Informe de Misión, 3a etapa, versión preliminar. San José, Costa Rica: CADESCA-CEE. Programa de Seguridad Alimentaria del Istmo Centroamericano.

Maxwell, Simon J., and H. W. Singer. 1979. Food aid to developing countries: A survey. *World Development* 7:225–47.

Mellor, John W. 1988. Food policy, food aid and structural adjustment programmes. *Food Policy*, February, 10–17.

Merino M., José Gerardo. 1987. Utilización de harinas compuestas en Centroamérica y Panamá. *Boletín de Ciencas Naturales y Agrarias* 2, 1(March): 29–36.

Miles, Sarah. 1986. The real war: Low intensity conflict in Central America. *NACLA Report on the Americas* 20, 2(April–May): 17–48.

Montes, Segundo. 1984. La situación de los salvadoreños desplazados y refugiados. *Revista de Estudios Centroamericanos (ECA)*, December.

Moore, Emily C., and Jim Fitzpatrick. 1988. *Project food aid: A classification of its uses as a development resource*. New York: CARE.

Moore Lappe, Frances, and Joseph Collins. 1979. *Food first: Beyond the myth of scarcity*. Rev. and updated. New York: Ballatine Books.

Morgan, Dan. 1979. *Merchants of grain*. London: Weidenfeld and Nicolson.

Morrell, James. 1977. The big stick: The use and abuse of food aid. *Food Monitor*, December, 8–10.

Murga, E. Victor M. 1986. El INDECA y las relaciones jurídicas sobre la comercialización de granos básicos. *INDECA: Organo Informativo* 1, 1(September): 3–5.

Naciones Unidas. 1983. *Derechos humanos: Recopilación de instrumentos internacionales*. ST/HR/Rev. 2. New York.

Nairn, Allen. 1986. Low intensity conflict: One hit, two misses. *NACLA Report on the Americas* 20, 3 (June): 4–11.

Naylor, George, ed. 1983. *The United Farmer and Rancher Congress*. Congress held 11–13 September in St. Louis, Missouri. Ames, Iowa: North American Farm Alliance.

Newfarmer, Richard S. 1986. The economics of strife. In *Confronting revolution: Security through diplomacy in Central America*, ed. Morris Blachman et al. New York: Pantheon Books.

North American Farm Alliance. 1985. Peace and agriculture. Ames, Iowa. Collection of photocopied documents.

Norton, Roger D., and Carlos A. Benito. 1987. *An evaluation of the PL 480 Title I*

Program in Honduras. Report prepared for the AID mission to Honduras. N.p.: Winrock International.

OIT (Organización Internacional de Trabajo). PREALC (Programa Regional de Empleo para América Latina y el Caribe). 1983. *Producción de alimentos básicos y empleo en el istmo centroamericano*. Santiago: OIT.

———. 1985. *Guatemala: Pobreza rural y crédito agrícola al campesinado*. Santiago: OIT.

OIT. Programa Mundial de Empleo. 1981. *Pautas para la organización de programas especiales de obras públicas*. Geneva: OIT.

Olivares, José. 1986. Programa alimentario nicaragüense. FAO/ICBF. Paper presented at Segunda Mesa Redonda Internacional sobre SISVAN de América Latina y el Caribe, 1–5 December 1986, Bogotá.

Oxfam. 1985. *The field directors' handbook: An Oxfam manual for development workers*, ed. Brian Pratt and Jo Boyden. Oxford: Oxfam.

Oxfam America. 1985. The appropriateness of PL 480 as a development tool. Testimony prepared for the United States Senate Committee on Agriculture, Nutrition, and Forestry, 4 April 1985.

———. 1986. Third World debt: Payable in hunger. *Facts for Action* 16.

Oxfam Health Unit. 1984. *Oxfam's practical guide to selective feeding programmes*. Rev. ed. Oxford: Oxfam.

Paarlberg, Robert L. 1986. *United States agriculture and the developing world: Partners or competitors?* Final report of United States Agriculture and Third World Development: The Critical Linkage. Washington, D.C.: Curry Foundation.

———. 1988. U.S. agriculture and the developing world: Opportunities for joint gains. In *Growth, exports, and jobs in a changing world economy: Agenda 1988*, ed. J. W. Sewell and S. K. Tucker. Overseas Development Council, U.S. Third World Policy Perspectives 9. New Brunswick, N.J.: Transaction Books.

PAVA (Programa de Ayuda para los Vecinos del Altiplano). 1984. Final Report: 1. Guatemalan displaced persons needs summary covering Huehuetenango, Quiché, Western Petén, Playa Grande. 2. Proposed relief operation. USAID Project DR-520–84–04. Guatemala City.

Payne, Philip. 1983. Maximizing nutritional impact of feeding programmes. *Food Policy*, August, 249–51.

Pines, James M., Joyce King, and Janet Lowenthal. 1988. *Evaluation of Guatemalan PL 480 programs*. Prepared for AID under IOC Contract PDC-0262-1-00-7150. N.p.: John Snow.

Polos de desarrollo. 1986. Guatemala City: [signed by J. A. de P. T. and G. V. de M.]. Typescript.

Price Ledogar, Eleanor, and John W. Townsend. 1984. Supplementary feeding programs for school age children: Evaluation of a Guatemalan program for sponsored children. Unpublished manuscript.

Programa de Seguridad Alimentaria del Istmo Centroamericano CADESCA-CEE, Eje III Comercialización. 1987a. *Comercialización de granos básicos (primera fase)*. San José, Costa Rica.

———. 1987b. *Propuesta de síntesis de la primera fase (recopilación de información)*.

Programa Mundial de Alimentos. 1986. *Conclusiones y recomendaciones de la misión de evaluación y apreciación del proyecto Nicaragua 2536: Asistencia a grupos vulnerables y a niños pre-escolares*. Rome.

———. 1987. *Ayuda alimentaria: Políticas y programas*. Rome.

Programa Mundial de Alimentos. Committee on Food Aid Policies and Programmes. 1985. *Examen de algunas experiencias nacionales con programas y políticas de ayuda alimentaria: La experiencia de Honduras*. Nineteenth Period of Sessions, 20–31 May 1985, Theme 7. Rome.

———. 1986. *Informe resumido de evaluación provisional sobre el proyecto Honduras 2523: Alimentación a grupos vulnerables y promoción de actividades de desarrollo a nivel familiar*. Twenty-second Period of Sessions, 20–31 October 1986, Theme 11. Rome.

Programa Mundial de Alimentos–El Salvador. 1986. *Análisis de la problemática y costos actuales del sistema logístico de los proyectos de apoyo alimentario en El Salvador y alternativas de solución*. Vol. 1. *Documento básico*. Elaborado bajo la responsabilidad de Otto Eric Vidaurre Maldonando y José Arnulfo Sandoval. San Salvador.

Programa Mundial de Alimentos/Gobierno de Guatemala. 1982a. Plan de operaciones . . . para "Producción de alimentos básicos por pequeños agricultores," Proyecto no. 2587. Guatemala.

———. 1982b. Plan de operaciones: Capacitación femenina para el desarrollo comunal (CAFEDESCO). Guatemala.

Programa Mundial de Alimentos–Honduras. n.d. Resumen de las actividades del Programa Mundial de Alimentos en Honduras.

Proyecto de Cooperación Regional en Materia de Seguridad Alimentaria CADESCA-CEE. Eje de Trabajo 1. 1987. *Lineamientos metodológicos de una estrategia de seguridad alimentaria*. LC/MEX/L.49. Mexico City: CEPAL.

Ray, Daryll E., and James S. Plaxico. 1988. *The economic structure of agriculture:*

Rhetoric vs. reality. Study jointly commissioned by the National Farmers Organization and the National Farmers Union. Washington, D.C.

Refugees and food aid. 1986. *Refugees* 28 (April).

Repopulation 1986–1988: Vying for control of the journey home. 1988. *Central America Bulletin*, December, 4–8.

Report of the National Bipartisan Commission on Central America. 1984. 0–430–367. Washington D.C.: GPO.

Reutlinger, Schlomo. 1983. A fresh look at PL 480 Title II. *Food Policy*, August, 246–49.

Robert R. Nathan Associates, Inc. 1984. *An inventory of policies affecting agriculture in El Salvador: Main report.* Vol. 1. Selected policy issues and alternatives. Prepared under contract DAN-4048-C-00-3087-00 for Rural Development Office, USAID-El Salvador. San Salvador.

Rodríguez C., Lidia. 1986. Avances del SISVAN en Costa Rica. FAO/Colombia, ICBF. Paper presented at Segunda Mesa Redonda Internacional sobre SISVAN de América Latina y el Caribe, 1–5 December 1986, Bogotá.

Roemer, Michael. 1988. The macroeconomics of counterpart funds. Development Discussion Paper 262. Cambridge: Harvard Institute for International Development.

Rogers, Beatrice Lorge, and Mitchel B. Wallerstein. 1985. *PL 480 Title I: A discussion of impact evaluation results and recommendations.* AID Program Evaluation Report 13. Washington, D.C.: AID. (Views are authors' not agency's.)

Roque Castro, Francisco. 1986. Ayuda alimentaria en El Salvador: Importaciones y manejo. San Salvador: PMA.

Ruiz Granadino. 1986. Crecimiento de la producción agropecuaria y cambios en la estructura social rural. Proyecto: Crisis y Alternativas Centroamérica. Documento de Trabajo. San José, Costa Rica: ICADIS.

Sandoval V., Leopoldo. 1986. El problema de la estructura agraria de Guatemala en la conyuntura de un nuevo régimen constitucional en 1986. Guatemala City: ASIES.

Sanford, Jonathon. 1989. *Central America: Major trends in U.S. foreign assistance, fiscal 1978 to fiscal 1990.* CRS Report for Congress 89–374 F. Washington, D.C.: Congressional Research Service.

Schneider, Hartmut. 1978. *Food aid for development.* Paris: OECD, Development Center.

Seligson, Mitchell A. 1986. La economía política del desarrollo agrario de Honduras, In *Honduras: Realidad nacional y crisis regional*, 313–24. Tegucigalpa: CEDOH.

Sen, Biswajit. 1987. NGO self evaluation: Issues of concern. *World Development* 15 (supplement):161–67.

Shaw, John, and Hans Singer. 1988. Food policy, food aid, and economic adjustment. *Food Policy*, February, 2–97.

Shepard, Lucy. 1986. El Salvador: The national plan. U.S. Government Memorandum 10 39/86. San Salvador: USAID.

Sheperd, Philip. 1987. *The Honduras crisis and U.S. economic assistance.* Boulder, Colo.: Westview Press.

SIECA (Secretaria Permanente del Tratado General de Integración Econúmica Centroamericana). 1987a. *Centroamérica: Comercio intra y extraregional de granos básicos—maíz, frijol, arroz y sorgo—período 1975–85.* Guatemala City: SIECA, DAG.

———. 1987b. *Centroamérica: Consumo aparente per capita anual de los granos básicos (maíz, frijol, arroz y sorgo) durante el período 1975–1985.* Guatemala City: SIECA, DAG.

———. 1987c. *Centroamérica: Producción de granos básicos—maíz, frijol, arroz y sorgo— durante el período 1975/76–1986/87.* Guatemala City: SIECA, DAG.

———. 1987d. *Centroamérica: Resumen del volumen y del valor del comercio intraregional y con terceros países de granos básicos durante el período 1975–1985.* Guatemala City: SIECA, DAG.

SIECA. CCMEP (Comisión Coordinadora de Mercadeo y Estabilización de Precios de Centroamérica). 1985. Protocolo especial sobre granos (Protócolo de Limón). Guatemala City: DAG/SIECA/CCMEP.

———. 1987a. *Acta número treinta y siete.* Trigésima Reunión Ordinaria, 9–10 April 1987, San José, Costa Rica.

———. 1987b. *Resoluciones de la comisión coordinadora de mercadeo y estabilización de precios de centroamérica (CCMEP).* Guatemala City: SIECA, DAG.

Simon, Jean Marie. 1988. *Eternal spring: Eternal tyranny.* New York: Norton.

Singer, Hans, John Wood, and Tony Jennings. 1987. *Food aid: The challenge and the opportunity.* Oxford: Claredon Press.

Smith, Gayle. 1987. Ethiopia and the politics of famine. *Middle East Report*, March–April, 31–37.

———. 1988. Rethinking humanitarian aid. *Food Monitor*, Spring/Summer, 20–21.

Spiro, Howard M. 1977. *Clinical gastroenterology.* 2d ed. New York: Macmillan.

Stalker, Peter. 1979. Food confusion. *New Internationalist*, December, 22–24.

Stevens, Christopher. 1979. *Food aid and the developing world.* London: Overseas Development Institute.

Stoll, David. 1990. *Is Latin America turning protestant?* Stanford: University of California Press. Forthcoming.

Sukin, Hope. 1988. U.S. food aid for countries implementing structural adjustment. *Food Policy*, February, 98–103.

Tarrant, J. R. 1980. *Food policies*. Chichester: John Wiley.

Thiesenhusen, William C. 1989. The economic contributions of peasants are underestimated. *Choices*, (second quarter), 30–32.

Thomas, John W. 1986. Food for work: An analysis of current experience and recommendations for future performance. Development Discussion Paper 213. Cambridge: Harvard Institute for International Development.

UCADEGUA/UPAGRA/FEDAGRO. n.d. *El plan del maíz*. San José, Costa Rica: Centro Nacional de Acción Pastoral.

United Nations High Commissioner for Refugees. 1987a. *Overview of UNHCR activities: Report for 1986–87*. Submitted by the High Commissioner to the thirty-eighth session of the UN General Assembly, A/AC.96/696. New York: United Nations.

———. 1987b. *UNHCR activities financed by voluntary funds: Report for 1986–87 and proposed programmes and budget for 1988*. New York: United Nations.

Universidad Nacional de Costa Rica. 1987a. La problemática del sector agropecuario: No solo el diálogo es permanente. *Situación Económica de Costa Rica*, November 1986–January 1987.

———. 1987b. Crisis sectoriales o crisis generalizada en el sector agropecuario? *Situación económica de Costa Rica*, May–June.

USAID (U.S. Agency for International Development). 1966. *The war on hunger: Guidelines for planning and programming AID assistance in agriculture and related sectors*. Washington, D.C.

———. 1978. *Agricultural development policy paper*. Washington, D.C.

———. 1983a. *AID handbook 9*. Washington, D.C. (Looseleaf notebook updated periodically with inserts.)

———. 1983b. *Guatemala project paper: Small farmer development (amendment)*. DLC/P-2137/1. Washington, D.C.

———. 1983c. *Land and labor in Guatemala: An assessment*. Washington, D.C.

———. 1983d. *Northern Zone Infrastructure Development Project paper*. 515–0191. San José, Costa Rica.

———. 1983e. *Programming PL 480 local currency generations*. Policy Determination 5. Washington, D.C.

———. 1983f. *Regional strategic plan*. Washington, D.C.

———. 1983–88. *Congressional presentation, fiscal year 198-*. Various years.

————. 1984. Country development strategy statement, FY 1986: Guatemala. Washington, D.C.

————. 1984. *Front lines*. Washington, D.C.: USAID.

————. 1985. La cooperación internacional de AID.

————. 1986a. *Annual budget submission, FY 1988: El Salvador*. Washington, D.C.

————. 1986b. LAC [Latin American and Caribbean] policy in support of military civic action in El Salvador. Washington, D.C.

————. 1987. Third World growth helps U.S. farmers. *USAID Highlights* 4, 2(Spring).

USAID. Bureau for Food for Peace and Private Voluntary Assistance. 1988a. *Monetization field manual: Title II and Section 416(b) programs*. Washington, D.C.

————. 1988b. *Voluntary foreign aid programs, 1985–1987*. Washington, D.C.

USAID. Bureau for Food for Peace and Voluntary Foreign Assistance. Office of Food for Peace. 1988. *Commodities reference guide*. Revised by the Pragma Corporation. Washington, D.C.

USAID. Bureau for Latin America and the Caribbean. 1984. *Displaced persons in El Salvador: An assessment*. Washington, D.C.: USAID.

USAID. Bureau for Private Enterprise. Office of Food for Peace. 1988. PL 480, Title I, Section 108 Workshop. Washington, D.C.: USAID.

USAID–Costa Rica. 1986. Action plan/Annual budget submission. San José, Costa Rica: USAID.

————. 1987. Program strategy summary. (handout)

USAID. ECONOMIC RESEARCH SERVICE. 1984. *FATUS: Foreign agricultural trade of the United States, January/February 1984*. Washington, D.C.: GPO.

————. 1986–89. *World food needs and availabilities, 198–* . Various years. Washington, D.C.

USAID–El Salvador. 1986a. *Amendment no.1 to the Memorandum of Understanding on the FY 1985 PL 480 Title I local currency program*. San Salvador, El Salvador: USAID El Salvador.

————. 1986b. National Plan briefing paper. Memorandum 39/86. San Salvador: AID Information Office.

————. 1986c. *Report to the Congress on progress in carrying out the provisions of agreements with the Government of El Salvador governing the use of local currency receipts generated under FY 1985 ESF and PL 480 assistance*. San Salvador, El Salvador: USAID El Salvador.

————. 1986, 1987. El Salvador Title I and Title II PL 480 food programs. Briefing papers. San Salvador.

———. 1987a. El Salvador: Agricultural recovery. Briefing paper.

———. 1987b. *Memorandum de entendimiento sobre el programa de moneda local de la Sección 416, del año fiscal 1987/Memorandum of understanding on the fiscal year 1987 Section 416 local currency program.* San Salvador.

———. 1987c. *Memorandum de entendimiento sobre el programa de moneda local de PL 480, Título I, del año fiscal 1987/Memorandum of understanding on the FY 1987 PL 480 Title I local currency program.* San Salvador.

———. 1988. El Salvador: Agrarian reform program.

USAID–Guatemala. 1984a. *Food production plan to participate in the Caribbean Basin Economic Recovery Program.* Guatemala City.

———. 1984b. *Evaluation of the Ixcan colonization project (520-T-026) Guatemala.* Office of Rural Development Report 9. Guatemala City.

———. 1986a. *Agricultural sector policy analysis.* Draft version. Guatemala City.

———. 1986b. *Briefing book.* Guatemala City.

———. 1986c. *FY 1987/88 action plan.* Guatemala City.

USAID–Honduras. 1984. *Project evaluation summary: PL 480 Title II Food for Peace.* Tegucigalpa.

———. 1987. Overview of the PL 480 Title I and Title III local currency allocations. Tegucigalpa. (Informational handout.)

AID. Latin America Bureau. 1983. *Regional strategic plan for Latin America and the Caribbean.* Washington D.C.

USAID. Office of Planning and Budgeting. 1989. U.S. overseas loans and grants, obligations and loan authorizations, July 1, 1945–September 30, 1987. Washington, D.C.: USAID.

USAID. PVA/PPE. 1985. *PL 480 Title II evaluations, 1980–1985: The lessons of experience.*

USAID. Regional Inspector General for Audit. 1984. *Monitoring dollar and local currency resources under Economic Recovery and PL 480 Title I and III programs in Honduras.* Memorandum Survey Report 1-522-85-1. Tegucigalpa.

———. 1985a. *Audit of private sector support program and PL 480 local currency generations USAID–El Salvador.* Audit Report 1-519-85-13. Tegucigalpa.

———. 1985b. *USAID–Costa Rica's monitoring of and controls over dollar and local currency resources under Economic Recovery and PL 480 Title I programs.* Memorandum Survey Report 1-515-85-8. Tegucigalpa.

———. 1986a. *Audit of idle United States donated dairy commodities observed in Panama.* Audit Report 1-525-86-29. Tegucigalpa.

———. 1986b. *Non-federal financial and compliance audit of Public Law 480, Title I funds in Costa Rica.* Audit Report 1-515-86-01-N. Tegucigalpa.

USAID ROCAP (Regional Office for Central America and Panama). 1985. *Technical support for food assistance programs.* ROCAP Project Paper AID/LAC/P-225. Washington, D.C.

U.S. Army. 1985. U.S. Army operational concept for low-intensity conflict. TRADOC Pam 525-44.

U.S. Comptroller General. 1975. Impact of food aid in agricultural production. In *Disincentives to agricultural production in developing countries*, chap. 9. Washington, D.C.: GPO.

U.S. Congress. 1979. *Agricultural Trade Development and Assistance Act of 1954, as amended: Public Law 480—83rd Congress.* Washington, D.C.: GPO.

U.S. Congress. House. Committee on Appropriations. Subcommittee on Agriculture, Rural Development, and Related Agencies. 1984. *Agriculture, rural development, and related agencies appropriations for 1985.* 32–939. Washington, D.C.: GPO.

U.S. Congress. House. Committee on Appropriations. Subcommittee on Foreign Operations and Related Agencies. 1987. *Hearings on foreign assistance and related appropriations for 1988.* Part 3. Washington, D.C.: GPO.

U.S. Congress. House. Committee on Foreign Affairs. 1983. *Hearings on the world food situation.* Washington, D.C.: GPO.

U.S. Congress. Committee on Foreign Affairs. Subcommittee on Western Hemisphere Affairs. 1988. *The implementation of the humanitarian assistance package for Central America.* Hearing held 2 June 1988. Washington, D.C.: GPO.

U.S. Congress. House. Committee on Government Operations. 1988. *Poor management is impeding the Food for Peace program.* 100th Congress, 2d session, House Report 100–537. Washington, D.C.: GPO.

U.S. Congress. House. Select Committee on Hunger. 1985a. *A review of selected studies on world hunger.* Staff Report. Washington, D.C.: GPO.

———. 1985b. *Food aid and the role of the private voluntary organizations.* Hearing before the House Select Committee on Hunger, 18 April 1985. Washington, D.C.: GPO.

———. 1985c. *Special report on applying United States food surpluses to the problems of hunger.* Washington, D.C.: GPO.

———. 1987. *Enhancing the developmental impact of food aid.* Hearing before the International Task Force of the House Select Committee on Hunger, 18 June 1987. Washington, D.C.: GPO.

U.S. Congress. Senate. Democratic Policy Committee. 1987. *Foreign aid to Central America, FY 1981–1987.* Washington, D.C.

U.S. Congressional Research Service. Foreign Affairs and National Defense Division.

1986. *Trends in foreign aid, 1977–1986.* Study prepared for the House Select Committee on Hunger. Washington, D.C.: GPO.

———. 1989. *El Salvador, 1979–1989: A briefing book on U.S. aid and the situation in El Salvador.* CRS Report for Congress 89–369F. Washington, D.C.: Congressional Research Service.

U.S. Congressional Research Service. Office of Research Coordination. 1989. Background information on CONARA and U.S. food assistance in El Salvador. (Brief summary compiled by Mark Hopkins, intern.)

USDA. 1982. *Farmline.* Washington, D.C.: USDA.

USDA. ASCS. 1982. Commodity Credit Corporation. ASCS Background Information 2. Kansas City, Mo.

———. 1985. Explanation of PL 480 Title II operations, procurement and shipment. Kansas City, Mo.

USDA. FAS (Foreign Agricultural Service).

———. 1980–86. *Food for Peace, 198– annual report on Public Law 480.* Washington, D.C.

———. 1981. Public Law 480 sales program: Brief explanation of Titles I and II. Washington, D.C.

———. 1984a. CCC Export Credit Guarantee Program GSM-102: To expand United States agricultural exports. Washington, D.C. (Pamphlet.)

———. 1984b. *PL 480 concessional sales and food for development programs: Terms and conditions, planning and implementation procedures.* USDA, FAS. Foreign Agricultural Economic Report no.212; supersedes 1977 Report 142. Washington, D.C.

———. 1984–85. Title I, Public Law 480 agreement with the government of Costa Rica: Summary. (Various agreements and amendments, dated 19 November 1984 and 29 November 1985.)

———. 1984–86a. Title I, Public Law 480 agreement with the government of El Salvador: Summary. (Agreements dated 1 November 1984, 29 January 1985, 20 December 1985, 8 August 1985, and 27 June 1986).

———. 1984–86b. Title I/III, Public Law 480 agreements with the government of Honduras: Summary. (Agreements dated 24 February 1984, 26 July 1984, 21 June 1985, 15 March 1986).

———. 1985–86. Title I, Public Law 480 agreement with the government of Guatemala: Summary. (Agreements dated 9 August 1985, 6 June 1985, 2 July 1986).

———. 1987. Section 416 of the Agricultural Act of 1949, as amended. (Fact sheet.)

USDA. FAS. Agricultural Attache–Costa Rica. 1987. Costa Rica grain and feed annual: Report to USDA, FAS. (Not official USDA data.)

———. 1989. Costa Rica agricultural situation annual, 1988. Attaché report CS9007. San José, Costa Rica. (Not official USDA data.)

USDA. FAS. Agricultural Attache–Guatemala. 1987. Honduras agricultural situation. Report to USDA, FAS. Guatemala City. (Not official USDA data.)

———. 1988a. Attaché report, Guatemala—8005. Guatemala City. (Not official USDA data.)

———. 1988b. Attaché report, Honduras—8004. Guatemala City. (Not official USDA data.)

———. 1988c. Attaché report, El Salvador—8003. Guatemala City. (Not official USDA data.)

———. 1989a. Guatemala—Agricultural situation. Attaché report GT-9002 (1 March 1989). Guatemala City. (Not official USDA data.)

———. 1989b. El Salvador—agricultural situation. Attaché report ES-9002 (31 March 1989). Guatemala City. (Not official USDA data.)

———. 1989c. Honduras-agricultural situation. Attaché report HO-9002 (31 March 1989). Guatemala City. (Not official USDA data.)

U.S. Department of State. AID/OMB (Office of Management and the Budget). 1987. A plan for fully funding the recommendations of the National Bipartisan Commission on Central America. Special Report 162. Washington, D.C.

U.S. Department of State. Costa Rican Embassy. 1987. SPR 004: Economic trends report, Costa Rica. Department of State Airgram, 22 October 1987.

U.S. Department of State. Guatemalan Embassy. 1988. SPR 004: Economic trends report, Guatemala. Department of State Airgram, 10 August 1988.

U.S. Department of State. Salvadoran Embassy. 1988. SPR 004: Economic trends report for El Salvador. Department of State Airgram, 8 November 1988.

U.S. Embassy–El Salvador. 1985, 1987. *Agreement between the government of the United States and the government of El Salvador for the sale of agricultural commodities/Convenio entre el gobierno de los EEUU y el gobierno de El Salvador para la venta de productos agrícolas* (20 December 1987 and 22 May 1987). San Salvador.

———. 1987. *Agricultural commodity foreign donation agreement (Section 416), country: El Salvador.* OGSM/416 DDP. San Salvador.

U.S. GAO (General Accounting Office). 1977. *The World Food Program: How the U.S. can help improve it.* Report to the Senate Committee on Governmental Affairs. ID-77-16. Washington D.C.

———. 1981. *Food for Development program: Constrained by unresolved management and policy questions*. Report to the Congress. Washington, D.C.

———. 1982. Cargo preference requirements add to costs of Title II Food for Peace programs. Report to the Honorable Millicent Fenwick, United States House of Representatives. GAO/PAD-82-31.

———. 1983. Political and economic factors influencing economic support programs. GAO/ID-83-43. Washington, D.C.

———. 1984a. *AID needs to strengthen management of commodity import programs*. Report to the administrator, Agency for International Development. GAO/NSAID-84-47. Washington, D.C.

———. 1984b. Funding of joint combined military exercises in Honduras. Letter to Representative Bill Alexander, 22 June 1984.

———. 1984c. *Monitoring dollar and local currency resources under economic recovery and P.L. 480 Title I and II programs in Honduras*. Memorandum Survey Report 1-522-85-1. Washington, D.C.

———. 1984d. *U.S. economic assistance to Central America*. GAO/NSAID-84-71. Washington, D.C.

———. 1985a. *Providing effective economic assistance to El Salvador and Honduras: A formidable task*. GAO/NSAID-85-52. Washington, D.C.

———. 1985b. *USAID/Costa Rica's monitoring of and controls over dollar and local currency resources under economic recovery and PL 480 Title I programs*. Memorandum Survey Report No.1-515-85-8. Washington, D.C.

———. 1986. *Foreign assistance: U.S. use of conditions to achieve economic reforms*. GAO/NSAID-86-157. Washington, D.C.

———. 1987. *Foreign aid: Potential for diversion of economic support funds to unauthorized use*. Acc. 132074. GAO/NSAID-87-70. Washington, D.C.

Volke, Gary. 1987. *Economic growth, agricultural trade and development assistance*. Agricultural Information Bulletin 509 (March). Washington, D.C.: Economic Research Service.

Waghelstein, John W. 1985. Post-Vietnam counterinsurgency doctrine. *Military Review*, May.

Wallerstein, M. B. 1980. *Food for peace: Food for war*. Cambridge: MIT Press.

Weeks, John. 1985. *The economies of Central America*. New York: Holmes and Meir.

Wennergren, E. B., et al. 1986. *Solving world hunger: The U.S. stake*. Cabin John, Md.: Seven Locks Press.

Wessel, James, with Mort Hantman. 1983. *Trading the future: Farm exports and the concentration of economic power in our food economy*. San Francisco: Institute for Food and Development Policy.

————. 1982. The case for food aid. *World Food Programme News*, October–December.

————. 1983. *Food works: Twenty years of food aid for development, 1963–1983*. Rome.

————. 1984. Project summary: Honduras 2742, forestry development. Rome.

————. 1987a. *Ayuda alimentaria: Políticas y programas*. Rome.

————. 1987b. *Status of development projects and emergency operations*. Rome.

————. n.d. *198– in review*. Rome. Various years.

WFP (World Food Programme). 1978–87. WFP shipments by recipients for development projects and emergency Operations. Rome.

WFP. Committee on Food Aid Policies and Programmes. 1984. Project summary: Guatemala 784 (Exp. II) Community Development. Rome.

Wheaton, Philip. 1982. *Inside Honduras: Regional counterinsurgency base*. Washington, D.C.: EPICA Task Force.

Whittemore, Claire. 1981. *Land for the people: Land tenure and the very poor*. Oxford: Oxfam.

Wijga, Alet. 1983. *The nutritional impact of food-for-work programs: Report of a state of the art study*. Wageningen: Netherlands Universities–Foundation for International Cooperation.

Williams, Robert G. 1986. *Export agriculture and the crisis in Central America*. Chapel Hill: University of North Carolina Press.

Wing, Harry E. 1987. *U.S. food aid programs and the Guatemalan experience*. Office of Rural Development Report 22. Guatemala: USAID.

Winrock International. 1987. *Implementation and impact evaluation of PL 480 Title II program*. Prepared on contract for USAID–Honduras.

Working Group on Food and Farm Policy. 1984. *Beyond crisis: Farm and food policy for tomorrow*. Washington, D.C.: Rural Coalition.

World Bank. 1986. *Poverty and hunger: Issues and options for food security in developing countries*. Washington, D.C.

————. 1987. *World development report, 1987*. New York: Oxford University Press.

Woodruff, Calvin W. 1978. Intolerancia a la leche. In *Conocimientos actuales de nutrición*. Guatemala City. Instituto de Nutrición de Centro América y Panamá (INCAP)/Archivos Latinoamericanos de Nutrición (ALAN).

Worthington, L., ed. 1982. *Who's involved with hunger?* 3d ed. N.p.: World Hunger Education Service.

Index

Agency for International Development. *See* U.S. Agency for International Development (AID)

Agricultural Trade and Assistance Act. *See* PL 480

Agricultural Market Institute. *See* Grain stabilization institutes

Agriculture: disincentives for, 65–67; overproduction and food aid links, 6

Balance of payments, 19–24, 61–63, 206 n.4

Basic grains, 42–45; PL 480 and, 52; structural adjustments in, 83–86, 211 n.5

Bellmon amendment, 56–59; evaluation of, 189, 213 n.22

Block, John (secretary of agriculture), 50, 51

Breast-feeding, 223 n.50

Bumpers amendment, 67

CARE (Cooperative for American Relief Everywhere), 101–3; agroexport incentives, 88; distributive aid, 99; educational program, 128; ESF funding of, 105; evaluation of, 106–7, 110; food-aid sales, 69; food-for-work, 134, 142–43; in Guatemala, 218–19 n.16, 220 n.21; in Honduras, 181; missions, 120; monetization, 106; in Nicaragua, 178; and USAID, 219 n.17; and World Relief, 220 n.19

Cargo Preference Act, 34

CARITAS, 19; food-for-work, 134; in Guatemala, 175, 176; in Honduras, 181

Catholic church: and the displaced, 155; and food-for-work, 143

Catholic Relief Services (CRS), 100–101, 119; and AID, 154; distributive aid, 99; in Honduras, 64–65; program evaluations, 106–7; Section 416 arrangement, 175

Central America: agricultural protectionism, 93–94; agricultural system, 43–47; agroexports, 87–94; balance of payments, 22–24, 61, 63; campesinos, 43–44, 77; dietary changes, 59–60, 110–12; food aid, 203 n.3; food aid coordination and monitoring, 70, 121–24; food exports, 41; food import dependency, 42, 55–59; food security, 41–43, 70–71, 76–77, 211 n.1; malnutrition, 106–12, 211 n.4; private sector aid to, 76–77; rural poverty, 45; U.S. farm commodities exports to, 47; wheat consumption, 63

Central America Food Security Program (CADESCA), 89

Central American Nutritional Institute (INCAP), 121–22

Central Intelligence Agency (CIA), and contras, 181

Cheese, 111, 113–14

Christian Broadcasting Network, 119

Churches, use of food aid by, 6

Church World Services, and AID, 99

CONADES (National Commission for Aid to the Displaced): and the displaced, 151–56, 229 n.19; monetization, 71, 115; and World Food Programme, 168